HOW MOVIES HELPED
SAVE MY SOUL

FINDING SPIRITUAL FINGERPRINTS IN CULTURALLY SIGNIFICANT FILMS

GARETH HIGGINS

FOREWORD BY TONY CAMPOLO

HOW MOVIES HELPED SAVE MY SOUL

FINDING SPIRITUAL FINGERPRINTS IN CULTURALLY SIGNIFICANT FILMS

Published by Relevant Books
A division of Relevant Media Group, Inc.
www.relevantbooks.com
www.relevantmediagroup.com

© 2004 by Gareth Higgins

Design: Relevant Solutions
www.relevant-solutions.com

Relevant Books is a registered trademark of Relevant Media Group, Inc., and is registered in the U.S. Patent and Trademark Office.

For information:
RELEVANT MEDIA GROUP, INC.
POST OFFICE BOX 951127
LAKE MARY, FL 32795
407-333-7152

Library of Congress Control Number: 2003093115
International Standard Book Number: 0-9714576-9-7

    04 05 06 9 8 7 6 5 4 3 2

Printed in the United States of America

Dedicated with love and affection to:
My Mum Fay, who showed me what good acting is,
my Dad Iain, who took me to my first film,
and my brother and sister Brian and Caryll, who put up
with me hogging the video recorder when we were kids.

ACKNOWLEDGEMENTS

THIS BOOK EXISTS BECAUSE I WROTE IT. BUT THAT only happened because: Al Spence introduced me to "real" cinema by taking me to the QFT and more than anyone else, gave me the love for film that this book is about. Roy Samuelson and Jeff Ham showed me what L.A. is like. Neill Whiteside and Andrew King went to the movies with me seemingly every week when we were teenagers.

Mark McCleary bought me my first *Halliwell's Film Guide*. Mike Blythman, Cary Gibson, John Kyle, Jennie Taylor, Tim Magowan, Phil Harrison, Keli Harrington, Keith Patrick, Suzanne Patrick, Bart and Marty Campolo, Gavin Harper, Jeremy Bond, Irene Milliken, Jonny Clark, Trevor Henderson, Jenna Galbreth, Ewan Gibson, Steve Hill, Amy Ornee, Pete Rollins, Brian Edge, Bill & Linda Kervin, Davy & Betty & Shannon Kidd, David Templeton, Derek Poole, Pete & Ellen Allely, Terry & Gerrie Hogg, Johnny Clark, Caroline Orr, Craig Sands, Rose Riddell, Dave Schulz, Glenn Jordan, John Kyle, Mark McCleary, Mervyn McCullagh, Neil Brittain, Niall Brown, Steve Hill, Stuart Mullan, Stephen & Jenny Hamilton, Kellie Turtle, Bill Roy, Johnny and Susan McEwen and Jackson, Ella and Charlie, and especially Jude Adam let me indulge myself by reading endlessly from this book when it was a work in progress.

The good people of Relevant Books, especially Cameron Strang who took a risk in even agreeing to publish this, and the majestic Cara Baker who edited me with grace and patience, put up with my interminable pedantry over words, and even laughed at my jokes.

John Brewer took me under his wing, kept me sane during my postgraduate study, and taught me how to write right.

Malach O'Doherty, who published some of my "early, funny" works, and kept telling me he thought I was a natural writer. That meant a lot.

William Crawley gave me the subtitle and endured my insecurities. Eolath Magee helped me do something about those very same insecurities. David Dark made me think about the absence of secular molecules in the universe. Bruce Main a) helped show me what it means to be a Christian and b) kept asking me "How's the book going?"

Nick Thorpe, Ali McBride and Adrian & Janice McCartney, made me feel someone might actually want to read this book. Mike Riddell's words are so lyrical, and his friendship encouraged me to write.

Tony Campolo first helped me to see spirituality in popular culture and wrote a wonderful foreword. Steve Stockman told me to go for it, and, more than most, has helped Northern Irish Christians take pop culture seriously. The members of the Club du Cinema (near and far—in Belfast, London, Edinburgh, and Nashville), stayed to the end of the credits every time. And my parents didn't force me to get a "real job."

These people are treasures. They share the credit (and I guess that means they also share the blame) for how I think and write. You would like them.

FOREWORD

THE BIBLE TELLS US THAT IF WE FAIL TO DECLARE God's Gospel, "the very rocks will cry out" the message. Gareth Higgins picks up that theme and finds messages in moving pictures that God wants us to hear—messages that are either seldom heard from church pulpits or, when preached, expressed with insufficient drama. For Gareth, going to the cinema is often going to what George MacLeod called "a thin place—a place where the line between harsh reality and the transcendent is so subtly blurred that it is difficult to tell one from the other." Gareth, a religious guy, filters what he sees on the silver screen through the grid of his faith commitments and experiences.

Some years ago, as a university student, I took a literature course in which the professor went to great lengths to explain the host of symbols and allegories that he saw in his reading of Herman Melville's novel, *Moby Dick*. After several lectures in which the professor went on in a seemingly endless proclamation of the Gospel according to Melville, a friend in the class leaned over to me and whispered, "I think he's getting more out of *Moby Dick* than Melville ever put into it."

If my friend's judgment was correct, it can also be added that this is what we are all entitled to do with art. When we engage with art, whether it be a piece of literature, a painting, or a movie, we have every right, and even an obligation, to read into it truths and insights that go beyond anything that the artist intended. In the context of the critiquing of post-modernists, it is not even necessary for us to ask what the artist intended to communicate because as deconstructionist Jacques Derrida and his followers would tell us, once the words are written, the painting painted, or the movie shown, that which was produced by the artist takes on a life of its own, independent of the creator. Then, we who engage these works of art are free to create the meanings they have for us.

Whether he would agree with me or not (and I think he does), Gareth Higgins is this kind of post-modernist, so do not argue with his interpretations of what he finds in the movies of our times. What Gareth offers us is not so much a series of interpretations as it is a methodology for engaging movies. He calls upon us to engage films with hungry eyes, and he echoes Jesus in saying that those with eyes to see will see truths in films that speak to the existential conditions of our times and to the spiritual conditions of our souls.

Gareth calls us to go to the movies to hear and see sermons. Unlike the didactic messages that are heard from many pulpits, he senses the messages coming to him through movies as sermons that are not so much heard as they are "overheard." Soren Kierkegaard called such forms of communication *the indirect method*. This Danish philosopher (though he himself would disdain any such title as "philosopher") contended that most of us reject messages that are direct. Kierkegaard tells us that if we are to really hear the Gospel, it will be because we overhear it spoken to someone else and realize indirectly that what is being said powerfully relates to us and what is going on in our own lives. To make this point, Kierkegaard noted that the Pauline Epistles were written to people in first century churches, yet, when we hear them read, we sense that what they say is about each of us—individually.

In another illustration, Kierkegaard tells us that it is like waiting with a crowd of people on a street corner for a break in the traffic that will allow you to cross that street and overhearing two people in front of you gossiping. The two of them are oblivious to your presence, and, to your shocked dismay, you realize that they are saying revealing things about you.

For Gareth Higgins, like Kierkegaard, church sermons are too direct, and therefore, those in the pews are able to prepare defenses against them, whereas in movies, those who make the movies do not even know who the viewer is, but indirectly communicate to him or her those messages that the viewer needs to hear.

The author of this book is a young man, and for his generation, movies like *The Matrix* and *Field of Dreams* speak prophetically and offer themes for spiritual analyzation; I know he would have liked to come of age when the likes of Federico Fellini were around. In the 1950s, we went to the movies with expectations of receiving messages from the oracles of the age. Films like *La Dolce Vita* explored the superficiality of our sensate culture, and films like *The Seventh Seal* portrayed the sufferings of those "Knights of Faith" (as Kierkegaard would call them) who were willing to struggle with the forces of darkness in their desperate quest for certainty about God. It was impossible to view those movies without coming away with deep feelings of angst, usually followed by long discussions of what life was all about.

"Great art is revolutionary, in that it reveals what is absent and hence makes us discontent with what is," the social philosopher Herbert Marcuse said. Indeed, great movies prove that point. Some of them help us to sense the loss of community in contemporary society and long for a better place for our homeless souls. They highlight the absence in our everyday lives of the mystical, or what the philosopher of religion, Rudolf Otto called, the *mysterium tremendum*. They make us aware that life, as we are living it, is not what it was meant to be. Movies give us a glimpse into the future in ways that those prophesying preachers, who claim to have figured out what the Bible tells us about the end of the world, never could. Hence, movies may offer us an eschatology that is closer to biblical truth than those exegetical experts in scriptural hermeneutics can ever approach.

The most prominent theologian of my time (and I am an old man now) was Paul Tillich. It was Tillich who taught us that theologians are called to answer the questions posed by the philosophers of the day. He argued for what he called, "an answering theology." If Tillich were with us today, he might say that theology should be responding to the questions raised by the movies of today. Given the death of contemporary theology, as it has gotten sidetracked into logical positivism, linguistic analysis, and, of late, deconstructionism, it may have fallen to those who make movies to raise the questions that are of ultimate concern to most of us. Gareth Higgins obviously thinks so, and if he is right, then this book is most definitely worth the time you take to read it.

TONY CAMPOLO, PH.D.
PROFESSOR EMERITUS
EASTERN UNIVERSITY
ST. DAVIDS, PENNSLYVANIA

TABLE OF CONTENTS

INTRODUCTION

"In reality, every reader is, while he is reading, the reader of his own self. The writer's work is merely a kind of optical instrument, which he offers to the reader to enable him to discern what, without this book, he would perhaps never have experienced in himself. And the recognition by the reader in his own self of what the book says is proof of its veracity."
—Marcel Proust, c.1910

"Some people can read War and Peace *and come away thinking it's just a simple adventure story, other people can read a chewing gum wrapper, and unlock the secrets of the universe."* —Lex Luthor, *Superman,* 1978

LET ME TELL YOU A SECRET. I WAS BORN JUST before it started to go sour. It was the middle of the most important decade in cinema, the years of *Taxi Driver, Night Moves, Nashville,* and *Jaws,* but only a heartbeat away from *Star Wars,* which pretty much ruined everything. The great American critic Pauline Kael said she lost it at the movies, and I started to lose it too at the time—around 1989—I realized there was more to film than *Superman, The Goonies,* and *Back to the Future.* Thank God for the Queen's Film Theatre in Belfast—that museum of light which I credit with getting me through my university finals, but now I recognize it as being far more important than that. Film is so wrapped up with the fabric of my life that, along with the community of friends and family with whom I'm blessed to travel, I simply cannot explain myself without it. That's probably what this book is really about—explaining myself.

I began it by thinking I'd just write a few reviews, partly for friends who kept asking me what films they should see, partly for the simple pleasure of having to watch the films again, but mostly because so much of what passes for film criticism is a waste of space, not to mention that so many so-called "film guides" tell us as much about how a movie *feels* as a wine list does about how a ripe Chilean merlot tastes. Indeed, the traditional "capsule review" probably does nothing more than give people an excuse not to search beyond the tyrannical borders of the corporate Hollywood stew. I wanted to write about films in a way that encourages people to actually *think about* them. Anything else is like buying a road map without ever going anywhere. But as I have explored the territory of films I have come to deeply appreciate, I realize that in writing about them, I am revealing a great deal about myself. I remember reading a review of *Field of Dreams* in which the critic wrote that she could never love anyone who didn't love it. The difference between her and I is that she has the decency to limit herself to one film. Those of you who know me may therefore see this book as a kind of joint apology/explanation for my idiosyncrasies. Those of you who simply want to be prodded in the direction of films that may make a difference to you, or that will at least open you to the possibilities of what this art form can do, will, I hope, find something of worth on these pages.

Before we go any further, I better tell you how to use this book:

It basically consists of sixteen chapters on the meaning of cinema, organized according to themes like "war" and "love" and "quest." (My friend Jennie wanted me to write a chapter devoted to *Dirty Dancing*, but I need this book to sell more than one copy, so I had to reluctantly demur. Sorry, Jennie.) I've tried to write about themes that have some resonance for people who want to make sense of their own lives, of our place in the world, of the need for an encounter with God to heal us. So I deal with anti-heroes (the ambiguous morality of being human), brokenness (how depression and the pain of our lives needs to be brought to the light if we are to survive), conspiracy (how we so often feel alone in a field where all the weapons of the world are trained against us), death (because, along with taxes and telethons, it's the one thing that will happen to us all), community (the human race has lost something to do with being present with each other, and we need to find it—quick), fear (it's the place most of us seem to live, most of the time), God (I couldn't really write a book about spirituality in cinema without a chapter called God), justice (one person's justice is another person's revenge), love (because I'm pretty sure we need help to know what love actually means), outsiders (because it seems that most of the important things that happen in this world involve outsiders), power (because the Church is full of the wrong kind, and we need to learn that the path to true power is through our own disempowerment—we need a regime change), quest (the journey is the destination and all that good stuff), war (what is it good for?), and *The Matrix* (because I don't know what category to put it in).

Most of the pieces here are better read after you have seen the film, but you may wish to still read the piece as an encouragement to see it. Each piece includes reference to other films you may be interested in after seeing it and attempts to locate it in a context of cinema history and style. As availability on DVD and video changes on a weekly basis, I recommend you check such availability on the web. As for the "authorship" of a film: For too long, writers have been penalized by the convention of referring to films as "made by" their directors. As a meager contribution to redressing this imbalance, this book frequently lists films and the names of their directors and writers as "co-creators." Writers deserve nothing less, and any director worth their salt will not deny this.

ONE LAST THING BEFORE WE BEGIN: WHAT CAN FILM DO FOR YOU?

Godfrey Reggio, director of the magnificent *Koyaanisqatsi*, said that film is "a method of getting information to the public in a manner that's almost unavoidable." And, at its best, as the most immediate, inescapable art medium, film can transport you to what the founder of the Iona Community, George MacLeod, called a "thin place," where the line between harsh reality and the transcendent is so subtly blurred that for a moment, or if you're lucky, moments, you find it difficult to tell the difference. The comment by Proust that opens this introduction refers to literature, but tells the truth about film as well. *Life* itself may be given to us in a flash of celluloid light, as the very human desire to live vicariously through characters and circumstances removed from "real life" overwhelms with its all too easy charms. And your heart is lifted, or squeezed, or torn down, as you imagine what could be, or weep for what is, or fear for what is threatened. Who among us has not felt at least in microcosm the anguished courage of a William Wallace in *Braveheart*, or identified with the last minute redemption of a Lester Burnham in *American Beauty*, or suffered the torment of a Michael Corleone in *The Godfather Part II*, on realizing that what we thought we controlled was actually controlling us? Film, in the final analysis, can do for you what all great art does—irritate and heal, challenge and affirm, inspire and sadden. It can, in the case of a film like *Magnolia*, truly give you more life, or as in *Wings of Desire*, make you believe in God, or as with *The Wizard of Oz*, tell you the truth about your own existence.

Film should be treated with the same respect as church or poison, for it can change your life. People of faith have always been at the pioneering edge of art, from Michelangelo's Sistine masterpiece reaching up to heaven, to Bach's attempt at honoring the creativity of God with mathematically profound sonatas, to Blake's lyrical appreciation of the mystic world, to more recent stumbling worshipers and wounded prophets such as Van Morrison, Martin Scorsese, Joni Mitchell, and John Irving. These people understand what my friend David Dark meant when he wrote the following provocation, which could serve as an adequate summary of the message of this entire book: "There isn't a secular molecule in the universe."

Despite this, contemporary Christianity, at least in its institutional forms, often seems reluctant to recognize, much less embrace, the wonder of human creativity on the spiritual journey. So I hope that this filmology—a small contribution to the understanding of film, an appeal for its location in the pantheon of life-enhancing art, and a defence of the idea that in a God-breathed universe, there can be no sacred-secular division—may be a worthy travelling companion on your pilgrimage. I make no claims for the comprehensiveness of this book—I freely admit that it's just about as biased as they come; the films I write about are here because I want to talk about them; I guess that means I also think they need to be talked about. But there could just as easily have been a hundred others here instead. I don't have the only "right" interpretation of any of these (apart from *Field of Dreams*, of course); I just want to encourage you to watch more.

Let's begin by having a look at the first film I remember seeing.

THE BLACK HOLE
(GARY NELSON, DISNEY, 1979)

What is Satan doing in a Disney film? I saw this classic cheesy camp sci-fi adventure in 1979 at what was then the ABC cinema in Belfast, opposite the Irish Presbyterian Church HQ— an appropriate enough location, for Martin Scorsese summed it up when he said that he had a hard time telling the difference between going to the movies and going to church. The ABC is a hotel now, but for a few years, it was where Dad would take my brother Brian and I to Saturday matinees and even the odd weeknight showing. Dad used to be very coy about taking us to the cinema; we did it from time to time, and I'm sure he enjoyed it. Part of the enjoyment was to keep it secret from us—both what we were going to see, and even the fact that we were going at all. Thus I remember being in the car in the summer of 1984, halfway to the Ormeau Road, when he said, "What's this film called—Mickey Mouse and the Stone?"

Now the most-wanted film of that summer was the Michael Douglas/Kathleen Turner adventure comedy (and homage to Spencer Tracy/Katherine Hepburn, although of course I didn't know that then), *Romancing the Stone*. Disney's old Camelot picture *The Sword in the Stone* was on re-release at the same time, but Brian and I, in spite of our usual fondness for animation, most emphatically did *not* want to see Merlin merrily mythologizing when what looked like the greatest film since *Raiders of the Lost Ark* was showing on another screen. Thankfully, Dad was just kidding, but I don't think he told us until we heard him ask at the box office for tickets for the film we really wanted to see; that was a moment of relief matched only in later life when I discovered I didn't have the potentially fatal e.coli virus on a trip abroad. You can see that I take my films seriously.

Anyway, back to *The Black Hole*. What is Satan doing in a Disney film? Indeed, what are Anthony Perkins, Ernest Borgnine, and Maximilian Schell doing in the same film if it's not a psycho-thriller/second-world-war/cowboy-film hybrid? This movie is about a mad scientist who has killed his entire crew on a deep space experimental mission (well, he's actually turned them into androids, but they might as well be dead). Our hero, Robert Forster—later to be rediscovered and nominated for an Academy Award in Tarantino's *Jackie Brown*—arrives with the magnificently named Yvette Mimieux and Joseph Bottoms, along with journalist Ernest Borgnine, the cute—possibly gay—robot Vincent (with the voice of Roddy McDowall), and just-in-it-to-be-the-recognizable-character-actor-who-dies Anthony Perkins, to investigate the massive ship (a ghost?) stagnating on the edge of the eponymous inverted galaxy (that's what a black hole is, you see). There follows some cod-philosophising and laser fire as Doctor Schell reveals his Machiavellian (Max-imilian?) scheme, to take the ship through the black hole and become something new.

He is dead-set on this, and just to prove it, he has a big scary red robot with rotating knives for hands (which he uses imaginatively on someone holding what looks like a phone book). And—oh! The irony—the robot belonging to the mad scientist played by Maximilian Schell is named—wait for it—Maximilian! Much laser fire and cute robot-bashing later, and our heroes have made their escape through the black hole, inexorably following the good doctor and his unfriendly hench-robot. The final image of the film has the mad scientist *inside* Maximilian, surveying a scene evocative of *Dante's Inferno*.

Who would have thought that a kids' film would evoke Jung and Freud and end on such a sour note? *The Black Hole* is by no means a great film; in fact, it's not even a *good* film, but it's fun, and for the contrast of ambition and target audience, not to mention John Barry's epic score (and an overture which reminds me of a sadly missed element of going to the movies), it's definitely worth seeking out. A good film with which to begin a life-long pilgrimage into cinema. That journey is the story of the rest of this book. Welcome aboard.

CHAPTER ONE

DR. HIGGINS' ROSETTA STONE

HOW TO READ A FILM IS THE TITLE OF A FAMOUS— and quite brilliant—guide to highbrow criticism by James Monaco. Published in 1977, it's never been out of print, and rightly so. It's pretty much a bible for serious film students, particularly of the academic kind who never use the word "movie," and don't go to the cinema with anyone but their most trusted fellow scholars in case the experience is diminished by Philistines seated on either side, who may commit the most grievous sins of popcorn-eating or—*the horror*—talking during the credits, or indeed, enjoying the film as it is. You should read it if you want to become an academically minded film scholar. I'm not an academically minded film scholar (although I once was an academic, and you can still get my utterly fascinating Ph.D. thesis about apocalyptic beliefs from the Queen's University Belfast library), and I usually only go to the cinema with friends who will appreciate the film, but there is such a thing as a quality *movie.* "Film" is sometimes the most appropriate word, but not always. I mean, one of the most entertaining experiences I had in a cinema in the past few years was on the opening night of *Armageddon*, which most certainly does not satisfy the definition of a quality "film." Sorry, I'm departing from the script here. Stephen King—that most cinematic of novelists—says that when you write, you must take out everything that isn't *the story*, but I quite like this paragraph, so it's staying in. I beg your indulgence. You don't have to read any further if you don't want to. Just put the book neatly back on the shelf where you found it (unless, of course, this book has been successful, in which case it's in the window display. Come to think of it, if it's not in the window display already, you could do me a favor and put it in there, just in front of the new John Grisham.) If you're reading this on the web, then I question the wisdom of my publishers in allowing *this* to be the sample page used. It's hardly the best writing in the book (I think that comes in the section on death, but you can make your own mind up.)

Now, where were we? Ah yes, the Rosetta Stone. Those of you who have even the vaguest memory of elementary school history will know what I'm talking about here—a piece of granite, discovered in Egyptian sand in the nineteenth century. Although only partially complete, the stone led to a quantum leap in the interpretation of hieroglyphics, which meant, among other things, that *The Ten Commandments* and *The Prince of Egypt*, and even the quite monumentally bad '80s "thriller" *Sphinx* could at least pay lip service to semantic accuracy. But the stone has more relevance to our appreciation of film than that: I want to encourage you to construct your own Rosetta Stone, with which you will interpret the hidden treasures of cinema, films, movies—whatever you wish to call them. Call it a template, call it a toolbox, call it what you will, but if you don't make a conscious effort to become informed about film, your watching will be impoverished. No film exists in a vacuum, and even a minimal attempt at preparing yourself to watch can greatly enrich the experience. Now I don't want to turn film-going into a dry and dusty, almost meaningless academic exercise. That's what university film studies courses are for (ouch). But I do want to encourage people to learn the tools of watching. In much the same way that the poetry of Philip Larkin is best appreciated with some background knowledge of industrial Britain in the 1960s-1980s, or the preservative art of Damien Hirst with reference to consumerism and transcience in the 1990s, or the architecture of the pyramids with an understanding of ancient paganism, or Jennifer Lopez's pop videos with a pair of ear plugs and a pair of binoculars, film is best encountered with a little understanding of the context which birthed it. There's no reason why we should not seek to be better informed about what we are watching; and its potential meanings. So, to that end, I propose the following:

- Subscribe to a decent, intelligent but accessible film magazine and read it, even the articles about Polish agricultural cinema of the 1950s. There are only a couple of magazines like this, but they're not paying me, so I won't name them.

- Don't read reviews before you see films (it will stop you from seeing the good ones; you can read the reviews afterward, and find out if you were right). But do read wonderful film lit like Derek Malcolm's *A Century of Cinema*, Martin Scorsese's *Scorsese on Scorsese*, Norman Kagan's *A Stanley Kubrick Film*, David Thomson's *A Biographical Dictionary of Film*, and the annual *Projections* series edited by John Boorman and Walter Donohoe. You should probably also read Joe Queenan's reviews in *Movieline* magazine. You won't learn much about films, but you'll laugh really hard.

◆ Don't expect or ask for "realism" as a mark of a film's quality. If you grew up in New Zealand and you dislike *The Piano* because it's always raining, that's your problem. Likewise, if Nicolas Cage's breathing from a respirator as he allows a dying man to pass in *Bringing Out the Dead* strikes you as medically impossible because you're a doctor, don't assume that Scorsese got his facts wrong; the character's hallucinating, for goodness' sake. And just because people generally don't burst into public song at the drop of a hat doesn't mean that musicals can't be either extremely entertaining or have profound things to say (*Dancer in the Dark, Moulin Rouge,* and *Rocky Horror Picture Show,* to name just three[1]).

◆ Do not eat popcorn when watching films. It's bad for a) *your* health and b) *my* ability to hear the film if I'm sitting beside you.

◆ Find one or two friends who are willing to join you on a journey of discovery in cinema. Watch some movies together with strong coffee, and then talk about the films over a meal. Food and drink grease the wheels of conversation like nothing else.

◆ Approach films as you would a novel, an art gallery, or even a contemplative spiritual encounter. Take your time. Give the film your full attention. If it's a slow film, all the better; that means more time to let it wash over you. However, this means you should avoid diuretics beforehand. How coffee-gulping film fanatics like myself

---

[1] Well, fair enough, I was kidding about *Rocky Horror,* but I needed three examples and was tired when I wrote this.

can resolve the incompatibility of their two major loves is the subject of my next book.

◆ Don't ever let me catch you using "slow," "violent," or "arty" as value judgments on film. A film may be *unnecessarily* slow, or *gratuitously* violent, or *pretentiously* artistic, but it may also be gloriously languorous, morally conservative in its violence, or as beautiful as anything by Monet or Gehry. *Yi-Yi*, a three-hour long Taiwanese film, flew by, while I aged several years as I suffered the ninety minutes of *Tomb Raider*.

◆ Look at the film. Watch it. Observe how the camera moves, and take care to look around the screen for things you may have previously missed. *Blade Runner*, for example, is filled with images that are visible at the edges of the screen and are hardly ever shown in close-up. This is linked to the next rule:

◆ Do not watch any film made since 1950 on television unless it is shown in widescreen. The advent of widescreen video and DVD has meant that, among other things, we can see Ned Beatty eavesdropping on Lily Tomlin while she talks on the phone in *Nashville*, Nicolas Cage and Laura Dern seated beside each other in a car in *Wild at Heart*, and that when Robert de Niro says his famous line "This is *this*!" in *The Deer Hunter*, he's pointing at a gun, not at thin air. These are but three examples of where the filmmaker's vision has been distorted or even destroyed by the practice of butchering films for broadcast on the idiot box (technically known as "panning and scanning for television," but I'm not in a generous mood).

◆ Consider what the difference between a good and a bad performance is. Marlon Brando in *On the Waterfront* is a key example of the former, while Marlon Brando in *The Island of Dr. Moreau* is one of the best examples of the latter. You need to work out why for yourself, because I certainly don't know.

◆ Ask yourself *what* is being said, *how* it is being said, and *why* it is being said. Reflect on the possible journey that led the filmmaker to produce what you have just seen. Think about what its consequences might be. This is a complex question, as in the case of a film like *Reservoir Dogs*. It was clear to me but not everyone I saw it with that it is an anti-violence film rather than a comedy about torture. It is a simple question, however, for a film like *Swordfish*, wherein *the filmmakers try to make us think* the mass murder of anyone who disagrees with U.S. foreign policy is justified because *we're supposed to believe* cluster bomb mines look cool on screen, and *they clearly hope that showing Halle Berry topless will make us forget* our complicity.

◆ It is universally acknowledged that there are only seven basic stories in the history of cinema. They can be paraphrased by the names of the seven dwarfs, but I can't remember the names of the seven dwarfs, so we'll have to just pretend we know what the seven universal stories are. Sad truth is, most American cinema is obsessed with only one of these stories—the individual's triumph over adversity. But that may not be too bad a thing, as long as we realize that the "worlds" in most films are not analogous to our own. They may inspire us in general terms, but we will never build a barn as quickly as the

Amish in *Witness*, or teach like Robin Williams in *Dead Poets Society*, or fall in love as quickly as Jack and Rose in *Titanic* (some of my friends would doubt this, but I'm in a grumpy mood today, so I'll let it stand and hope that someone proves me wrong someday).

- It is sometimes difficult to find good movies at the multiplex—as Paul Schrader said: "Most books are bad, most painting is bad, most everything is bad. Why shouldn't most movies be bad?" But you should never permit yourself to be found guilty of saying, "*Field of Dreams* is a piece of sentimental crap"; "Black and white films are boring"; "*Gladiator* is my favorite film"; or "I miss Adam Sandler movies."[2]

- Listen to Miles Davis records from the 1950s and early '60s as often as you can. This will turn you into a more reflective person and give you something to do late at night when you come home to your empty house (you will, of course, need to choose between film and the love of a partner).

- Don't talk during the credits. Just enjoy the opportunity to reflect on the film. Be conscious and alert, even if you didn't like the movie. The person sitting beside you may have been deeply affected by it. The last thing they need is for you to tell them that it was, in your eloquent terms, "crap," although this does sometimes make for memorable

---

[2] I wrote this before I saw the outstanding *Punch-Drunk Love*, which made me reassess pretty much everything I thought about love at first sight. As for Mr. Sandler, let's hope lightning strikes twice.

moments. My childhood best friend, not a fan of serious cinema, was asked after *Rain Man*—not a masterpiece, but a deeply emotional and sad film—what he had thought. In a statement that has resonated through the ages, well at least over the past fourteen years since the film was out, my mate pronounced: "Ah, there were a few funny bits in it." And after my third viewing of Terrence Malick's unquestionable work of genius and compassion, *The Thin Red Line*, as soon as the credits began to roll, I was conscious of the sound of my own epiphanic breathing for half a second before the bloke behind me said to his wife in a voice loud enough to drown out the parting of the Red Sea, "That was the biggest load of shite I've ever seen in my life." I think I've made my point. Don't talk during the credits.

◆ Observe the Ten-Minute Rule™. This was first established in November 1997, when my good mate (whom I shall call Mr. X because he denies the veracity of this story) and I had been to see the wonderful French concoction and *Vertigo* homage, *L'Appartement*. It's a thrilling film, and I was on the edge of my seat both with anticipation and sheer wonder at the scope of what was on screen. It was, without contest, my favorite film of the year. I had experienced cinematic euphoria, which is better the less you have it, and fully expected Mr. X to feel the same way. So when I asked him what he thought of the movie, he said, "It didn't really have a story, did it?" I hope I did lovers of film a service that night by declining Mr. X's offer of a lift and walked home alone, so as not to transgress my non-violent philosophy. From that point on, I instituted the Ten Minute Rule™, whereby I will not discuss the film for that period of time after the credits have finished.

By that time, your emotional response to the film will have begun to integrate itself into your psyche and will be protected from attack by the ignorant. Or they will have gone home and you can enjoy the memory of the film by yourself. As the Native American proverb says: Do not believe that you understand an enemy until you have walked a mile in his moccasins. Then you will be a mile away from him, and can keep his moccasins (I'm paraphrasing). Whether or not you have any friends left after a year or two of following the Ten Minute Rule™ is a moot point. I mean, what's more important, celluloid visions or human community?

Okay, that should get you started on constructing your own Rosetta Stone. If you don't want to sweat over it too much, all you need to remember is Dr. Higgins' key rule: "Film is Your Friend." This is a universal truth that should help you through much adversity. With that in mind, we can proceed to the main feature.

CHAPTER TWO

ANTI-HEROES
THE GUYS WE LOVE TO HATE

HERE'S A TRUISM THAT WILL STAND THE TEST OF time: Harrison Ford is not an interesting actor (although his presence is reassuring, like a cinematic comfort blanket). Tom Cruise is not an interesting actor, most of the time (although evidently easy on the eye). Harvey Keitel is a very interesting actor.

Ford's films since *Star Wars* struggle to maintain any tension or interest simply because we know he's always going to win. Nothing can stop Harrison Ford. His choices have been so predictable that we always know what to expect; and when, as in *What Lies Beneath*, he tried to pull the rug out from under us, the shock value of Harrison-as-bad-guy was so overplayed in the trailers that even that came as a whimpering conclusion to an incredibly derivative film. Tom's not much better, although at least with *Eyes Wide Shut* and especially *Magnolia*, he bared his soul a little.

As for Harvey, well, he's an entirely different fish. A man so committed to the "truth" of his characters that for a while there I wondered if I would see a Keitel film *without* his naked body writhing in psychological agony; he's one of the most courageous actors around (if you doubt me, just try spending a couple of hours with him in *Bad Lieutenant*). His is not a life dedicated to "career development," and he rarely seems to make films for the money alone (*Monkey Trouble* was an honest mistake). Even weak films are lifted by his presence. His female counterpart is probably Ellen Burstyn, whose performance in *Requiem for a Dream* set a new benchmark for taking character seriously. Keitel and Burstyn are first among equals in the portrayal of anti-heroes. Actors often say that they are more attracted to parts with shades of gray rather than staple Hollywood perfection ice-cream concoctions—you know, like all the parts Brad Pitt played before he was in *Se7en*. It's no wonder because, frankly, we live in an age where people are more fascinated by darkness than light. Ian McKellen's Magneto in *X-Men* was far more intriguing than Dr. Xavier, the Joker more than Batman, and The Man With No Name is more interesting than Luke Skywalker. The devil doesn't just have all the good music; he can be found at the movies, too.

HIGH PLAINS DRIFTER
(CLINT EASTWOOD, ERNEST TIDYMAN, 1973)

"Do not forget to entertain strangers, for by so doing some have entertained angels without knowing it." —Hebrews 13:2

What is Satan doing in a Clint Eastwood film? Or existentialism, for that matter? If you think you know Clint, if you think all he amounts to is a relatively dumb gunslinger and occasionally laughable romantic hero, *High Plains Drifter* will change all that. When *Unforgiven* was released in 1992, almost twenty years after *High Plains Drifter*, it was striking how much talk there was of it being the ultimate revisionist Western, with its "realistic" depiction of the vagaries of frontier life and murder. But Clint had done this all before. *High Plains Drifter* is the story of a monumentally politically incorrect avenging angel with no name, and it makes no concessions to the audience's taste for heroes.

It all starts pretty conventionally: Stranger rides into town, townsfolk stare him out, Stranger goes to bar for a drink, townsfolk stare him out, Stranger asks barber for a shave, townsfolk stare him out, Stranger kills three men and rapes a woman who looks at him the "wrong way"; townsfolk ask him to be their sheriff. (Don't you find it amazing that no one bats an eyelid in Western towns when this kind of stuff happens? Or that cinema audiences are so numb to it that they don't either? Thank God real life ain't like the movies ...) We know there's something awry when we see the overhead shot of the town—called Lago—it's a different kind of town than we have become accustomed to in westerns. For one thing, it's right by the beach—a sort of "Sodom by the sea," as one wag put it—for another, it's totally isolated from anywhere else. It seems that Lago just appeared from nowhere, perhaps arising out of the ground as some Native American cultures believe, perhaps landing from the sky. What is clear is that there's really no one else around; once the Stranger comes, there's only one show in town and only one town to have it in.

There's a clue to the path the film is going to take in the name of the town. Is there any significance to the word Lago? I think it has something to do with the old English word for jail—Gaol—people imprisoned in their own guilt; as the Stranger moseys moodily into town, one of the first things he sees is a native standing inside the frame of an unbuilt building, like a jail cell. And as I've said, within five minutes of his arrival, our anti-hero has shot three men and raped a woman who appears to enjoy it. This is not a film that could be made today. The Stranger arrives quietly, talks quietly, and quietly tears the place apart. It's difficult to say more about the plot without giving too much away, so I will have to be satisfied with saying that this is a dark, vicious, violent, very serious film. It's about the incarnation of a revenge fantasy, possibly from beyond the grave, and is a supreme example of a director's discipline—there is no dead weight in this picture. It touches (lightly) on racism against Native Americans; a scene where the Stranger gives blankets and sweets to a father and his children could have been sentimentalized, but Clint plays it subtly—this is not "Robin Hood goes to the Wild West." The Stranger marks out his territory by befriending the only other outsider, a dwarf, and we see that there is something very dark in the town's past which may have led the Stranger there (nice use of elliptical flashbacks for this, by the way).

The Prophet Isaiah says that the sin of Sodom was inhospitality—the people of Lago harbor a guilty secret that is nothing if not an example of such exclusion. They say they're God-fearing folk, which the film suggests means they keep themselves to themselves, are racist, and refuse to take responsibility for either their own actions or the needs of others: Clint Eastwood is definitely not a fan of the church. His character quickly brings the people under his spell and gets them to attend to his every whim, to the point of redecorating the entire town his way, with a brand new color scheme; but, fear not, this is not a surrealist cowboy version of *Trading Spaces*—and this Stranger is not the Martha Stewart of the "Gothic Western World of Venegance," although he does paint the town red. There's characteristic Clint-esque humor, too, as exemplified when he enquires of the local minister regarding a group of people who have found themselves homeless:

"Are all these people your sisters and brothers?"

Minister. "They most certainly are."

The Stranger. "Well, then you won't mind if they all come and stay at your place."

The film is pervaded by a sense of strangeness; and there's an excellent moment as the townsfolk realize that the Stranger is leaving them to die at the hands of those whom they had turned in for doing their own dirty work. And, lest we forget, there's brilliant framing in Bruce Surtees' cinematography—especially when the Stranger stands in front of a burning building and the blur gives him the appearance of having horns. But, how should *we feel* after seeing this? I fear that we may feel justified in our delight that the town is punished rather than reflective about our own share in responsibility for the mistreatment of others. We all have guilty secrets—from the bullying or name-calling we participated in during grade school to our complicity in global social inequality. A telling line in *High Plains Drifter* says, "You don't want anything to happen to your town. But you won't do anything about it." This is often true, but unfortunately the Stranger's antidote to such apathy and irresponsibility is to kill those who wronged him. Walter Wink, the theologian of non-violent resistance, would hate this movie—it is the myth of redemptive violence writ large—but there is a suggestion in it that revenge is not a good idea: The Stranger has made no peace by the end of the film and merely moseys away from the town, much as he had moseyed in. Is he on his way to another site of revenge? Or has his spirit been freed to go to its final resting place? The film does not tell us. Also, as so often with Clint, it's easy to accuse this film of misogyny, but I'm not so sure that it's not simply cynical about *everyone.* (If you don't agree, then have a look at the fully rounded female characters played by Meryl Streep in *The Bridges of Madison County* and Rene Russo in *In the Line of Fire* as counter-evidence for Eastwood's hatred of women.)

I first saw *High Plains Drifter* on late night Friday television, with the picture being the only light in the room—the story is so dark that it was just as well the light in it is so great; cold, but breath-taking. It's a cruel film, but its values are not much different to the way we sometimes live today. Early in the movie, one of the characters who least wants to see the Stranger says, "It couldn't be worse if the devil himself had ridden right into Lago." Actually, *High Plains Drifter* couldn't be better.

HANNIBAL
(RIDLEY SCOTT, STEVEN ZAILLIAN, DAVID MAMET, 2001)

FBI Director: "What are you doing there in the darkness?"
Clarice Starling: "Thinking about cannibalism."

This is what happens when you give an art student a big budget. The opening credit sequence of "Hannibal" is a blatant rip-off from *Se7en* (but then again, what credit sequence since 1995 *hasn't* been?): CCTV cameras overlooking Florence, which give the impression of lacerating their subjects. As *Hannibal* begins, we may be forgiven for thinking that we're about to be assaulted by yet another "psycho-chic" thriller, of the kind so popular in the late 1990s (although it does have a great look to it, and the music is so romantic). After two-and-a-half viewings, I still don't know what to make of this film. It's not a film with much to say, but it's nicely put together—a dark and fleshy love story between two people who are more similar than anyone else in the film's world. And it is, quite frankly, the nastiest film from the Hollywood mainstream in a very long time.

Everybody knows Hannibal Lecter by now; we last saw him in *The Silence of the Lambs* having escaped the torments of Dr. Chilton's regime at his Baltimore hospital, preparing for a hearty meal at the same Dr. Chilton's expense. FBI Agent Clarice Starling had just been commended for her courage in bringing Jamie Gumm to American justice (which of course meant a bullet in the chest for Jamie), but now it's ten years later. She's unjustly under a cloud at work, while Lecter is on the ten most wanted list but making his home indulgently as a medieval librarian in Florence, how and where we might imagine he always wanted to live. So he wears a natty hat and cape and lectures on great Italian poets—you'll never guess which one preoccupies his particular psychic inferno—thoroughly pleased with his new, magnificently cultured and highly calibrated life. He obviously lives in a world where nobody has seen *Silence*, for he has made little effort to change his appearance—he's a few pounds heavier but appears ignorant of the advantages plastic surgery would give him if he wants to avoid detection. All seems well, and the good Florentines have little to worry about if they allow their guest to spend his days buried in five-hundred-year-old manuscripts and his nights reciting a Bach sonata on his opulent piano.[1] People are safe as long as they leave him alone or don't allow their mobile phones to go off during his lectures; as his former nurse says, "He told me he preferred to eat the rude—free range rude he called them." If only a pesky Italian cop hadn't stuck his nose in where it wasn't wanted. This new character, Detective Pazzi, is nicely ruffled, harking back to earlier ethnically esoteric movie cops—perhaps a bit like what Popeye

---

[1] Which reminds me that one of the best things about Lecter films is that they introduced me to the world of the great Canadian pianist Glenn Gould; there is something redemptive about cannibalism after all.

Doyle in *The French Connection* might have become if things had gone worse than they did. Pazzi is after the reward offered by the horribly disfigured Mason Verger, one of Lecter's earlier victims, played here with camp callousness by Gary Oldman, for the return of Hannibal. Verger claims to be a Christian, and like all good movie Christians, he wants to feed his worst enemy to killer pigs. Verger says, "I have immunity from the risen Jesus—and nobody beats the Ris …" [sic]—this is a cheap joke, but not surprising; it's been chic for a few decades to attempt to make Christianity look bad by refusing to engage with its better examples. (Although this type of film is not without an ironic symmetrical pair—there are plenty of films out there that try to make Christianity look good in a cheap way.)

The film stands as a good example of how different directors respond differently to the same material. There are now four Lecter films—*Manhunter, Silence, Hannibal,* and *Red Dragon.* Whereas *Silence of the Lambs* (Jonathan Demme, Ted Tally) was a tight procedural thriller, with its focus on the ticking clock and rescue of a Senator's daughter, and its precursor *Manhunter* (Michael Mann) [and its recent remake *Red Dragon* (Brett Ratner, Ted Tally)] was as much about the trauma of Will Graham, the man who first brought Hannibal to book as the thriller narrative, this nasty little story dwells on the darkness at the heart of Clarice—she is unable to shake off her past, and even by the end of the movie, she is in exactly the same position as before—married to her work and desperate to satisfy the ghost of her father. Scott's film uses broad brushstrokes, Mann is cold and clinical, Ratner provides a Hollywood thrill machine, and Demme focuses on the tension—four utterly distinct films.

It is difficult to discern whether or not this is a deeply cynical film, for it appears to raise questions to which it proposes inconsistent answers. Its philosophical values are incredibly immature—with one character first being sympathetically portrayed as kind to dead birds, then revealed as a collector of the memorabilia of psychopaths; also, the way in which we are meant to accept a qualitative moral difference in the violence of drug dealers, Verger, the FBI, and Lecter respectively; and the irresponsibility of making death by gun violence look like ballet. One of the more disturbing aspects of the film is the way Julianne Moore as Clarice is photographed—are we supposed to *look* at her the way Hannibal *talks* about her? The film doesn't reveal, as the book does, the roots of his cannibalism—and this may be the most ill-conceived interpretative decision of all. The author, Thomas Harris, tells us that Hannibal was a Hungarian child refugee at the end of the Second World War and that his beloved sister was killed and eaten by fleeing Nazis; therefore, his own cannibalism is a kind of macro-revenge. In reading the book, this elicited my sympathy, but the film ignores it altogether, which raises the question of who has the right to determine a character's psychological history and development—the author or the adapter? This is a question as old as cinema itself—from Sherlock Holmes to Dracula (another point of reference for Hannibal—he's a kind of vampire, and Ridley Scott cleverly makes him look like Max Schreck's Nosferatu in the scene where he is captured by CCTV filleting an Italian.)

The film is ravishing to look at and entertaining on a certain level (a blood red post box on a cold grey background and a thrilling little chase in a train station stand out as respective examples), but it is also problematic, for it wants to make evil attractive but knows that it can't go too far. It's okay, for instance, for Hannibal to kill an FBI director because he was part of the process, whereby Clarice has been undermined by the very authority she swore to uphold. Ridley Scott has underlined the film's amorality, saying that "Hannibal is pure in his own way— he only punishes those who deserve retribution." We may query how this "deserve" is defined, but I fear that the tyranny of the

Hollywood conveyer belt, serving up junk food blockbuster product after junk food blockbuster product, every month of the year, will squeeze out any space for reflection on this film. But we really need to ask how it could be that the most popular entertainment character of the 1990s was one of the most evil? Eugene Peterson once wrote that there is no one around whose actions are either good enough or evil enough to be interesting; *Hannibal* may challenge that statement, but the film does not have the intelligence to provoke an audience's mind. It evokes Dante but doesn't understand Dante; it wants to both horrify and entertain; to seduce us into enjoying a certain kind of evil and showing abhorrence to another; to find psychopathy attractive and legitimate authority repellent; in other words, *Hannibal* wants to have its cake and eat it too, preferably with a nice Chianti.

CHANGING LANES
(ROGER MICHELL, CHAP TAYLOR, 2002, CERT.15)

This is an important film. Perhaps the most serious examination of ethical dilemmas in a mainstream Hollywood film for several years, *Changing Lanes* tells the story of a chance meeting between two men, who crash their cars and spend the rest of the film attempting to undo each other's lives in revenge. Samuel L. Jackson and Ben Affleck attack their roles with gusto, and Sydney Pollack proves why he should devote more time to appearing on the screen than working behind it. It's tightly directed by Roger Michell, who made *Notting Hill*, but this is about as far away from Hugh and Julia's intelligent love-fest as you can get.

We are thrust during the opening titles onto a New York freeway and introduced to our two protagonists—an ambitious lawyer and recovering alcoholic. The lawyer is on his way to lodge some duplicitous documents in court, while the recovering alcoholic is hoping to gain shared custody of his children. Busy traffic changes their lives as they crash and one refuses to help the other. Saying more of the plot would spoil the film, so our analysis will have to begin here.

There are vast themes in this film—from doing the right thing, to racism, to selfishness, to addiction and the damage it does to families. The lawyer has to confront a key question, best summarized by his ex-girlfriend (Toni Colette), who serves as a kind of Greek chorus when she says: "Do you want what's right? And what's right is your job, your wife, your life?" He has to decide if the simple, ostensibly challenging pleasures of career and status and trophy wife and yacht are worth the price of amorality they are beginning to cost him. And later, the recovering alcoholic who has just beaten up two strangers begins to face up to his state in life when he sees himself as no different from the lawyer—who seemingly has power, but is in fact a hopeless case like the rest of us when left to our own devices: "He's a man of no honor. But that's okay because no one else has any honor either," as one character says.

The question of power is exemplified when one character finds himself bankrupt "because the computer says you are." The film has him throw the computer through a window, which may well be a natural response but does nothing to change the character's financial circumstances! He is locked into a system over which he feels he has no control, but the film leads him to a place where he can finally assert his own moral choices, in spite of the pressure to "join the crowd" and do the wrong thing.

Changing Lanes makes much of the theme of mentoring, with William Hurt's AA sponsor providing the moral anchor for Jackson's character, in much the same way that Colette brings clarity to Affleck's situation. A key scene has one character defending his theft of charitable funds by asserting: "I can live with myself because at the end of the day I think I do more good than harm. What other standard have I got to judge myself by?" But thankfully, the film does not let this comment rest without analysis. In fact, its final moments made it—for me—much more worthwhile than going to church the week I saw it: "The reward is doing the right thing" appears to be the film's manifesto, which makes it more like the Sermon on the Mount than much of what is proclaimed from many (tragically) self-help-hungry pulpits.

A PRIMER IN ANTI-HEROES

So here's some of the cinema's finest (or should that be darkest?) anti-heroes for your viewing pleasure: I recommend you start with Harry Lime in the wonderful British film from the late '40s *The Third Man*—this man fed poisoned penicillin to children, but we still laugh at his jokes—a bit like Pacino's Richard III, in *Looking for Richard*, who not only "can smile, and murder while I smile," but makes us smile while he's at it! (Check out Ian McKellen's version of the same character in *Richard III*). Another slyly humorous guy who kills people is George C. Scott's U.S. Army General George Patton in the Schaffner-Coppola film of the same name from 1970, but this book has hardly started, so I won't get too politically controversial yet. There's more bloodshed, too, in 2000's Brit gangster black comedy *Sexy Beast*, wherein Ray Winstone's world weary ex-gangman Gal Dove (geddit?) is seeking to live a quiet life but is forced by the monstrous Ben Kingsley to revisit his old ways before he can (literally) bury the past.

Cinema seems especially suited to the articulation of anti-heroic sentiment; you don't have to look too far to find one that appeals to your particular tastes. Robert de Niro's woefully conflicted gangster in Sergio Leone's 1984 masterpiece, *Once Upon a Time in America* shows how the basest desires (theft and the taking of life) can so easily co-exist with the highest ideals (love and service). Hitchcock's *Vertigo*, indisputably one of the greatest films ever made, provides a disturbing look into the life of a man whose necrophilia is all the most disturbing because he is played by James Stewart, that icon of the wonderful life, to whom we would previously have entrusted our very children. For another down home anti-hero, seek out the underrated *The Talented Mr. Ripley*, which shows how easy it is to descend from loneliness into psychopathy. I did not feel comfortable in my own skin after watching this.

For anti-heroes with a '90s twist, look no further than *Reservoir Dogs*, which to my mind is a far better film than its younger brother *Pulp Fiction*—its attitude to violence is profoundly moral, for one thing, and it isn't anywhere near as self-important. I could hardly breathe after seeing it; my mate Al and I drove home, and he said, "I wouldn't mind having that kind of lifestyle for a while. Without the violence, of course." I'm not sure what he meant, other than the potential coolness of wearing dark suits and dark glasses, but this masterpiece of nihilistic gangsterism went through me like a bullet. Not one for the Sunday school picnic, though. *The Usual Suspects* comes from a similar stable, but its story of Keyser Soze, the greatest anti-hero of them all, has a great deal more humor (but don't miss the opening two minutes like I did the first time I saw it; I hadn't a clue what was going on. And for those who still dispute who Keyser was, think long and hard about his initials.)

For anti-heroes with less violent tendencies, we should look to the suburbs. It seems almost redundant to iterate praise for *American Beauty*, but for all its popularity, it maintains the power to engross and surprise as we squirm through the decline and are given hope by the redemption of Lester Burnham, another wonderful Kevin Spacey evocation. Robert Duvall's *The Apostle* is a mostly undiscovered gem, wherein he kills a man and preaches the Gospel and almost convinces us he can do both with integrity. Another suburban anti-hero with spiritual resonance is Christopher Walken's Johnny in *The Dead Zone* a masterful, tragic thriller from David Cronenberg—one of the most important directors to seek out if you want to understand North American movies today. Walken always seems like he's either about to burst into tears, song, or gunfire, and Johnny is gifted/cursed with second sight. We see how such a burden would destroy its steward (and get to see Martin Sheen playing the anti-Bartlett). It opens beautifully with the fragmentation of suburban images growing progressively colder, and it is one of the most resonant, moving stories of tragic love and dangerous power. Cronenberg also directed the 1986 version (the good version!) of *The Fly*, with Jeff Goldblum decaying before us— the antithesis of the all-American, squeaky-clean sexmobile.

The Stranger in *High Plains Drifter* comes from a long and dishonorable line of Western anti-heroes, and it is, of course, a moot point to mention his heritage in films such as *A Fistful of Dollars, For a Few Dollars More*, and *The Good, the Bad, and the Ugly*. But you'll also find his antecedents in John Ford's magnificent *The Searchers*, where John Wayne clearly doesn't realize the damage he's doing to his image as he wreaks havoc in the search for his niece. Perhaps the best anti-heroic story in westerns is in Leone's *Once Upon a Time in the West*, which has three iconic anti-heroes to choose from: Charles Bronson as a harmonica-playing, gun-toting guy with a vengeance, Jason Robards as a crook on the run with a soft spot for the ladies, and Henry Fonda—of all people—as an assassin who doesn't think twice about shooting a child and tries to seduce a woman by raping her. There are vast themes in this film, not least of which is the ambiguous moral choice between three amoral men. A similar theme is found in Peckinpah's *The Wild Bunch*, made in the same year as Leone's film but with a distinctly different tone. It's about the end of an era, while the Leone deals with the beginning of one. Peckinpah is evidently in love with his violent men, and his film is wildly misogynistic, but as an elegiac testament to a (thankfully) bygone age, *The Wild Bunch* is in a class of its own. *Heat* is a kind of postmodern Western in that it focuses on a driven thief and his honorable pursuer; as the thief engages in that old chestnut, the "last job before I retire"; the parallels between thief and cop—both use violence to get their ends, both cannot maintain meaningful relationships, both have their own unusual code of honor—are possibly the strongest points of the film. It's near-namesake *Heist* by David Mamet is another thoroughly enjoyable slice of the underworld, with Gene Hackman explaining his method of wisdom thus: "I'm not very clever, so when I need to do something smart, I just think about what somebody cleverer than me would do, and then I do it." A metaphor for discipleship, perhaps? (And Kubrick's wonderful thriller *The Killing* makes a great companion piece for *Heist*.)

If Peckinpah's film tickles your fancy, and you want to see some more testosterone-fueled, angst-ridden violence, then *Fight Club*'s your show. Fincher's pulpy analysis of the condition of the postmodern male—he who has nothing to live or kill for—would work as a neat double bill with Clint's *Unforgiven*, in which he appears to atone for earlier sins of the *Man With No Name*. Perhaps the greatest name of all anti-heroes is the one I (and probably most readers of this book) grew up in awe of— Darth Vader. While I opened this story by disparaging *Star Wars*, and I still feel pretty much the same way, there is something to be said for *The Empire Strikes Back*, with its mythic revelation of Vader's true identity. Another larger than life anti-hero from the past, but this time with historical evidence to support his existence, is Antonio Salieri in Milos Forman's over-egged but still astonishing Mozart biopic, *Amadeus*. It is a testimony to F. Murray Abraham (where is he now?) that we miss him when he's not on screen, even after he (maybe) *kills* the hero. *Quills* is a dark little film (some would describe it as extremely disturbing) about the Marquis de Sade's battles with the Church; I found it remarkable for its witness to the value of human freedom and to how the institutional representatives of God so often corrupt the Gospel. When, in the final scenes, de Sade swallows a crucifix while lying naked and bruised, chained to the wall of a church-funded cell, we realize that although he may be rejecting the Church, he is embracing the divine.

For anti-heroes closer to (my) home, look no further than Richard Harris' finest characterization, that of the Bull McCabe in John B. Keane's tale of Irish land-idolatry *The Field*, wherein blood and right and tradition mix to disastrous ends. Jack Nicholson's full-blooded performance of Randall McMurphy in *One Flew Over the Cuckoo's Nest* brings to life another character trying to balance two communities—this time it's patients and nurses; he makes the mistake of being "different" in a rigid world and pays for it with his life—which perhaps makes him a cousin to Deckard in *Blade Runner*, who finds that he is not master of his own destiny when he sees an origami unicorn.

James Bond deserves a chapter to himself, but I couldn't face watching all the films again, so I'll just suggest that it may be worth reflecting on why such an amoral character who murders with impunity and treats women with the same disdain as an empty Martini bottle—a throwaway commodity—could inspire such popularity and get away with it?

Then we have anti-heroes in films about the media and politics. Anthony Hopkins may not look much like him, but his portrayal of *Nixon* brought out both the malevolent machinations and inner brokenness of this man—the scene in which he prays with Henry Kissinger should be textbook material for filmmakers wanting to learn how to film hypocrisy and truthfulness at the same time. Robert de Niro revealed his fine comic skills in Scorsese's undervalued *The King of Comedy*, wherein the textbook for celebrity stalkers is delineated with biting humor, and the end presents a satisfyingly bleak future for the media. This future is echoed in Sidney Lumet/Paddy Chayefsky's *Network*, as Peter Finch's neurotic anchorman encourages the American people to rise up and declare the fact that not only are they are not "totally satisfied with our service," but that the world has gone mad and that they aren't going to take it anymore. Of course Finch's character dies at the end; we could hardly have a happy outcome for a prophet. *Citizen Kane* is, of course, the archetypal anti-hero in the media, and it's well nigh impossible to write something new about it. I'll just say that, while not the greatest film ever made, it is everything else you've heard about it. And it's surprisingly compassionate for a film usually associated with attempts at destroying the reputation of William Randolph Hearst. Anti-heroes can be redeemed, in real life, and even in the darkest of films.

If those gems aren't enough for you, then try your luck with the following:

Both versions (1962 and 1991) of *Cape Fear* are worth watching; it describes revenge as the natural outcome of oppression and is intelligent enough (in the Scorsese re-make at least) to portray the victim family as being morally ambiguous. *Dirty Rotten Scoundrels* is, of course, not a very serious film, but these guys whom we end up loving are really a nasty piece of work. Just like the bad guys in *Fargo*—it's painful to watch William H. Macy's character descend further into hell all because he needs money and feels he has nobody he can ask for it (and Minnesota really *is* that cold). It's cold in Alaska, too, the evocative setting for *Insomnia*, where Al Pacino once again proves his brilliance at dealing with morally ambiguous characters but is met with more than a match in Robin Williams' character's troubled soul in a story of how one lie needs to build on another.

We don't often think of T.E. Lawrence as an anti-hero, but look again at the scene in *Lawrence of Arabia* where he struggles to cope with the fact that he has just killed a man—he says, "I enjoyed it"; we may fear that might be our reaction, too. *Miller's Crossing*—Why do we love people who kill so much? (Also has the best use of "Danny Boy" in a film.) *The Offence*—Sean Connery as his most realistic—a cop gone sour, beating a confession from a child murder suspect. This is the underbelly of "justice." *Raging Bull*—This is regularly acclaimed the best film of the '80s, but I'm not sure about that. Having said that, Scorsese's film of a boxer pummeled emotionally by his inability to let people in is dark and beautiful, but a little too "perfect" for my tastes.

Rope—This is one of Hitchcock's '40s thrillers and is notable both for the style (each scene was shot in a single take) and the substance (guys who kill someone just to see if they can get away with it). *Runaway Train* is a blustering explosion of a chase film, with Jon Voight's escaping criminal as the anti-heroic axis; he's trying to get out of the tundra and eventually straps himself to the front of a speeding train in a last act of defiance— and the audience is still rooting for him. *Rushmore*—Perhaps it's not the most obvious choice for this section, but Max Fischer, the failing high school student, is one of the most engaging anti-heroes in cinema. Jason Schwartzman and Bill Murray make this a lighter but deep film about loss and love, and it should mean a lot to anyone who was always chosen last for the team at school.

In Woody Allen's *Sweet and Lowdown*, Sean Penn plays

the musical anti-hero who can only express his love through music—everything else is rage and selfishness. I imagine he's a bit like a non-violent version of the protagonist of *Taxi Driver*, which plunges us into the tunnel of darkness in the soul of Travis Bickle, not so much played but *inhabited* by de Niro. It's a shame that his "You talking to me" monologue has become the stuff of frat party jokes because this movie is probably the most valuable exploration of the nihilistic impulses that can be triggered by loneliness—the kind of things that the Church exists to transform—but there is finally no healing for Travis because nobody cares enough to look at him until he has killed someone. If, after all this, you still have time for some more anti-heroic men on quests, then spend a weekend with *Barry Lyndon*, *Bugsy*, *Sleuth*, *Sling Blade*, and *A Clockwork Orange*. And, finally, I want to include *Topsy-Turvy* at this point, not simply to end this dark chapter on a lighter note, but because Mike Leigh's Gilbert & Sullivan biopic says more about both the consolations and struggles of the creative mind than you would ever expect. It doesn't lionize its heroes but simply paints what real life is like. So let it work its magic in you. It's easy to watch movies about anti-heroes and judge the protagonists, but hopefully we will remember the line between good and evil doesn't run between different people, but goes through the center of us all.

THE WRAP

Do we need anti-heroes? What do they *do* for us? Why are we so interested in the darker side of our nature? Are we simply bored with the blandness of everyday life? Is there a universal human impulse to explore what's crawling underneath the rock of our being? Artists in all media have thrown such questions around for millennia, from the author of the biblical story of

Saul, to the Jewish Golem myth, to Goethe's *Faust*, to Picasso's *Guernica*, to Harry Lime in Graham Greene's *The Third Man*, to the dastardly Montgomery Burns in *The Simpsons*. There's no reason to believe that they have exhausted the possibilities for an answer. Carl Jung believed that the human psyche could only be fully whole if it was *integrated*—that is, reconciled—to each half, light and shadow making peace with one another. The anti-hero myth is most helpful when applied to such attempts at integration. The honesty of declaring that we are all capable of both extraordinary good and extraordinary wickedness is in short supply in much popular art. When we see it, we are grateful, for such honesty presents us with an opportunity—to see our own reflection, or at least the reflection of our darkest potential, and to consider the possibility of change. Dishonest art portrays evil as something "outside" the rest and the best of us, something which we exclude and deny. Nowhere is this more striking than in American popular westerns and war films of the immediate post-Second World War period. The ideologically pure John Wayne archetype (if you're a political animal, for J. W. today, read George W. Bush) defeats the nefarious (and usually ethnically distinct) enemy, often employing the pseudo-religious justification of "a body for an eye, a country for a tooth." The audience is never allowed to consider the gray areas of the hero's psyche. The hero myth is ironclad protected from questions of moral ambiguity. Dishonest art perpetuates dishonest living. But honest art can be a gift, a lens through which human beings can see the possibility of psychic integration. As a member of the most psychologically disintegrated generation in history, I can't do anything else but welcome this.

CHAPTER THREE

BROKENNESS
IN WEAKNESS WE ARE STRONG

HANDS UP WHO HAS NOT BEEN CLINICALLY
depressed? Depression is the key psychological trait of our time,
and I believe it is one of the few areas where the insight of some
filmmakers is generally strong. Perhaps this is due to the well-
worn theory that creativity and melancholy are two sides of a
coin; maybe filmmakers are more likely to understand depression
from the inside … While it is the case that recent Hollywood
cinema has produced its share of whimpering characters who
claim that their "pain" at not having a "big enough" house
is equable with depression, there are plenty of more honest
examples of emotional darkness available. *Paris, Texas* is one of
those few films truly worthy to be called a masterpiece. The
film is centered on one man's inability to be centered himself.
However, many other Hollywood productions which claim to
"say something" about depression put me in mind of the article
published by *The Onion*, the hilarious/offensive prophetically
satirical web newspaper, describing the mid-life crisis of a
fourteen-year-old Sudanese army veteran: "I've already lived

half my life, my kids will eventually be conscripted themselves, and in fighting the civil war, I've done everything I planned to in this life. What am I going to do now?" But these films are not discussed here. There's a new one out every other week, so you don't need me to tell you what they are.

The relationship between creativity, spirituality, and depression has probably been over theorized, so here's my two cents worth.

THE PLEDGE
(SEAN PENN, 2001)

"A prophet is not without honor except in his hometown and in his own household." —Matthew 13:57

Sean Penn is often spoken of as a Hollywood rebel, as if the studio system is a military junta or dictatorial machine. There is some truth in both of these assertions, and *The Pledge*, his third film as director, is nothing if not a challenge to the sensibilities of an audience that wants only to be pleasured by explosive action, racy smut, and easy endings. This is a dark, compelling, and terribly depressing film about the kind of man we see every day on street corners, not smelling great and mumbling to himself. These folk are easy to step around or over, but *The Pledge* reminds us why we must never judge by outward appearance. A story of two murders—of a child at the start and of a man's soul throughout—this is impressive and significant cinema, and we should be grateful that Penn has not delivered on his earlier promise to retire from the movies and that his star, Jack Nicholson, is still prepared to take risks on camera.

When it opens, everything tells us that something isn't as it should be. Images of Nicholson's character Jerry Black mumbling drunkenly to himself, cold snow scenes, overhead shots of an ice-covered lake—the music and opening atmosphere are just right. It is so difficult to get an audience's attention without resorting to gunfire or sex, but Penn draws us in with beautiful blends between Jerry's face and black birds circling—a portent of things to come. Nicholson appears to trust Penn more than other directors and is prepared to do things for him that others aren't and things that he isn't willing to do for others. Nicholson is a towering figure in popular cinema who has not been disciplined enough with his choices; we're not used to seeing him not in control, but *The Pledge* divests him of this, taking him a million miles away from the pretensions of "You can't handle the truth!" in *A Few Good Men*. He plays a soon-to-be-retired cop who seems to have nothing in his life other than the job and fishing. He's a "two-time loser" in marriage and has no family except his colleagues, but even they want to see him gone. He glances out of his office window and sees an elderly couple struggling to walk down the street; this is what awaits him, and the rest of the film is about his attempt at providing himself with an honorable legacy. At his leaving party, he is clearly unhappy, and Penn frames him in the middle of a crowd of dancing celebrants, alone, the only person not having a good time. (This is representative of Penn's beautiful visual flair, as when a missed plane elliptically moves away from the concourse, or when we follow Jerry's four by four on a mountain drive.)

A child has been murdered, and Jerry chooses to stay involved in the case after telling the bereaved parents of their loss. They're good Christian folk, and, as is so often the case in the movies, these Christian folk do more to destroy than edify. After asking in anguish, "How could God be so greedy?'" the girl's mother makes Jerry swear "by his soul's salvation" that he will find the killer and makes him look at a cross when he does so. She is—however unwittingly—cursing him, and he is damned from this point. Jerry finds new purpose in investigating the case, closed by police bureaucracy and legalism, which in movies, of course, rarely gets to the heart of the matter; he becomes another in the long cinematic tradition of rebels who challenge the system. With its main character undermined by his former colleagues, shrinks, and bureaucratic pedantry, this kind of film usually seems to be saying that only the offbeat can find the truth, but they also tend to end with the vindication of the hero. But this is a different kind of film … He visits the father of another child victim, played by Mickey Rourke, proving himself to be more adept at investing even a cameo role with deep emotion than a hundred bigger stars; he weeps his paternal guilt, saying, "We just used to hold each other. I should have been able to protect her." He buys a gas station centrally located between the sites of similar murders, befriends local woman Robin Wright Penn (another Hollywood risk-taker), and waits. One day he sees a fishing program on television that encourages the use of live bait to catch bigger fish; it's a small moment, easily missed, but on this "hook" hangs the future of the protagonist. This is his undoing—to think that the impossibility of the oath he swore as a young cop can somehow be fulfilled, that he could protect the innocent from the chance of evil being done in a world where there is no community.

Three scenes stand out as exemplary of the director's craft: Penn blends the voices in Jerry's head with the psychiatrist's questions, with him perspiring just as she asks him if he has had sudden bouts of perspiration. There is a beautifully shot and acted scene of tentative love between two broken people, more poignant when we remember the director is married to one of the actors in the scene. This is soon followed by a quite brilliantly tense scene as Jerry races to the church where he believes the next murder is about to take place. But this film is not weighed down by beauty or tension—in spite of glorious photography and one of Hans Zimmer's best scores, it is not the aesthetic that lingers in the mind but the tragedy of a good man brought low by circumstance, fear, the mental disintegration of the post-modern world, and unfulfilled expectations.

There are nice little touches throughout the film, like a woman doing her toenails in an office, an orange peel ashtray, cutting to a clock with Jerry's failing to process a credit card transaction, the slow motion turning of a petrol dial as his madness begins to descend. Now *The Pledge* is not a perfect film: I would question for instance the use of "name" character actors—too many is distracting. I mean, I *want* to see Vanessa Redgrave and Sam Shepard and Helen Mirren, but they deserve to be given some meat to chew on rather than the character actor scraps here; nonetheless, it is a pleasure to see them when possible. We may also think that some of this film is a little too obvious—the fact that Jerry's surname is Black and the circling ravens as a portent of doom, for example, but the glass is most definitely half full. As I watched it with some of my closest friends, there was that rare sense of a collective experience, especially as our breath was taken by Mickey Rourke's character's anguish over his daughter's death. This kind of mutual emoting at the behest of film is one of life's rare gifts, and I am grateful that there are still films around capable of producing moments like these.

But why is it important to have films so dark and unrelenting? So hopeless and fearful about life? Because it reminds us who we sometimes are, what human nature can really be, why we must never stop living in the hope of what life can really be like. This film subverts our expectations; we know something bad is going to happen, but it isn't what we expect—it's a brave film, for it has the courage of its convictions. With one of the most depressing endings in a Hollywood film for a long time, *The Pledge* does not pull its punches or concede to our perceived need for catharsis—just like real life. The song over the end credits includes the line, "Watching goodness die a thousand deaths, we just turn our eyes away"; Jerry chose not to do this, and it killed him. Is this really what the reward for goodness is? I hope not, but it is good to have films like this once in a while as an antidote to the enervated, hermetically sealed, antiseptic, multi-nationalized leftovers casserole Hollywood usually serves up. It has believable characters and an involving story, and it touches on themes that are much bigger than the sum of its parts. It is a testament to Nicholson's skill in that he actually makes us believe he needs to look for furniture in what his character calls the "not-too-expensive to poverty-stricken range." For an hour or two, he ceases to be "Jack," the iconic figure who evokes a thousand Jokers of the past, and becomes ordinary Jerry Black, a fearful, tragic man who may remind many of us a little too much of ourselves. There is, finally, not a lot of hope in this film, and we are left with a sense that it seems to be agreeing with the ancient shibboleth that a prophet in his hometown is without honor, but a prophet may be anointed and also be mad. I suspect Ezekiel would recognize himself here.

MAGNOLIA
(1999, PAUL THOMAS ANDERSON)

"If you refuse to let them go, I will plague your whole country with frogs." —Exodus 8:2

Film, music, and literature are reflections of human values. This much is true; this much is a cliché. It may then be assumed that forgiveness will appear in these media in broad proportionality to its appearance in real life. I cannot produce statistics to confirm this or otherwise, but I suspect it isn't true. American popular cinema, in particular, reinforces what Walter

Wink calls the myth of redemptive violence—proposing that all problems should and can be solved quickly—and without any kind of moral consequence—by a loud thump (human or atomic, it doesn't really matter) from Herr Schwarzenegger. But there are treasures to be found, if we know where to look.

Magnolia is my second favorite film (*Wings of Desire* is the first, but we'll get to that German postmodern expressionistic film about angels becoming human later). For now I'll concentrate on this magnificent epic journey into the psyches of a few Los Angeleans over the course of one rainy day. It's impossible to explain this film to someone who hasn't seen it; come to think of it, it might also be impossible to explain it to someone who *has* seen it. But I'll try. The film begins with a discussion of the theory that there are no coincidences, that everything works together as part of a seamless, providential whole. Life is too strange to think otherwise, don't you agree? We are then thrust into a tale of trauma and redemption. A man lies dying from lung cancer, tended by a male nurse, while his much younger wife appears to be swayed by the neurosis of her looming grief. A boy and his father prepare for the boy's latest appearance on a combative adult/kid quiz show that makes the circus freak-shows of the past seem tame by comparison. The quiz show host is shown having sex with his secretary, before telling his producer that he also is dying. His wife waits at home, nursing the first of many large whiskey tumblers that she will need that day. His adult daughter picks up a trick in a bar and takes him home for a rough encounter that will pay for the rest of the day's cocaine. A self-help guru begins his seminar for the day, expressing his repellent sexist views on how to "trap women." A journalist arrives to interview him, sure that she knows more than we do. An electric goods salesman drives his car into a shop window and talks about his plans to have corrective dental surgery, even though there's nothing wrong with his teeth. A cop prays by his bed after listening to his own personals ad on the phone, and sets off for work. And the weather's not looking good at all …

There's a storm brewing at the heart of *Magnolia*, but before the catharsis of the remarkable downpour that climaxes the film, we get to spend a long time in the company of these broken people. Each of them has been responsible for causing pain to others, each of them has experienced their own trauma, each of them needs a shock to change direction. The film takes us into the heart of darkness, and it feels unpleasant, wrenching, painful to be there. This kind of darkness is all too often invoked as the excuse for Christians not to engage with such films. But I would contend that the contrary is true. Darkness and trauma and pain are the story of so much of our world. While it is not helpful for us to be weighed down by the sense of trauma that often surrounds us, it is irresponsible on the other hand to ignore this. I remember some friends telling me that they did not want to see *Schindler's List* because it would upset them too much. Well, that may well be the case, but perhaps there are occasions when the *only thing* we *should do* is to swallow our sense of self-protection and *allow ourselves to be upset.* Oprah Winfrey once told Steven Spielberg how she empathized with the "pain" it must have caused him to spend time making that film and asked him how he coped with it. His answer was succinct and affirmed his honesty: "Well, yes, it was painful to make that film, but not as painful as it was to live through the events that we were portraying." I think he would affirm *this* question: Is our sense of personal comfort more important than taking the pain of life seriously and perhaps being encouraged to *do something about it*?

Back to *Magnolia*. It would be unfair of me to tell you the whole story, so I shall just concentrate on one aspect. William H. Macy plays "Quiz Kid Donnie Smith," a man in his early forties who achieved temporary fame as a child on the very same quiz show/display cage that the other contemporary character endures in the film. He works in an electric goods shop and only has the job because of his long-lost celebrity. When he crashes his car and asks his boss for a loan to pay for his new braces, the employer, ironically named Solomon Solomon (the law of diminishing returns applies: twice the name = half the wisdom) fires him. Donnie makes his way through the driving rain to a plush bar, where he drinks tequila and observes from afar Brad the bartender, the object of his affection. Brad has braces, which look funny on an adult male but lend pathos to Donnie's dilemma. He wants Brad to love him and even explains that he's getting his teeth fixed to win his heart, but Brad's embarrassed, and a Machiavellian elder statesman at the bar interferes to prevent Brad and Donnie's relationship from going any further. We next see Donnie borrowing another car from a kindly, elderly lady and driving to his former place of employment, where he uses a key copy to break in and steal wads of cash from the safe. He has to shimmy down a telegraph pole to make his getaway, and while he's doing so, something very strange happens. Frogs fall from the sky, thousands of them. Some of them hit Donnie, and he falls to the ground, smashing his teeth in. A passing cop—the one we saw praying earlier, picks him up, dusts him off, and sits with him under a petrol station roof while the frantic din of the frogs drowns out their conversation.

Once we can hear it, we catch Donnie saying, through tear-stained eyes: "I really do have love to give. I just don't know where to put it." Then the two new friends silently return to the electric store, where the cop helps the thief return the money he stole. The cop gives Donnie his number and makes sure he gets home safely before returning to his tasks on the beat. The film ends with his voiceover:

A lot of people think this is just a job that you go to … But it's a twenty-four-hour deal, no two ways about it, and what most people don't see is just how hard it is to do the right thing. People think that if I make a judgement call then that's a judgement on them, but that is not what I do. And that's not what should be done … Sometimes people need a little help. Sometimes people need to be forgiven. And sometimes they need to go to jail. And that is a very tricky thing on my part, making that call … You can forgive someone. Well, that's the tough part. What can we forgive? Tough part of the job. Tough part of walking down the street.

Some people need to be forgiven. It is rare in a Hollywood film to see the guilty be treated in such a fashion. Donnie is representative of so many of us, with his anguished cries about where he should put his love, and his desperation for community, and his anxieties about the future. He doesn't like or love himself because he has been shown so little love by others. And when he reaches what he thinks is the point of no return, of irrevocable immoral choice, by stealing from Solomon, it is not with a sense of triumph that his financial problems are solved. He steals the money with one hand, while the other is metaphorically covering his eyes because he can't face what he's done. But the intervention of God (what else could the plague of frogs mean?) should not be read as a punishment. Rather, in much the same way as a parent will slap their child's hand away from the fire, it is God's mercy that sends this torrent. Donnie falls to the ground—much like we have fallen as a race—but the divine allows him to be caught by grace. In this sense, Donnie is everyman. The "Christian" response to Donnie may be to initially despise him; but he is me and you and all of us. Where do we put our love? Does anybody truly understand us? Don't we *all* need to be forgiven? In other more mainstream films, Donnie would be a peripheral character, or would not appear at all. He would not be considered interesting or exciting enough; no four-star babe will want to bed him. So we will have to put up—yet again—with more flaccid, superficial eye candy and the myth of redemptive violence. *Magnolia*, thankfully, is wiser than most. We see a man like us, and we see him being treated with dignity. "What can we forgive?" is the question posed by this film. And while its answer seems to be "Most, but not everything," it comes closer to a piece of Christian prophecy than most sermons I've heard. There are universes of life inside this film, and we would do well to see ourselves within it, too.

PARIS, TEXAS
(1984, WIM WENDERS, SAM SHEPARD)

I used to think that Thomas Merton, that saint of real life mysticism; who left this earth too soon, was too wise to have lived in the twentieth century. But then I saw his character pop up in Robert Redford's excellent little horror film *Quiz Show* and realized my mistake—his was a profoundly modern spirituality, with the gift of connecting ancient truth claims with contemporary reality, just what we need in these troubled times. Merton said that no one can find true life "unless you have risked your mind in the desert." There's something about the truth of Sam Shepard's writing in *Paris, Texas* that leads me to believe Shepard must be familiar with Merton, and not just because it's about a man wandering in the kind of desert that has real sand and baking sun. This movie is about that most common of modern malaises (and my soapbox)—community breakdown, but before we get to that, let's have a moment's silence in honor of great opening title sequences ... This one is red on black, and it somehow fits right in with the burning drama of one man's broken heart and the starkness of what happens when people break faith with each other. Whoever coined the phrase "the desert of the real" (and I'm pretty sure Morpheus got it from someone else) may have stolen it from this movie, which opens with exceptionally beautiful shots of a lonely man appearing out of nowhere in a barren landscape, watched by a hawk. The metaphor is not strained, but we're gradually made aware that this man is troubled by how deep the talons of his past have sunk into his soul. He almost looks like a cartoon character—evocative of the Road Runner's nemesis, Wile E. Coyote, after a nervous breakdown. Then when we see his face in close up, we realize that it's Harry Dean Stanton and know that his story must be even worse than that poor animated wolf's inglorious end. It isn't long before he's on a hospital gurney, looking like Jesus. (Wile E. Coyote, Harry Dean Stanton, and Jesus—now there's a triumvirate to make up a *very cool* dinner party.) Stanton's character, Travis, is mute, unlike the guy in real life (especially if you go to see him play with his jazz combo in L.A.'s Mint night club on a Saturday night—the poor man has what I might generously call an "interesting" sense of what singing is, but he certainly runs a tight band). His face is heartbreaking for the audience—when he looks in a mirror he has to run away—and I wonder if that experience is closer to home for more of us than would like to admit it.

Something BAD has happened to him, as he says, "A lot can happen to a man in four years. All kinds of trouble." And his experience has made him different—his shoes are "one size bigger," but that's just the tip of his iceberg; we're watching a dead man walking, trying to find out if he can ever go home, staring into the long distance, searching for "her," or freedom from the past. Which, I suppose, is what all of us, to some degree, at some points in our lives, are looking for.

So, anyway, his brother comes to pick him up, showing both real grace (he'd rather have him confess to horrible misdeeds than to say nothing) and an aptitude for making Travis feel worse about himself (he has the perfect wife and work and wealth, while Travis has nothing but the past). In the early scenes between them, we see how brothers—whether biological or spiritual—can unwittingly bring both love and a sense of competition. Travis joins his movie namesake, Mr. Bickle from *Taxi Driver*, on a journey inward, into his own heart of darkness, and we're privileged to join him. We follow him to where he meets and bonds with the son who is too young to remember him, and we discover that something bad happened to break their relationship. It's mysterious, but not a mystery film; it's set in the West, but it's not a western; it's funny in places, but it's not a comedy. *Paris, Texas* is well nigh uncategorizable, if indeed such a word exists. We see that Travis owns a piece of land, but he says he can't remember why he bought it. This made me think of how we sometimes get to the stage of forgetting why we did certain things that were important in the past, but not anymore, lost in the mists of time. Of course, buying fields is an honorable biblical activity, whether it be those that host pearls of great price or those that hold the dead bodies of broken traitors. Maybe Sam Shepard was thinking of such plots of land when he wrote this. There's something about land in the history of our faith that resonates with the deeper emotions of the human spirit, so it's easy to understand how Travis' plot gives him dignity, in spite of it being little more than a small patch of dust bowl.

Aside from the land, we discover that Travis has also lost the love of his life, who—thanks be to God!—is played by Nastassja Kinski at her most realistically beautiful. The film paints the depth of their love by screening an old home movie, the camera dancing round them as they play on the beach with their son. This is one of the great cinematic scenes of what true love is really like—the audience may resonate with or feel envious toward the way the characters touch each other's faces and lips. The son says, "Is that my mom?," and Travis replies, "It's not really her, it's only her in a movie." Probably the most appropriate answer, for in a sense this scene is about the power of cinema to touch us. Travis and the boy travel to meet the mother, who is working in a kind of brothel for people who don't touch each other. Travis talks to her through a screen, like a bank teller to a customer. A long scene ensues where Travis breaks our hearts with the story of their love and how it broke; he retells how their affair ended: "He just lay there in bed and listened to her scream … he didn't feel anything anymore, all he wanted to do was sleep. He wished he were far away in a deep vast country where nobody knew him."

The two lovers are relating through a screen, which is not unlike how this generation uses computers to relate—this reminds me that we need to take care that we don't stop touching each other. Travis is letting her go by telling her of his love, but also telling her that he realizes he cannot be an adequate father to their child. The regret for things past—and the idea that dependent love can trap—is palpable. They have to turn away from each other to communicate the deepest thoughts, and the scene is so uncomfortable that I wanted to turn away from the screen, too. And we, the audience, become so caught up in the story of their love that we want the closure of them ending up together—which I suppose represents our desire to forgive them both for their failures, for being too much like us, really.

There are so many riches in this film, from the evocation of fatherhood with a dad having fun with his kid by walking backward down the street, to Ry Cooder's music, which is so good I don't want to say anything about it because it deserves to be allowed to speak for itself, to the drive-thru bank that somehow looks like a spaceship, to Robby Muller's poetic use of color (red for lifeblood, which eventually moves from the background to consuming everything at the moment of redemption), to the lifetime of pain that is etched onto Harry Dean Stanton's face. As we travel along with Travis, the film provokes us to think about the injustice of the U.S. healthcare system (Christians really *should* have something to say about this) and how owning a little bit of land can grant dignity, and it even manages to evoke how small-town America actually *feels*. This is not a film to escape into but one that is more real than most about brokenness and suffering—just like family life. It speaks of the resurrection of a dormant soul and is a good model of what I might call "healthy non-closure"; by which I mean it is honest about the loose ends that we often find ourselves left with.

There is no total closure other than God—if those who hunger and thirst for righteousness will be filled, then so will Travis, who wants to put things right and move on with his life. Depression, brokenness, and being an outsider so often give people better vision—they see the truth more clearly, or, as someone has said, "Thinking people don't sleep as well." And I guess this is the curse of the prophet—people of faith who want to see the truth and build the kingdom of God will often find themselves struggling deeply with their own sense of happiness and self-esteem. It is important not to become overwhelmed by the "birth pangs" of creation, the "groans" for redemption that St. Paul speaks of; but it is more important to listen for them and to respond by helping yourself, and others, to become more human. Sometimes this means "losing" in the short term, but true humanity takes the long view. Four years in the desert for Travis is a blink of an eye for God, and God, of course, will not let you be tested beyond what you can bear. There is more than enough grace in the universe to cope with your brokenness and mine, whatever its source or consequences. The strangest moment in this film has Travis pass by a man on a bridge, shouting shibboleths at the interstate traffic below like the war veterans we have all seen in urban America: "There will be no safety zone," rhymes his portent of doom. Travis quickly passes by, perhaps not to be "infected" by whatever demon has possessed this brother. But there is a look of recognition between them, as if Travis is saying, "I know where you have been."

Earlier, Travis tries to drive in the right direction after getting lost and indicates the antidote to such meta-pessimism, and this may be *Paris, Texas'* greatest gift to us, the broken audience: "I don't know where I turned off, it didn't have a name ... but I can find our way out again." The prophet on the bridge may sound too close to home when he says, "There will be no safety zone"; maybe that's where you or I are at right now. We may not know where we turned off the road, but we can find our way out again. There is a safety zone for the broken. If the grace of God isn't enough for Travis, a man who once tied his wife to a stove, then it isn't enough for me. The film ends with mother and son reunited and Travis bathed in a green light—almost like he's going to be taken to space. It's a fresh beginning, and he allows himself a satisfied smile—he has forgiven himself, done something right, and perhaps will again. Surely this is the meaning of redemption—not what we've done, but how we respond to it when we receive grace? If so, Wenders' and Sheperd's film is worth our time and attention. It's a slow journey, but it might just change your direction.

A PRIMER IN BROKENNESS

If you like travel and don't mind a bit of grief, *The Accidental Tourist* might be just what you need, as William Hurt and Kathleen Turner express their loss at the murder of their son, and Anne Tyler reminds us why she's one of those writers everyone needs on their shelves. There's more death and grief on this screen than is comfortable, but love—real love—is shown to conquer all, in the subtlest of ways. Love makes the difference to the broken in *Leaving Las Vegas*, although this doesn't have a happy ending; but if you want to face up to the realities of alcoholism, then Nicolas Cage's performance will imprint itself on your mind. Illness and addiction tread their tragic paths through some great films: You could make a start with *Naked Lunch*; the deeply moving *Longtime Companion* (the first mainstream film to take HIV/AIDS seriously, well before *Philadelphia*); Ken Loach's painfully true *My Name is Joe*; and the film with Michael Keaton's best performance, *Clean and Sober*.

It's become a cliché that the Academy will always reward actors who play people with emotional or physical challenges to surmount. The fewer mental or physical faculties, the more golden statues seems to be the logic. If we get past the cynicism, there are a few such films worth taking a couple of hours of your time. *Scent of a Woman* may not be the most honest of films, but demands to be seen for the family dinner scene at which Al Pacino's angry blind man offends everyone; this is a painfully embarrassing scene, which may resonate with us all. Personally, I have a soft spot for *Rain Man*—people who know tell me that Dustin Hoffman's portrayal of an autistic man is note perfect, but I admire this film mostly for what it says about forgiveness between siblings. *My Own Private Idaho* was little seen even after River Phoenix died, but his narcoleptic character is one of the most moving performances in recent cinema. *Memento* is a cool little film about a man with amnesia—if we can't remember what we've done wrong, are we still responsible for it? *The Butcher Boy* is probably my favorite film about Ireland, and it uses a psychologically disturbed young man as the lens through which it examines the pain of my country's history (and has a few trenchant things to say about the institutional Church's propensity for distorting the Gospel).

Another Irish film with the Church at its center is *Lamb*, about a priest (played by Liam Neeson) trying to care for a troubled little boy, whom he finally kills to put out of his misery. The film ends with Neeson screaming in agony as he fails to take his own life—we can change things for others, but not always for ourselves. Similarly, the central character in *Bringing Out the Dead* is a paramedic who is dying on his feet as he tries to rescue others. He lives with suffocating guilt because he could not save one girl and cannot move on with his life. This is one of Scorsese's most explicitly religious films—it ends with the paramedic in the arms of a woman, as the sun rises upon them; they are obviously meant to look like Mary and her innocent child.

Slightly older kids appear in *Rebel Without a Cause*, which still has value nearly fifty years on; anyone who has ever been a teenager will identify with this one. *Naked* and *All or Nothing* (both by the great British writer-director Mike Leigh) deal with alienation among young people and their families and the damage that bad work does to people; one ends with the hero in worse straits than before, the other with signs of redemption. You need to watch them both, so I won't tell you which is which. (One of my few claims to fame is that Mike Leigh and I once found ourselves leaving early from a screening of one his films at the same time; pretty humiliating for me, and I guess he'd seen it before ...) Finally, to keep up with my attempts at ending chapters on happy notes, after you've immersed yourself in all this brokenness, do yourself a favor and watch *As Good as it Gets*, which manages to be both serious about the challenge of obsessive-compulsion and as funny as having a bath in chocolate.

THE WRAP

Christians often shy away from depression (at least in public); it seems not to fit with our belief in the redemptive properties of discipleship. Just pray like Jabez and all will be well. This is strange, because Jesus and Prozac are not the same thing, in spite of what the televangelists tell you. He is not a mystical anti-depressant, there to carry us through all our troubles and make us sleep well at night. Discipleship is not the antidote to feeling sad. In fact, we would do well to remember that even Jesus got so anxious about His destiny that He sweated blood. I've only seen that happen once—it preceded a major epileptic seizure in a friend; ironically, it was during a prayer meeting. It was not a pretty sight. It underlines the fact that people who sweat blood are experiencing just about the most intense emotional agony available in the range of human possibility. Jesus knew this pain. He was lonely. He was doubtful. He was afraid. He must have wondered at times if He was insane. He may well have asked Himself if He was just talking to a voice in His head when He was praying. And the other biblical figures whom Christian tradition holds up as examples, from Moses to Elijah, Mary to Paul to John, and the post-biblical heroes of the faith from Martin Luther to Dietrich Bonhoeffer to Dorothy Day have all known the creeping, chest-tightening adrenaline flow of fear and anxiety, or the baying of the black dog of melancholia at their doors.

In the church of my youth, we used to sing a song that had the line, *And in His presence, our problems disappear.* But that's a lie, or at least an unhelpfully exuberant way of putting it. Jesus will not make all your problems go away. In many ways, He is there to make your life *more* difficult! "Take up your cross and follow me" is hardly a recipe for emotional highs. No, following Jesus, or indeed, following any serious religion, is a difficult task. Our pain is real and may well stay real. Of course, there is healing, but I'm not sure it is the same kind of healing that some preachers proclaim. Lazarus, after all, died *again* after being resurrected. The real miracle of discipleship is that it can lift our field of vision to something higher than ourselves, and it should provide an organic community of fellow travelers to accompany us, bear each others' burdens, and lighten the load. Believe me, I've been carried a *lot* by my friends. And sometimes therapy or medication *is* a great idea, so don't ignore that if it's what you need (I, like pretty much every other Gen-Xer, can attest to the value of both friendship and the analytic couch). But I do wonder if the malaise of our generation is not largely influenced by us having far too great expectations of life; we are taught to expect a high-paying job and a fast car and a hermetically sealed detached house and hermetically sealed detached family, when these alleged treasures are really only available to the few. But we can build something much greater than material success if we commit ourselves to the spiritual community, do a little bit of sharing, and seek first the kingdom of God.

Our old friend Marcel Proust was no stranger to depression, spending much of his life in bed, weakened physically by various ailments, and near-paralyzed emotionally by the worst ailment of all: that of seeing the world as it is. He knew something that most of us shy away from—that we are from dust, and to dust we shall return. And, like so many great artists, he was able to find the kind of redemptive hope that does not deny the truth of our existence, but simply makes good use of the brief moment we have on earth. Marcel once wrote, "Aesthetically, the number of human types is so restricted that we must constantly, wherever we may be, have the pleasure of seeing people we know." If he had been around today, he might have been referring to movies about brokenness. And, at the risk of seeing yourself too often, I hope we might all be more attentive to the brokenness of characters we see on screen; this world needs all the compassion it can get.

In the final analysis, or at least in my mid-term conclusion, these films remind us that there is a need for human beings to be honest about their own brokenness. We're all broken people trying to keep our lives under control, and it seems that few of us know how to succeed at that task. If you do, write and let me know; as for the rest of us, maybe the best we can say is that Jesus was broken, too, and knew the importance of friendship enough that He always brought eleven with Him. So if this chapter, or more to the point, these films, stir up your own sense of brokenness, don't suffer in silence. There is a community of people somewhere near you who need the gift of your pain to make them whole. And the divine is as close as your heartbeat. Only you can take the step you need to in the direction of healing. But you don't have to take it alone.

CHAPTER FOUR

CONSPIRACY

IT'S NOT PARANOIA IF THEY'RE REALLY OUT TO GET YOU

GROWING UP IN NORTHERN IRELAND, IT'S HARD not to develop a conspiratorial mindset. There was a lot of death around when I was a kid; the fact that our long-term social conflict was significantly influenced by religion made it all the more confusing. I mean, why would Christians want to kill each other? One of those strange questions that you can only answer when you've plumbed the depths of pain yourself, I guess. Anyway, living where I do, it was easy to feel afraid of what might be around the next corner, or that my dad might be dead just because he was late coming home from work. "It's not paranoia," as the former host of *Politically Incorrect* Bill Maher once said, "if they're really out to get you."

There's something quite disturbing about the way that our generation is taught to fear, that to get ahead we must trample on each other because someone else is always planning our downfall. There is wisdom in being "wise as serpents, but innocent as doves," as Jesus would put it. But I would put the emphasis on the innocence—not naivety—a wide-eyed wonder at the world that is prepared to have faith in its beauty and in the others made in the image of God who inhabit it alongside us. This, I know, might get you killed, but I guess that's something people who want to follow the path of truth will just have to put up with. Can you imagine what life would be like if, instead of keeping up with the Joneses, or maintaining a stealth-like approach to our next-door neighbors to the point of letting our lives permanently run at DEFCON 4, we simply trusted in the goodness of humanity?

Having said that, I must admit that conspiracy theory movies are among my favorites; I love the sense of keeping up with a convoluted plot, of not knowing who the bad guys are, and of the final revelation, which in the '70s meant death or destroyed reputation for the hero, but unfortunately has to be tempered by a little more Hollywood sugar these days. There is a seemingly insatiable human need to be brought to the edge of our seats, allowing our pulses to race and our palms to sweat, as we are gripped by a hero's dilemma. The detonator clock ticking away precious seconds as Mel and Danny decide which wire to cut (it's always the blue one), the fugitive desperately trying to cut free from a bus crash just asking to be hit by a train, Jodie grabbing her phone before jumping into the appropriately named panic room before the bad guys see her, Indy ducking at just the right moment before ancient blades slice a millimeter above his head … these are some of the defining moments of popular cinema. And although—perhaps because—these kind of things almost never happen to "real people," we love them, we love to watch them, we love to feel just a little bit of vicarious adrenalin. It would be pessimistic to say that this is because we think our own lives are boring, but that may be the sad truth. However, just as the Christian mystery writer Dorothy Sayers thought that reading a good whodunit could release metaphysical tensions in ordinary people, perhaps preventing us from doing ill to our brothers and sisters, movie thrillers may just be able to do the same. So, let off some steam, and enjoy this brief sojourn through the conspiracy movie consciousness. And don't worry, the good guy (usually) wins. So, you might want to cast your eye over these treats. Just don't let them shape your view of the world too much.

MINORITY REPORT
(STEVEN SPIELBERG, SCOTT FRANK, 2002)

"If a man is considered guilty for what goes on in his mind then give me the electric chair for all my future crimes."

So said "the artist formerly known as the artist formerly known as Prince" [sic] in his *Batman* soundtrack. Prince was prescient, for this also is the theme of the new Spielberg/Cruise hybrid *Minority Report*, a beautifully structured future noir and a rich seam of theological argument. Based on Philip K. Dick's short story, we find ourselves in a dystopian future (is there any other kind in cinema?), where people are convicted of murders that they may commit later, whether premeditated or not. Three "pre-cogs," genetically modified humans, gifted and cursed with the ability to see the future (like particularly neurotic charismatic Christians) form the key to this system. The "pre-criminals" are doomed to end up in their own personal hells, trapped in physical and mental limbo for eternity. The logic that leads them there is foolproof (evidenced by the fact that it is controlled by Max von Sydow, the most serious of Ingmar Bergman's leading men) until our hero (flawed and broken, to be sure, but still played by Tom Cruise, so ironically we know the outcome of the film in advance—Cruise has yet to end a film on an unhappy note), is named as a future killer and must go on the run. Cue a great deal of astonishing action set pieces and much Cruiseian angst, until a fairly predictable but nonetheless gripping denouement (including rural peace for the pre-cogs, like a permanent country retreat for the prophecy-anxious) lets us leave the theater with some degree of closure.

The film seeks to examine the age-old question of free will vs. predestination, and although it leaves most of the philosophizing to the audience, it still provides some striking moments, particularly when characters realize they have a choice about their futures. As for its "message," *Minority Report* assesses an American state where government interference in people's lives has gone into overdrive. Citizens' every movements are monitored unless they sacrifice their eyes—nice irony here, as the powers that be seem to say, "You can see as long as we can watch." The film's Attorney General echoes recent disturbing developments in actual U.S. policy when he defends this extraordinary abuse saying, "That which keeps us safe will also keep us free."

I needed a Spielberg film in this book, and although *Minority Report* is not my favorite, spiritual resonance abounds here, from the comment that the pre-crime police are "more like clergy than cops" (Fuller Seminary even gets a name check), to the use of Bach's "Jesus, Joy of Man's Desiring" to keep the pre-criminals soothed in their prison. The government is playing God, using an all-seeing eye to prevent murder. The rub comes in the fact that one character has killed another to allow the system to proceed—committing a grievous crime to avoid further grievous crimes. We are faced with the question of how free we should be—if such a system as pre-crime actually existed, should Christians support it? Or should we be free to choose, even if that choice includes the possibility of murder? If the alternative were a system that punishes people's intentions, whether or not they commit a crime, what would John Calvin say? The Attorney General says, "Even if the system is perfect, we are not," which could also be a description of the Garden of Eden. However, God's response to this, thankfully, has been the offer of mercy, not to judge our misguided motives and temporary anger. Some say that Spielberg has only faced up to darkness in his films since he got older and stopped being one of the so-called movie brats. I disagree—the shark in *Jaws*, the government in *Close Encounters* and *E.T.*, and the husband in *The Color Purple* are all deeply drawn representations of what might face us in the night. But I do think that he has developed a clearer focus and critical faculties. Although *Minority Report* does not deal with its own arguments in any kind of detail, it does at least raise important questions. It is intelligent enough to provoke me to think that while human intention cannot be disregarded, the predictable future is not the actual future if we act to change it. The real minority report is the narrow path—that when the chips are down, rather than be selfishly bent solely on our own survival, choose to love mercy, and to do justly, and to walk humbly with our God. *Minority Report* is mature enough to allow the audience to make its own choice.

NORTH BY NORTHWEST
(ALFRED HITCHCOCK, ERNEST LEHMAN, 1959)

I have a problem with Alfred Hitchcock. His films have so comprehensively entered the popular consciousness that it is impossible to come to them fresh, even if we have never seen one before. Something about *North by Northwest* prevents it from being a tense experience for me; similar to the fact that our folk knowledge of what happens in *Psycho* prevents us from feeling excited or scared. Even if we have never seen it, we know who did it, and why (s)he did. Thankfully, this doesn't at all inhibit our delighted wonder at these works of genius. *NXNW* is perhaps Hitch's most perfectly realized marriage of thrills and laughs, as a flamboyant anti-hero (Cary Grant) is mistaken for a spy and spends the rest of the film running from (and into) James Mason's heavies. His character's name is "Roger O. Thornhill"—he says the "O" stands for nothing, and this is one hollow guy. I think this is a none-too-subtle way of representing the ROT of the upper-middle class that Hitchcock, the working-class miner's son, despised. He has a perfect tan and handmade shoes, like Grant himself; he's a "little more polished than the others."

The story is at once simple and convoluted—Thornhill is mistaken for a spy and kidnapped by some nefarious bad guys led by James Mason and his "special friend" Martin Landau. There are two chases—by car and plane (the buildup to which is a masterpiece of editing and mise-en-scene)—a couple of fights, some spectacular set-pieces, a femme fatale (or is she?), a government conspiracy, and our hero gets the girl. What more could we want? But I think it is a mistake to see *NXNW* as a simple action comedy—it's riddled with metaphorical bullets and aesthetic pleasures. For one thing, the dialogue is some of the most sparkling Hitch ever worked with. We discover that there is "no such thing as a lie, merely the expedient exaggeration." Mason has a marvellous moment of villainy when he says, "The least I can do is afford you the opportunity of surviving the evening." I was reminded of how funny it is on a recent viewing when, for example, Cary says, "Not that I mind the odd case of abduction once in a while but I've got tickets for the theater tonight," or responds to "I'm a big girl" with, "Yes, and in all the right places." The story is beautifully structured, building mystery and tension (in spite of Grant's inability to play drunk in a key scene; he's clearly having a lot of fun, and so are we.) But there is much more than humor and action here—I think Hitchcock is using Grant's character as a commentary on modern superficiality and relationships.

Thornhill is an advertising executive, and I guess some might think you can't get much more superficial than that. He runs away from his mother while being chased by people who want to kill him, so we get some of Hitch's trademark misogyny and distrust of parents; the romance between Grant and the divine Eva Marie Saint is totally unconvincing—Cary can't kiss for toffee. He's so cold and dispassionate that if I thought Hitch were more cynical I would say he's trying to make a point. This same point is alluded to in the relationship between Landau (one of Hitch's stereotyped gay villains) and Mason—there's all kinds of weird sexual stuff here, from Mason accusing Landau's character of jealousy and saying he's flattered to the downright crass—but hilarious (the use of a train speeding through a tunnel as a saucy metaphor).

So, *NXNW* isn't a particularly profound film, but it does present an archetype of the anti-hero as cad. Thornhill is morally without foundation; he's selfish and a user of women, but he's enormous fun to be around (in small doses). The icy blonde is portrayed as far stronger and more intelligent, and Grant is obviously older than the actor playing his mother, so it's pretty clear that Hitchcock doesn't particularly like his protagonist. He's the kind of guy you'd invite to a cocktail party but never go on vacation with. *NXNW* is a story based on coincidence upon accident upon downright naïve construct switching back through predictable denouement, but still thoroughly entertaining. The use of soundstages is pretty awful—the trees even shake in one scene, and if this had been directed by somebody else, I'm almost certain it would not have the reputation. Still, for what it is, the breeze that blows through *NXNW* is a refreshing one, while its central character is a reminder of what we can be like if we lack a moral compass.

THE CONVERSATION
(FRANCIS FORD COPPOLA, 1972)

Francis Coppola's *The Conversation* has a beautiful opening shot with a very strange angle, looking down on people, a Big Brother's eye view of what's happening. This, in itself, is the whole point of the film—that someone may always be watching us, we never know who or when or where. The first image we see of bugging equipment is very sinister—it looks like a gun, and this reveals Coppola's negative view of snooping early on. I remember thinking that this could be a brilliant political thriller as soon as I first saw the moustachioed guy with the earpiece who makes his appearance on the plaza where people are going about their business as we eavesdrop. I was glad to find that the film just gets better. This opening scene is a tour-de-force, as cameras flow everywhere, and we hear what the people buzzing around like flies hear. The protagonist, played by Gene Hackman, is called—in a slightly obvious irony—Harry Caul; he disagrees with the audience when, from inside the van from which he is carrying out the surveillance we're watching: *I don't care what they're talking about, all I want is a nice fat recording.* We gradually realize that we're following a couple walking in circles, carrying on an obscure conversation. They pass by a homeless man, sleeping on a bench, and the woman says, "He was once somebody's baby boy." (Look at the subtle response in Hackman's face when he hears that again—we learn something more about him in that moment; he's obviously given to loneliness, and there's something of the lost "baby boy" about him, too.) We follow Harry home along sharp camera angles and find that his warehouse apartment is about as vacant as he looks. He makes a phone call in which we discover the measure of the man—he talks to a person who sent him a birthday present, thanking her, but asking her not to do it again. His paranoia is evident: "How did you know it was my birthday? I'd be quite happy to have all my personal belongings burnt up in a fire because I don't have anything personal."

We discover that there's rivalry in the bugging field, and learn that businesses (and therefore politicians) make substantial use of the buggers (Harry is referred to as "the guy that told Chrysler that Cadillac was getting rid of its fins"). These guys are professional liars, very unusual people; Harry's merely the most neurotic of a very neurotic bunch. I better not say any more about the plot—the pleasure of this film is in not knowing what happens before you see—or, more accurately, hear—it. So I'll underline that Coppola's skill in the writing and direction in this film is just about unrivalled—the moment when Harry hides from nothing at the top of the stairs of his girlfriend's house took so much imagination to create, and there is real pathos when she tells him, "When I heard you coming down the stairs my toes were dancing under the covers, but I don't think I'm going to wait for you anymore."

In its fragmentary journey, *The Conversation* unsurprisingly focuses on one conversation, and takes in the banality of killing (as one clearly murderous character offers another "some nice Christmas cookies"), the need to listen closely to what others are saying and the soullessness of doing things for the sake of money alone. It's the best kind of thriller, revealing layers at just the right unexpected moment, and there is a richness to be found in watching it again once you know (or think you know) what's going to happen. (Another thing to love about this film is the fact that the central character is a jazz musician, but I guess that's my personal prejudice creeping in again. I really must stop that.) There's great use of piano only on the soundtrack—stark, crisp, frightening, just like the life of Harry Caul. It's a sad experience to watch this film because we're engrossed in the story of a man so broken by his own guilt (for a death he thinks he could have prevented), paranoia, and loneliness that he says of his own near-death experience, "I remember being disappointed I survived." He also says, "I'm not afraid of death, but I am afraid of murder," and has only one moment of enjoyment in the whole film, when he blows on a little sign. His life seems to have passed into nothingness, as if meaning has passed him by like a person who bumps into you while walking on the street. And, when all is said and done (but not always heard), the master bugger can't find the bug in his own house. So he sits and plays his saxophone, perhaps finding solace in the only thing he seems able to do without hurting people. We watch him, and may feel no better than the eavesdroppers we've seen earlier in the film. I'm not sure what "spiritual" message I want to draw from *The Conversation*; perhaps it's just the sum of its parts—and therefore a magnificent contribution to cinema. But I am tempted to say more; that it is a salutary lesson about defining yourself in terms of your job, and how meaningful skills can be put to bad use. You don't have to be a surveillance operative to do this; many of us work in everyday contexts that abuse the poor, or make life difficult for others in some way or another. The question that faces us may well be centered on our ability to act, unlike Harry, to change the context of our lives, to refuse to prostitute ourselves to the highest bidder. There is, of course, a message in here about the power of words, and particularly of gossip, to shape our lives, but I don't imagine that good Christian people need a lesson in that.

A PRIMER IN CONSPIRACY THEORY

Politics is ripe for conspiracy theory, so we'll start there. There has rarely been a film with such contemporary relevance as Barry Levinson and David Mamet's *Wag the Dog*, a hugely entertaining riff on the blend between Hollywood and politics. De Niro does one of his few '90s performances worth the admission price. Dustin Hoffman is a delight, and the film would make us far more cynical if we weren't already.

The textbook '70s political thriller is *All The President's Men*, which shows just how to build a story from one tiny fact upward, has some very nice close-ups and deals with the banality of how the Watergate scandal was unraveled—one police car went to the hotel to investigate the break-in because the one that received the original call was getting gas. What Woodward and Bernstein were dealing with blows my mind, and reminds me of the vast chasm between most American news media today and the courage of others who were willing to question the powers that be. It's also honest about the messiness of a journalist's house, so I feel quite at home with it! (And it has a hilarious '90s counterpart in the satire *Dick*, which tells the same story in a very different tone.)

Roman Polanski's *Chinatown* (from 1972) is not really a political thriller in the same sense, but it does deal with the corruption of L.A. city council in the 1940s; however, it's much more interesting than that makes it sound. *L.A. Confidential* works alongside *Chinatown* as another story of Californian corruption and things not being what they seem, as well as being an example of how much the boundaries for screen violence have widened since Jack Nicholson's Jake Gittes was investigating adultery in Polanski's film.

Further up the coast from L.A. is that sloping city San Fransisco, the setting for one of my favorite conspiracy films, *Vertigo*. Purists may balk at Hitchcock's greatest masterpiece being claimed for the conspiracy genre rather than the love story, but there is a conspiracy at the heart of it, and it is this that destroys Scotty's (James Stewart's character) psyche. Scotty is destroyed to much the same degree as another poor Gene

Hackman loser, in Arthur Penn's *Night Moves*. He's another guy who thinks he knows what's really going on but is left with a look of wide-eyed shock when the truth is revealed (just like me when I first saw the film). There's another look of melancholic wonderment on one character's face in *Arlington Road*, one of the darkest mainstream Hollywood films of the '90s. If I say any more than that, I'll be giving the game away.

Two conspiracy films about the media need to be mentioned before we move on: *Manufacturing Consent* (a documentary about Noam Chomsky, the social theorist who somehow seems to be ignored in his home of North America) and *Quiz Show*, Redford's analysis of how TV companies in the '50s lied to their audiences about the "innocence" of game shows. It was said that this was the time America grew up; I wish that were true. We'll end with two hugely entertaining films that have major scenes about the meaning of words: *Marathon Man* (don't schedule a dental appointment for too soon after watching this) and Mamet's *House of Games* (in which the venality of theft and deception is explored, and one character is shown to be so full of himself that he would rather be shot dead than admit to weakness).

THE WRAP

Frederick Buechner, that great poet of the spiritual struggle, has so much to say about the kind of anxiety that Christians are perhaps especially prone to that I can't quote it in anywhere near enough detail. (But check out the entry for August 22nd in his "Listening to Your Life" anthology; it'll do you good.) Briefly, he says that because we can never predict the worst things that happen to us, we should live life in a more liberated way. The worst things—death, isolation, illness—will finally happen to us all anyway, so why not just make peace with that, and get on with your life? Life at the beginning of the twenty-first century is full of its pitfalls—real and imagined, from international terrorism to the cancellation of *Dawson's Creek*. We could be forgiven for thinking that life is like an icy lake—fun to skate on for a while, but ultimately out to get us. And, of course, the worst will eventually happen to each of us—we are all going to die someday. But the things that worry us tend not to be the things that end up happening, right? When things go wrong for us, they usually turn out to be the biggest surprises of all. If we could pre-empt pain by knowing about it in advance, then astrologers would be better paid than they are now. But even if we could tell the future, I'm not sure it would make us less afraid. The anxious people I know (and I'm fairly near the top of that list) spend so much of our time living in the unreality of the worst-case scenario that we never get on with making decisions about the here and now. We need to be more attentive to Morgan Freeman's words in *The Shawshank Redemption*: "Get busy living, or get busy dying." We need to recognize that, in spite of what Mr. Falwell and his ilk say, there is no grand conspiracy, no big dastardly plan to get rid of us, no threat round every corner, no demon behind every sneeze. There is only one meta-narrative: the story of God's redemption of the earth and the race of creatures He made "a little lower than the angels."

The poster for *Enemy of the State* said, "It's not paranoia when they're really out to get you," but that's just a humorous riff on a topic that, twenty years previously, was treated with the utmost seriousness in films like *The Conversation* and *The Parallax View*. No matter what you think, they're not out to get you. I know so many people, especially people of faith, who live in fear of what might happen if they put a foot wrong, or even if they put a foot right, or put a foot anywhere. But I don't think that's the way we're supposed to be. Isn't there something in the dim and distant, hazy memory of childhood Bible study about perfect love having some effect on fear? Even if it's not perfect (and God knows, what kind of love is?), there's something mighty calming about the love of the community that the Church should be. Of course, in real life, it doesn't always work out that way. Many of us find churches to be the most fearful places, rather than the safe spaces where we can be truly ourselves. And I don't know what the antidote is, other than to take the risk of being vulnerable with friends and hoping that they're honest enough to see themselves in you.

CHAPTER FIVE

DEATH
ALL GOOD THINGS MUST COME TO AN END

"It's a peaceful feeling when we surrender; and there is healing power in letting go." —Terence Trent D'Arby

THE PREVALENCE OF COSMETIC SURGERY (ESPECIALLY the kind that doesn't make any medical sense) is evidence for the charge that Westerners don't know how to face their own mortality. There are two kinds of people in the world—those who see death as a beginning, and those who see it as an end. I have usually fallen into the former group; although there are times when I have had to seriously consider the possibility that what we have on earth is all we can expect. Death in popular cinema, however, is rarely accorded the reverence it deserves; if art is to help us deal with the questions that face us, then its cinematic proponents have, on the whole, made it hard to find mortality raised as an issue. I would suggest that the reasons for this are both simple and obvious, although they should not be taken as a foregone conclusion. People who fund movies are not paid to think about death; most Western films are financed in

California, a state in denial of its own precarious mortality—as the recently completed but potentially earthquake-fatal L.A. subway system shows. Plastic people made by plastic surgeons (another example of death-denial) make the decisions about what gets made and what gets put into turnaround. So, most of the time, death in cinema is treated in a cursory manner (as in blockbuster body counts) or milked for all that the celluloid teat can squeeze out (as in schmaltz). Both of these types of films are as dishonest as each other, and one may be even dangerous. It seems to me that the onus is on filmmakers to *prove* to me that cinematic genocide *doesn't* desensitize us to real death.

But there are, thankfully, shafts of light at the end of the tunnel of cinematic portrayals of human mortality. Some filmmakers are prepared to take an honest look at death and dying, both in its natural and violent forms. Kieslowski's *A Short Film About Killing* shows just how horrifying it is to kill a person, with either criminal intent or at the behest of the state (and was instrumental in the abolition of the death penalty in Poland). The majestic *Magnolia* allowed us a privileged glimpse into Jason Robards' real process of dying, as the actor was terminally ill while he played a man on his last day alive. Both these films, and some others, are honest and unflinching as their characters experience one of the two things that every human being will. Neither of them [unlike the Julia Roberts-Susan Sarandon (a normally reliably truthful actress) hugfest *Stepmom*, for instance], makes us feel good about death, but both of them make us feel more appreciative of life. Having said that, there are films that cause me to actually look forward to my own death, in the most life-affirming way possible. *Wings of Desire* and *A Matter of Life and Death* are the very best of these.

I have long felt that the good life belongs to those who have made peace with their own inevitable deaths; "dying to self is the way to life" is not just a pithy religious teaching but simply an objective statement. This is neither nihilism nor long-term, slow-acting suicide. Losing yourself is the only way to be found. Cinema, on the whole, may not have a very mature attitude to this, but there is morbid wisdom in the celluloid valley where films go to die.

FEARLESS
(PETER WEIR, RAFAEL YGLESIAS, 1993)

"Unless a grain of wheat falls into the ground and dies, it remains alone." —John 12:14 (NKJV)

I miss my grandmother. She died in August 1995, after the long battle with cancer that it seems most of us will experience either directly or from the bedside. Her death changed my life; one of those moments when it's so clear that a chapter has ended, and there are no guarantees of a new one beginning. I miss my grandmother and still carry her photo in my wallet. She was close to me in life, as close as a blood relative can be I think, and she is close to me now that I cannot visit her anymore, or share a laugh or a cup of tea. I miss my grandmother, and there are times when I need to be comforted by the belief that I may see her again. Prayer and the gathering of my community of family and friends work most of the time, but every now and then I need to engage with a work of art, music, literature, or film that takes me to the deeper place. *Fearless* is one of those works of art. There are incredible treasures in this film, and like most treasures, they need to be searched for by the discerning. *Fearless*, while ostensibly a film about death, is really a life-giving piece of cinema, one of those cultural texts that come along once in a while, like Todd Greene's *Paw-Paw*, or Julie Lee's *Many Waters*, or John Irving's *A Prayer for Owen Meany*, or Gorecki's

69

3rd Symphony (which plays over the end credits), that stirs the spirit's depths, telling a dark story as if it's a tale of resurrection. If you want a Messianic metaphor in your films, then this is most certainly a contender. With *Fearless*, Jeff Bridges reminds us of his powers as one of the finest, most empathetic actors of contemporary cinema, and the director Peter Weir reminds us he is one of the finest artists in any medium, of any time.

Fearless opens with industrial noise and atmospheric light revealing a man appearing through what looks like jungle undergrowth, carrying a baby. In a biblical image that will resonate throughout the film, the first people he sees outside the "jungle" are men on their knees praying. Something terrible has clearly happened, and we are quickly shown the aftermath of a horrific plane crash in a cornfield. The man reunites the baby with her parents, having said in another image with biblical echoes, "I'm not the father, I've got to find the mother." As he wanders around the crash site, the audience sees what *he* sees: a screaming woman pulled from the wreckage, a child's shoe charred by the flames, men dressed like the government agents from *ET*, an unbroken champagne bottle rolling on the ground, one of the few intact survivors of this tragedy. He is asked if he was in the crash, but says "no." Weir's technique of using the protagonist's P.O.V. is a brilliant way to open the movie, revealing quickly—and shockingly—what's going on, in a manner that really makes us *feel* what it might be like to be in the midst of this horror. It's one of the most striking opening sequences of recent cinema—along with *Magnolia* and *Heat*. We are sucked into this story, and we must decide whether or not to let lose its grip.

The man, whom we recognize as Jeff Bridges, interrupts a taxi driver's camcorder voyeurism to ask to be taken to the nearest hotel, where he, in the first of many similar scenes, walks down a long, dark corridor. He showers and inspects his body, revealing a wound in his side (where Jesus' blood and water ran out) and telling his mirror reflection, "You're not dead." We next see him spitting on desert ground by his car and rubbing the sand between his fingers. Just as Jesus preceded his healing of the blind man with this strange act, Jeff's character, Max Klein, is about to receive *his* sight, and this is what the film is really about.

That afternoon, he puts his head out the car window to feel the breeze, goes to see an old lover, and eats strawberries that he thinks will kill him, served by a waitress called Faith. These are subtle, perhaps amusing but not clichéd moments—we are being drawn into Max's emerging spiritual and self-awareness, which he (and we) initially misread as fearlessness of death. This is underlined by the fact that he lives in San Francisco, where a cavalier attitude to mortality exists on the most populous faultline in the world. But Max has had an epochal, liminal experience that makes him a man who will face reality—he calls it a crash while the airline rep who comes to prevent him from suing can only manage to say it is "unpleasantness." This is a film about moving beyond such denial and becoming alert— alive—to the world.

The airline flies him home and sends a psychiatrist, nicely rounded by John Turturro, to befriend him and mitigate the damage he might do to their company, but this doctor is more neurotic than Max, like the other bureaucrats in the film. When he arrives home, with the shrink in tow, we first see his wife, played by the most marvellous Isabella Rossellini, ascending the stairs from the basement of their modernist house—a metaphor for where their marriage and his spirit have been before the crash. And thus we have a context for a life-changing parable of death and resurrection, played out by the quintessential "man on a quest." Max spends much of the rest of the film risking his neck walking out in front of rows of traffic, standing on the edge of tall buildings, eating strawberries when he can, and, in the film's most audacious scene, driving his car at high speed into a wall to heal someone by proving that sometimes you need to almost die before you can truly realize *some things are out of your control*. These moments are where the film resonates most with me. I have felt the same kind of exhilarated alienation—the sense of being so entirely different, so new, so alive that I could walk out in front of a whole motorway of traffic and not be harmed.

We follow Max as he befriends Carla, the screaming woman from the plane crash, who lost her two-year-old son Bubble, who is a deeply religious woman (it says "Jesus is my best friend" in Spanish on her bedroom door), who now says of God that "He hurt me forever, but I still believe in Him." The relationship between Max and Carla is not what it seems—we think his fearlessness and reputation as the "Good Samaritan" will lead her to make peace with Bubble's death, but Max also benefits from *her* role in *his* life. Before the crash, through flashbacks, we see that Max is a nervous wreck who doesn't like flying at the best of times, but the prospect of his own imminent death causes him to lose all his fear. Carla, however, has been nearly destroyed by the tragedy; enervated by the guilt of having been unable to stop Bubble from falling out of her arms, she blames herself for his death. She's guilt-ridden because she let go, although she could not possibly have saved him—and perhaps the worst kind of guilt is that which misrepresents the facts and blames the proponent for something for which he or she is not responsible.

Rosie Perez brilliantly *assumes* Carla's character, and when she breaks down into hysterical weeping, we are right there with her—this is a performance that everyone should identify with. Indeed, almost all the performances in this film are note-perfect, with the unfortunate exception of Tom Hulce's opportunistic, ambulance-chasing lawyer. His characterization is overblown—a bit like a juristic version of his Mozart in *Amadeus*, but out of place in such a serious film. The journey that the film follows Max on is redolent with spiritual metaphors—when he is asleep, his wife removes his slippers and kisses his feet; his son is called Jonah (who brought a message of salvation to those who would not normally listen—and it is Jonah's scrapbook dedicated to his father that leads to Max asking to be "saved"); Max tells Carla, "You go to church to talk to God—you gotta talk to somebody," and eventually realizes that there's no reason to love if there is no God. Max says the crash is the best thing that ever happened to him, but he does have to move on from this; the question is whether or not he has to physically die to become whole. Thankfully, the film resolves this quandary in a very un-Hollywood manner, which this essay will not spoil.

All in all, this picture is beautifully constructed, with almost every scene being worthwhile on its own; flashbacks to the crash are delicately introduced, and the writing is prosaic but not unrealistic or clichéd (When the psychiatrist says that Carla is filled with guilt and shame because she is an "old world Catholic," Max responds with, "I'm filled with guilt and shame, how is that old world?" Later he says, "People don't so much believe in God as they choose not to believe in nothing." Perhaps my favorite line in the film is, "This is America in the '90s, no-one apologizes anymore—they write a memoir.")

Watching this film for what must be the tenth time in eight years, I thought about what watching films analytically does to your enjoyment of them. I never really saw Max as a broken figure until this viewing—I had previously thought that he was a heroic character who brought healing to those around him. Now I realize that, while he helped Carla, he is a fairly selfish character who does not find his own healing until he admits his need, saying, "I want you to save me." As with the film versions of the lives of Moses and T.E. Lawrence of Arabia, *Fearless* exemplifies the adage that "unless a seed falls to the ground and dies, it cannot bear fruit." Max Klein thinks that he has been transformed by the plane crash—he says, "I walked away from that crash with my life—the taste and touch and beauty of life," but he is really only in limbo until he acknowledges his need for salvation. In acknowledging his need for his partner—the one who loves and knows him best—he can learn to live with his extraordinary experience in a way that allows it to make sense without destroying him or those around him.

The thing I like most about Peter Weir is the tone of his films—nothing else in contemporary Hollywood feels quite like them—with the opening and closing scenes and small moments between Carla and Max as examples of Weir at his best. I am so enthralled by this movie that it is difficult to write about. The film is simply too good for words, and if you talk during the credits rather than just allowing the film to rest a while, there may be something wrong with your sense of wonder. *Fearless* is a religious parable of great significance in an age of such apathy toward the deeper meanings of life and the devaluing of love and relationships, art and culture, beauty and truth. It is both a "sign" and a "signified"; as Roland Barthes might have it, an artefact of beauty which leads us on to further beauty. It belongs in the pantheon of great misunderstood works of art and would not be out of place in a cathedral, to the glory of God. *Fearless*, better than any other contemporary film, fleshes out the universal story of the prodigal, and envelopes us in a deeply moving portrayal of nothing less than the Christian message that "This son of mine was lost but now he is found, he was blind, but now he can see, he was dead, but now he is alive."

ONCE UPON A TIME IN AMERICA
(SERGIO LEONE, 1984)

This is another one of those films that's too big for me to explain. So I'll just say a few short words: It is amazing. A lyrical elegy for broken friendship, suffused like too much cigarette smoke with the aroma of imminent death, *Once Upon a Time in America* was Leone's final film, and the crowning achievement of a career dedicated to revealing all that is dark about masculinity. It's about four friends who begin careers as petty thieves when they're still supposed to be in school and grow to become powerful gangsters during Prohibition, that weird time in American history when the powers that be believed they could control people's thoughts. I don't want to tell you much more about the plot, because this one really is worth discovering for yourself. Suffice to say, De Niro plays a man broken on the wheels of his own indecision, refusing to grow, to take responsibility for his own life, who has spent most of his life hiding from the world. His is a living death, a warning about making selfish choices and blaming everyone else for what has gone wrong. I could go on, but I think this might just become a reason not to watch it. I'll just say that lots of people do awful things to each other, lots of people die, and it all ends in tears. But how brilliantly it tells this story. It's about the glorification of selfishness, fear of the past, the desire to move on, the limits of loyalty, the end of friendship, and the meaning of death itself. To my mind, there has been no better American film in the last twenty years.

FIGHT CLUB
(DAVID FINCHER, JIM UHLS, 1999)

Everything moves backward in the opening credit sequence to *Fight Club*, which, depending on your point of view, is either a work of benign fascism or a near-miraculous tract for our times. Nobody went to see it when it first came out in the dying embers of the 20th century (remember then?), but thankfully (for I am one of its disciples), DVD redeemed it. If you're reading this book (which you obviously are, otherwise I have just become the literary exemplar of a tree falling in the forest), then you've probably already seen it and might be looking for me to fall flat on my face by misunderstanding it. Hope not because it's too important to misunderstand. I recently read a "Christian" website review that said this film is "devoid of any redeeming content whatsoever: the cinematic equivalent of sucking on a bile duct," which is a bit like saying the Spanish Inquisition was defending the Christian faith, or that George W. Bush won the 2000 election fair and square—it depends on the way you look at it. My view is that this film is a wake-up call from our generation to the Church, and if we don't pay attention, we will remain as dead as its unnamed narrator is at the start.

Everything about this film is a surprise, from how the camera moves like a darting fish, to the use of Buddhist philosophy in the fight club's membership rituals, to the compassion it shows for the very people who are portrayed as victims in its self-help groups (not to mention the size of Meatloaf's breasts). Our narrator—let's just call him Gareth because he's supposed to be just like you and me—is shown suffering from insomnia, which he says means that nothing's real, everything's far away, everything's a copy of a copy of a copy …. He uses the IKEA catalogue like it's a *Playboy* centerfold and travels for an insurance company, so bored with life that he wishes for his plane to crash, because it would at least remind him that he's alive. His doctor responds to his requests for a cure by saying, "You wanna see pain? Swing by First Methodist church." (And where else would you expect to find pain but in a church?). He begins to attend support groups for people with terminal illnesses and other serious struggles to surmount ("When people think you're dying they really listen to you"), and reaches within himself to find the ability to sleep. He finds peace in another man's arms and cries his little heart out. He makes a habit of visiting the support groups—cancer, diabetes, male pattern baldness, it doesn't matter—and finds that "Every night I died, and every morning I was born again." He meets a stranger, Tyler Durden (with a name as silly as that he could almost be a celebrity Christian), who encourages him to start to fight, to fight to feel alive, to fight to stop "polishing the brass on the Titanic" (which he says is Martha Stewart's occupation). And so the fight clubs begin, with men meeting to strip to the waist and hammer life into each other. They are the fatherless generation, who have, by virtue of the heightened expectations placed on them and lowered resources offered to them, found no purpose in life other than web porn and expensive meaningless furniture, "working jobs we hate so we can buy sh-- we don't need."

But the fight club awakens them to something more alive than ever, with its pain as premature enlightenment. Guys thrash each other and themselves into seeing things as they really are. Ironically, the first guy they pick a fight with when the club is taken onto the streets is a clergyman, who is initially too timid to respond, but eventually joins in with gusto. That metaphor for the church's inability or unwillingness to take a stand does not go unnoticed. By me at least.

I heard Chuck Pahlaniuk—the author of *Fight Club's*

source novel—talk and read in Belfast in 2000. He was much more self-effacing than you might expect, but he had really cool hair, so that put my mind at ease. I remember him saying that some real fight clubs had sprung up across North America after the film came out. One of the biggest was at a Mormon university. The university tried to shut down the club, but its leaders insisted that nothing in the Book of Mormon could be used to ban fighting, which is an interesting use of a sacred text and put some ideas in my head for adult Sunday school classes. Everyone knows the first and second rules of the club, but one of the more neglected is: If this is your first night, you have to fight.

What a way to start a journey into becoming alive again—the postmodern equivalent of young pilots getting back into a Spitfire immediately after they crashed the first one. The narrator says that when the fight was over, "nothing was solved, but nothing mattered," but I beg to differ—the seeds of the redemption of the world are found in human beings awakening again to the death around them. If that means pain in the short term, then so be it. And anything that leads its participants to say, "By the end of the first month I didn't even miss TV," can't be all bad. The alarm bell that rings throughout this movie is so startling that I would suggest it should be required viewing for people who want to understand the world of the western male at this point in history. Its central theme—summed up by Tyler's simple adage, "You are not your f---ing khakis"—is a powerful riposte to the branding of the Church in bite-sized chunks that has emerged as a response to the failure of large-scale evangelistic initiatives. If you think that the challenges facing the Church will be met by changing the style of worship, your heart might be in the right place, but for God's sake, don't confuse style with substance.

And the wisdom of *Fight Club* goes further—in the

style of the monastic discipline of the Paper Street army, the contemplative injunction to "just let go" of the detritus that has subsumed yourself, the very question of the integrated self and how the traumatized mind can abuse you. I understand this film now more than ever—I have come from a spiritual closet that trapped my mind. I have been scared of God, of "letting go"; the pain of change has seemed too great. But, just as in C.S. Lewis' *The Great Divorce*—temporary pain is the corollary of spiritual growth—I now see that being "safe" (in the cheesy sense) is antithetical to being "good." Sometimes I want to go back to zero, and *Fight Club* ends on such a note, so I thank God for it. In one incredible scene, Tyler declares: "We are the middle children of history. We have no unifying cause. We have no Great War, no Great Depression. Our Great War is a spiritual war. Our Great Depression is our lives."

When I watch it, I want to shout "Amen! That's us, people." But the dark night of the soul isn't the end of the journey. Hitting rock bottom, giving in to a kind of death, as these guys do, is the beginning of resurrection, and the fight club is a kind of meta-level twelve-step program toward coming back to life. Movies like this are a mirror that we need to hold up once in a while; so go on, come out of your closet; you need to go beyond your numbness. Watch this movie and take the reality check that might just shock you into becoming more human.

A PRIMER IN DEATH

If you want to spend a few hours in the company of cinematic perma-sleep, have a look at these:

Se7en is a film about a man whose every moment must be a living death—the serial killer at the black heart of this film has truly given himself over to the dark side. We don't know why. He is paralleled in Morgan Freeman's wise detective, who himself is also a disciplined man, a lonely man, a truthful man. The unremitting darkness of this story is only moderately tempered by the final line of the film, when Freeman quotes Hemingway (which I'll paraphrase, although willingly concede that Hemingway was a better writer than I am—but then again, maybe I haven't spent enough time in Parisian cafés): "The world is a fine place, and worth fighting for."

The world is most certainly *not* a fine place in Abel Ferrara's Manhattan triptych *King of New York, The Addiction*, and *The Funeral*. These masterful films deal with a gangster trying to go straight, a newly unborn vampire adjusting to her un-life, and a criminal family inviting bloody apotheosis. Christopher Walken turns up in all three, but it's the priest's speech in *The Funeral* that shook me out of my seat. He is talking to a mafia wife and calls her on "talking the talk" of spirituality without living it. It's one of the most striking scenes of Christian authority in cinema. That whole film is a tragedy, and aptly named, for it's about the death of a way of being; and the final bloodbath is the only way one of the characters can see to purge the family of its past and make a clean break. *The Addiction* may seem like an obvious favorite for a former Ph.D. candidate, as the vampire—played by Lili Taylor—eats her dissertation panel when they put her through the ordeal of defending her thesis, but I'm much too charming to do something as vulgar as *that*. The film is much more valuable for what it says about the nature of spiritual power. When Lili is first approached by another vampire, she is given the opportunity to save herself. The vampire says, "Tell me to go away with authority and I will leave," but Lili is drawn to the allure of the un-dead and has to pay the consequences.

One of the finest performances ever committed to film is found in *Death in Venice*, where Dirk Bogarde's Mahlerian composer decomposes in front of our eyes, as he chooses to risk—and finally succumb to—cholera by staying where he can be near the most beautiful thing he has ever seen. This film is far too slow for postmodern sensibilities, and its storyline is hard to engage if you're averse to metaphor, but when I caught it late one night, I was transfixed. Maybe you will be, too.

Our ability to cope with death is analyzed in Ingmar Bergman's early film *The Seventh Seal*, which not only provided the inspiration for Bill and Ted's chess game, but raises the deepest of all questions: how to cheat mortality. *Japon*, maybe my favorite film of the recent Latin American revival, is a totally overwhelming, vibrant, vital film about a man's quest for his own death. I've never seen anything quite like it. I'll finish this selection with a surprising choice, but one that I—obviously—consider appropriate. *Star Trek II—The Wrath of Khan* is memorable for many reasons—William Shatner's receding hairline, Ricardo Montalban's ridiculous plastic chest, and the hilariously dated special effects to name but three. But it's here because it has the best death scene in popular cinema. And it's actually pretty profound, too. Spock's sacrificial death to save the crew of the Enterprise may be laying on the Christ metaphors a bit thick, but the scene is beautifully played by Shatner and Nimoy (never thought I'd say *that*, did ya?), and it still brings a tear to the eye.

THE END

It is one of life's mysteries that we spend so little time reflecting on the one thing that will happen to us all and that we will have eternity to experience and make sense of. Of course it's reasonable not to want to think much about death—it's messy, smelly, and sad. But all the spiritual wisdom of the ages teaches us that we can only truly live when we have made peace with our own inevitable deaths. This is not morbidity; it's actually the converse—truly joyful life can only be experienced when you take it seriously in the light of its temporary nature. I have a friend who used to pray every night that he'd be dead in the morning. He wasn't necessarily the most fun person to be around, but he had a point (and he's still with us, thankfully). He's made peace with the transience of life and is getting on with the business of being true to himself. And it's necessary for our own spiritual growth to die a few times, maybe a few thousand times. To die to fear, or to old paradigms, or old dreams, or guilt. Only when you have begun to make peace with the fact that everything around us is both growing and dying at the same time can you start to live with the kind of detachment from created things that seems to be at the heart of a real relationship with the divine. This does not mean being callous toward beauty or friendship. It does not mean being ignorant toward others in a pseudo-existential "we're all going to die anyway" fashion (and that way of being is all too often nothing more than *a fashion*, style without substance). No, dying to self (not that I've mastered that, of course, far from it) may just provide you with the key to living life as God intended. Death in movies can be an over-sentimentalized chocolate box or a horrific throwaway, but sometimes we are offered a privileged glimpse into what dying might actually be about, and what it has to teach us about life. Don't get too morbid, now ...

CHAPTER SIX

COMMUNITY

HOME IS WHERE THE HEART IS, OR IS THE NUCLEAR FAMILY JUST A TIMEBOMB WAITING TO EXPLODE?

"THEY F--- YOU UP, YOUR MUM AND DAD," SAID Philip Larkin, the British poet of melancholia. And they do, no matter how great they are. It's inevitable. Anyone who lives in close proximity to another human being for as long as the average parent to a child is going to make mistakes. You know those things your parents or siblings do that you're too embarrassed about to even remember? Like when your mum puts a silly hat on at Christmas and sings out of tune at the top of her voice? Or when your dad stuck a toilet plunger to his forehead and then removed it to leave a shocking great red circle that didn't go away for weeks? Or the time your brother listened to nothing but the *Teenage Mutant Ninja Turtles* soundtrack at dinnertime? Or when your sister declared to all and sundry that she was going to be an inventor and had an idea that would change the world? Or when you … on second thought, I don't want to give an example of what *you* might have done in case you make the obviously false assumption that I'm talking about myself and my own family. Remember those teenage times when you yearned for the day when you would be free of the shackles of your parents—who didn't understand you or the life you knew was right for you? Mine didn't understand that I was going to be an actor (or a lawyer) (or an astronaut) (or whatever the heck it is I am now). I felt squeezed, like the rest of my peers, into a box that wasn't made for me. And I hoped for the day that I could get out and make my way in the world.

Now, in my late twenties, I find myself returning home more and more often, seeking out my family's company, looking for their affection, realizing that, in one very important sense, they actually understand me better than anyone else I know. But my adolescence was a struggle. Probably no more or less so than yours, but mine may have involved more Polish agricultural documentaries. Part of the struggle was the fact that the biblical objective to honor parents was extremely difficult to put into practice when I was so certain that I knew better than they did (In fairness to myself, and I've been pretty hard on myself in this book already, so I think there's time for a bit of grace). I don't think this was entirely my fault. Christians often talk about "family values" as if Jesus had preached in favor of the two parents, two point four kids, and a dog template. But if we look a little closer at His words, we'll find that He had a very unconventional view of what family means—sons and fathers leaving each other for the sake of the faith, daughters and mothers breaking up, strangers being welcomed to live with—and treated as equal to—biological families. The concept of single people living alone was unheard of in His culture. But today nearly one third of Western young adults live in single-person households, which means good news for mortgage lenders, but bad news for human community. "Family values," in fact, is a term used to describe something that perhaps most readers of this book won't recognize, being the children of divorced parents. I don't think it's a coincidence that the kind of family many moralizing people seem to prefer is called the "nuclear" option. For more people than ever, especially of my generation, home was not where the heart was, and the nuclear family was just a time bomb waiting to explode.

As you know, Tyler Durden in *Fight Club* says of our generation that "We're the middle children of history ... Our Great Depression is our lives," and makes some fairly trenchant comments about how the nuclear family may have an automatic self-destruct mechanism. He may be right, you know. But the Church should be able to answer this with the incarnation of a true and truthful community, but all too often people leave their real selves at the temple door. "Community" might just be the term I use most (other than "It wasn't *my* fault!"). It's my soapbox, my favorite topic, and the source of most of my angst. The breakdown of community is one of the most pressing and dangerous social phenomena of our time. People live alone in greater numbers than ever before. We work in ever more isolated contexts, plugged in to call center headphones, or "relating" through computer screens, rushing everywhere, starving our souls of the company of fellow-travellers. I knew I had taken a wrong turn somewhere along my pilgrimage when I became so overwhelmed by work that I started referring to dinner with friends as a "meeting," as if the menu was an agenda and the coffee constituted "any other business."

But what does "community" mean? Some words spring to mind: non-nuclear, intentional, difficult, messy, true. We all have a positive need for belonging and to share our sense of identity with others, but this can all too easily become distorted in one of two ways—we either find so much belonging with one group that we exclude others, or we feed on each other to the extent that we are neither giving of ourselves nor attending to our own vital need for solitude. So we build churches based on "our" truth, or we spend most of our time with friends telling them about *our* needs, without ever seeking to participate in how they're doing.

The history of the Christian Church has often reflected what theologian Miroslav Volf called "exclusion" not "embrace," in which we welcome and accept people on the basis of how much they agree with us. You know the score—"I can't worship with you because you don't believe exactly the same as me," or "You can't teach me because you're not the same skin color or gender." At its worst, this kind of non-relating leads to the genocidal consequences of racism and sectarianism; at best, it narrows our field of vision so that we only ever experience the presence of "people like us," thereby forfeiting the gifts that diversity bring. Dave Andrews, a follower of Christ (he prefers the term "Christi-anarchist") who has pioneered a kind of communitarian example in urban Australia, called this the "closed-set" worldview. Volf and he both see openness toward others, whatever their differences from us, as being not only in the spirit of the Gospel, but as a key to the survival of the human race.

Some forms of "Christian" spirituality assert that we can only really accept those who agree with us—whether over issues of personal morality, cultural practice, or even theories of the Atonement. But this does not sound like the message of Jesus. He embraced people, not because they were *like* Him, but because they were human beings, created in the image of God. Before we are anything—male or female, big or small, athletic or tired, broken, bruised, or macho, from any faith tradition or none, we're *human*. When Jesus spent some time hanging out with the Samaritan woman by the well, He was not merely slaking His thirst but making a point about human community. According to the cultural and even legal niceties of the day, she was "untouchable" on at least three counts: she was female (for a man to talk to a lone woman in public was taboo), she was considered sexually deviant (and therefore the law of guilt by association would apply to Jesus, who was, of course, a rabbi with a reputation to maintain); and, worst of all, she was a member of the hated Samaritan people (with whom the Israelites experienced daily enmity). But Jesus chose to be with her, in public. I think this was partly because He wanted to show that being human is what brings us together. If you're a human being (and I suspect that most readers of this book probably are, although I have my doubts about some of my good friends), then whatever your culture or beliefs or mistakes, you have more in common with me already than simple doctrinal agreement will ever grant. We need to find some way to retrieve what we've lost of human community—we are not alone, but so often live as if our loneliness is all we have.

Movies about community sometimes present "perfect" families and friendship groups as if we should never find any conflict where there is community. But true community does not depend on lack of conflict; in fact, the opposite is true. Honesty and vulnerability and finding a way to resolve our conflicts non-violently must be the keystones of any community that expects to develop a real human life. This is a risk, because it is often easier to pretend to be something that we're not rather than face the challenge of conflict. Let's see what the movies have to offer ...

THE ROYAL TENENBAUMS
(WES ANDERSON, 2001)

There is no other film like this—epic in scope, intimate in focus, magisterial in structure; it's the truth of all our families and of the fact that not only does God have no favorites, but that everyone (and I do mean *everyone*) is welcome in the spiritual community. It's the story of one man's train wreck of a life and his attempts to win his family back, after realizing how much he needs them. It seems to take place in a world caught between the '40s and the '70s: People travel by steamship, wear fur coats, and listen to the Rolling Stones, but its heart is right up to date. It's easy to compare with Charles Addams and J.D. Salinger, but the comparison is entirely appropriate; *The Royal Tenenbaums* is a modern American masterpiece. In fact, if I didn't know any better, I might even say that this film *is* the great American novel. But I do know better, so I won't say that. Although I really must mention the art direction and production design are magnificent. The colors may have been drained from the characters' lives, but it's certainly on the walls of their house.

Royal Tenenbaum—I believe it so I'll say it right here: Gene Hackman's greatest performance—is a man so selfish and insecure that when his son complains that he's not a team player in a childhood game, he says, "There are no teams." And that's his problem—he thinks he's in this game of life alone. His kids are geniuses, but this means they can't be kids, and by the time they're adults, as the narrator says, "Virtually all memory of the brilliance of the young Tenenbaums had been erased by nearly two decades of betrayal, failure, and disaster."

These are people who have suffered major brokenness, like birds who have been kept in cages too long. Their father lives in a place called the "Lindbergh Palace," which itself is evocative of another family with tragedy on its memory. He runs out of money and decides to fake cancer so his wife will take him in. When she cries at this information, he finds he cannot initially sustain the lie, so he has not completely traded his humanity, but he still wavers back and forth between truth and manipulation because it's in his nature. So he moves in. And then lots of weird and wonderful and painful things happen. This is one film for which I'm going to preserve the plot, so I won't say much more about the detail. But as for the substance ... Anderson is a comprehensive wit—this film finds space for the eccentric stoned author[1], the lost lover, the wandering slut, the powerful but gracious matriarch, the doctor who's trying too hard to give his wife what he thinks she needs but does not want (obviously a tribute to the wonderful Oliver Sacks, author of *Awakenings* and much else, although I know nothing of his private life), the anxious son, the dog that brings people together, and even the good for nothing father. Wait—strike that, reverse it—in Anderson's world, nobody is good for nothing: Everyone has true value.

So, when all is said and done (and there's a lot said and done in *The Royal Tenenbaums*), what can it tell us about human community? Let's bring out the heavy artillery bullet points:

- This is a painful film to watch; because surely we must all be able to identify with some of it; it's such a knowing film. Aren't we all weird like this? I wouldn't know a "normal" family if it ran up and bit me.

- We're all nomads, too, in some sense (the film honors this part of the spiritual journey by calling its taxi firm the "Gypsy Cab Co.").

- Like two of the characters, some of us want to live in our childhood tents when we've grown up; the safety, coziness, and—quite simply—fun of being hidden from everything else is a powerful and reasonable attraction. This movie doesn't want us to grow up too soon—it knows that part of being truly human means becoming like a little child.

---

[1] I'm writing this at 2:03 a.m., so I know how he feels.

♦ The consequences of a lie can be liberating—Royal deceived his family when he said he was dying, but this ultimately brought him the peace and restored the family he didn't actually know that he wanted. He only realized that he *needed* them when he re-awakened to the human need for love. Making things right is painful, but better than letting them fester. Royal is a walking disaster, but he recognizes the need for a process to change—there is a beautiful moment when he faces this and lets his vulnerability take over, saying, "Do you think you could start forgiving me?" There is one point where he says to the family that he has enjoyed being with them, that "the past six days have been the best six days of probably my whole life." The narrator says, "Immediately after making this statement Royal realized that it was true."

♦ This example of being changed by the thing you don't expect is Royal's Damascus Road experience. I guess Royal's lie might be an example of what the biblical Joseph means when he said: Satan meant it for a curse, but God turned it into a blessing.

♦ Eli—the stoned writer—sends his press clippings to Royal's wife because he has no adequate parent. This movie recognizes that idolatry of the nuclear family lets millions of people slip through the net of community.

♦ Many of our families lurch from crisis to crisis, and many parents spend trying hours, days, weeks trying to work out where it went wrong. Everyone in this film is in desperation, looking for a needle in the hay that will resolve things. However, sometimes a crisis bears the seeds of hope. Things can often be put right—but even the putting right can be messy. Sometimes the worst does come to the worst, but this film shows how even divorce papers can be a gift.

◆ The family bird returns from a long journey with more gray feathers than before—it's been through something wild, like the rest of us, and has the scars to show it. When Jacob wrestled with God, he walked with a limp as a result—the gray feathers are exactly the same thing.

◆ Royal agrees to let his wife be free when he realizes that her fiancé is "everything that I'm not," and in this moment, he becomes the thing that he was not before—a good man. And you don't need a spiritual explanation of that.

I'm writing this in the early hours of a Wednesday morning, when I should really be in bed, but instead am in my parents' living room. (This book has also been written at my house, in cafés, on planes and trains—everywhere, in fact, except in my sleep. Although, after reading it, you may beg to differ.) My dad is on the other side of the room, falling asleep on the sofa, but somehow managing to hold his left hand under his chin while he enters the dreamland. I'm glad to be writing about *The Royal Tenenbaums* in this place. I don't know what your family was like. Mine was everything a family can be. Loving, safe, calm, rejoicing, funny, interesting, generous, grateful, as well as angry, insecure, deep in grief, boring, painful, unfair. Just like yours, I guess. Most of the challenges my family has faced could have been better met if people knew how to live in community better, to love one another, to not be afraid of vulnerability. Most of the gifts my family has could have been put to so much better use if human beings were more open to each other. Some families seem to be without such challenges; some seem only to make it through by the skin of their teeth. And, tragically, there are many that are not safe spaces, but crucibles of abuse and even death. We were not meant to live this way, detached from each other, too close for comfort, with strangers held at bay. This movie reminds us of the pain of being family and the need to widen our horizons and change our expectations if we are going to live together in peace.

It is so wise about life and the need for yet another chance to live again (*Give me second grace*, as Nick Drake sings on the soundtrack that seems to have been assembled with near-miraculous discernment). But it's not just its wisdom about being human that makes it a masterpiece in artistic terms—it's one of the most artful films I've ever seen. The universally wonderful ensemble cast acts in a beautifully paced context (remember that sometimes all good things come to those who wait), but it's the writing that knocks you for six. Unfortunately, like so many of the best films, *The Royal Tenenbaums* didn't grab a huge audience or eat up the box office receipts. But give this one time, and you'll be rewarded.

There was a family sitting in front of my friend Ewan and I (part of my own extended non-blood-related community) watching it together in silence to the end of the credits. I hoped that it had meant something to them. We see Royal's gravestone at the end of the film, and the inscription tells us that he: "Died tragically rescuing his family from the wreckage of a destroyed sinking battleship." And of course, that's exactly what he did. It may be true that there is room for a heck of a lot of failure, and one act of heroism in every person's life. But more than Royal's redemption, the film hopes that one day, all children will live together under the same roof. Now that is something worth hoping for.

THE BIG CHILL
(LAWRENCE KASDAN,
BARBARA BENEDEK, 1983)

Suicide is a fact of life. Emile Durkheim, one of the fathers of modern sociology, guessed that people kill themselves as a result of what he called "anomie." There is no adequate English translation of this word, which is appropriate, because it kinda means a lack of meaning in the world, a place of spiritual dormancy. It can occur at times of great social shift—like during wars or Christmas—or when nothing much at all is happening. What is clear is that there seems to be a relationship between suicide and society "losing its way." When things lose their sense of purpose, some people take their own lives. Maybe these people are the ones most closely in touch with what's wrong with the world and see this only too well. Maybe not. I'm not an expert, but like, I guess, many readers of this book, I have lost a friend to suicide. And it doesn't make sense. *The Big Chill* starts with a suicide that brings together old college friends, who have spent years apart forging professional lives, to regret the past they have lost. They were students when American life seemed ripe for radical change—Vietnam, free love, a time when young people were actually interested in politics (thankfully that time seems to have been resurrected). But the world didn't change. *They* did. In the wrong direction. They blame themselves for their friend's suicide, which is what most people do, but, after all, there was no reason. "We don't know why he killed himself but I don't know why I chose these socks," as one of them says. The movie has one of the best, most moving opening sequences ever; we follow the friends on the way to the funeral, and it tells us everything we need to know about the characters. The funereal organ is playing "You Can't Always Get What You Want," and that's really what this film is about.

We get to eavesdrop as they hang out together over the following weekend. They laugh and shout and sleep together and get angry and make mistakes and cry and say meaningful things. And we're right there with them. We want to be with these people. We are reminded of the friendships we ourselves yearn for, and how we really must slow our lives down so we can spend more time with each other. They seem both old and young at the same time, hanging onto the dreams of youth while resigning themselves to the likelihood of failure. But they are certain of one thing: As one of them says, "I feel like I was at my best when I was with you people."

They know that they have lost this sense of being *present* with themselves, never mind each other. They know that all the consolations of money cannot even begin to scratch the surface of the need for human community. And they are beginning to mature—"nobody said it was going to be fun" is the mantra that helps them face the reality of what it means to be an adult; although the film is much less pessimistic than this might make you think.

You feel like you want to be friends with these people— the honesty, the sense of what they lost, the need for a good argument to keep us alive, the ability to *be yourself* without fear. It helps that the cast is one of the best ensembles of actors ever assembled, including William Hurt, who might just be my favorite actor. He always underplays things, quiet, reserved, truthful, very alive without dominating the room. I've no idea what kind of man he is, but he seems to inspire respect in everything he does. He really understands the people he plays, and *The Big Chill* really understands the people in it. It's honest enough to say that fantasy wish fulfillment does not work, but that people *need each other*. At the funeral scene, the very stern minister asks, "Are not the satisfactions of being a good man among our common men not adequate for us anymore?"

And that's just the point. What does it mean to be "among our common men"? To be truly in each other's presence? What would we have to give up to rebuild the thing that we lost? Are we supposed to live detached lives once we turn 30 or have kids? Like one of the characters, "I'm not good at this conclusion thing," and maybe that's a good thing, because this film is about beginnings, not closure.

AMERICAN BEAUTY
(SAM MENDES, ALAN BALL, 1999)

American Beauty begins with a man saying of his middle class suburban life, "In a way, I'm dead already ... I have lost something—I'm not exactly sure what it is, but I didn't always feel this sedated." It's an amazing film, which most people think is about a mid-life crisis, and I initially wondered why, as a young man, I felt it was speaking directly to *me*, but I now think it has something to say to people of any age. The writer, Alan Ball, says it's about people who are searching for meaning in their lives, so I guess that means the six billion of us who currently inhabit this planet. Wide appeal indeed. I want to concentrate on three of its characters.

Kevin Spacey (has there ever been a more appealing actor who reveals so little of him*self*?) plays Lester Burnham, bored with his family, pissed off with his job, tired of life. His daily highlight is an early morning self-serve, and it's all downhill after that. He's spiritually dead ("this isn't life, this is just *stuff*"), but his salvation is found in the fact that he actually recognizes this and chooses to do something about it.

Lester's next-door neighbor is a family presided over by a former Marine Colonel, played by Chris Cooper (will someone please give that man more leading roles?). He is stern and angry and only manages to keep his rage at simmering point most of the time. Oh, and he's gay. Suburban (and probably ecclesiastical) suspicion has made him full of shame and bitterness and conflict at not being able to be himself. At the film's climax, he gives himself over to the part of himself that he's been fighting all his life; he tries to find himself. Tragically, he misjudges who to try this with. The rejection is too much for him to handle. And the fear of being found out leads him to kill someone to prevent what he thinks is his dirty little secret being discovered. The refusal of society to allow him to be himself means he feels ashamed just to be alive.

Then there's Angela, the quintessentially gorgeous high school cheerleader, who wants to be famous and boasts of her sexual conquests. The depth of her aspirations is summed up when she says, "If people who don't even know me wanna f--- me that's great because it means I really have a shot at being a model." We may wish to spurn her, to laugh at her shallowness, to mock the superficiality of this selfish little object, but the film brings us up short. We dare not objectify people, whoever they are. There are worlds of depth and pain under the shallowest-looking surface.

American Beauty isn't often thought of as a beautifully observed comedy of manners, but that's what it is. Let's face it: This is what the world is like for many of us. It's a story of resurrection, of how one man realizes his place in the world is found in connection to others, and how need for people is not a sign of weakness, but the path to finding yourself.

Angela is broken by the expectations this world places on young women. Her sense of self is only found in how great she might look on a magazine cover. No one is interested in who she really is. No one thinks she has anything to offer except the fulfillment of some sexual fantasy (and Mendes' *really* understands male sexual fantasy—any man who says he cannot identify with the dream sequences in *American Beauty* is either lying or has lost his memory). Like Shylock in Shakespeare's *The Merchant of Venice*, she is someone we might normally write off. But, "when you cut me, do I not bleed?" When Lester shows her some respect, she has begun the path of learning to respect herself. The Colonel, however, cannot respect himself, and at the end of the film, he has lost all dignity. Perhaps the most pressing need for society today is to admit its own weakness, its inability to save itself. To create opportunities for people to be honest with each other. To stop pretending that we're all "normal," or that "normal" *exists*, as if the amazing variety of human beings can be slotted into some pre-determined category. Paul said something about this when he declared that "in Christ, there is neither Jew nor Greek, slave nor free, male nor female." There should be no boundaries of human acceptability in the Church. Moral decisions are one thing; *people* are another. Whoever they are.

I have a friend who preaches a lot. He often reminds his audience that we're all broken people, and that if they knew the totality of what goes on his soul, they wouldn't listen to him; then he says that if he knew what was going on in *their* souls, he mightn't be talking to them! The path to healing the human race is to make people feel safe to be themselves. In this, the Church has often singularly failed. But it has the gifts to change. There should be no more Colonels, forced to suppress their true selves, never having a peaceful moment in life, and finally retreating to the shadows when the one chance at redemption is spurned. The final speech in *American Beauty* verbalizes Lester's redemption, with the revelation that there is a force in the universe that is entirely benevolent and more powerful than anything else. There is no more reason to be afraid of anything. The film asks us to re-examine our own attitudes and practices, maybe even our whole way of being. It woke me up, and reawakens me every time I see it. It encourages me to assert the right kind of control over my life, that nobody can tell me what to do unless I let them, to live in community, and to be myself. When his heart fills with the joy of simply *being*, he says, "Then I remember to relax and stop trying to hold onto it, and then it flows through me like rain, and I can't feel anything but gratitude for every single moment of my stupid little life." *Lester* only sees this for a moment, but that moment could help make *our* whole lives worthwhile.

A PRIMER IN COMMUNITY

We'll start with films about community where people recognize a good thing when they see it. *About a Boy* is not really about the kind of boy you might expect; it's Hugh Grant's manchild that learns to let other people in past his spoiled rich kid defenses through hanging out with a real kid. William Hurt's widowed writer in *Smoke* undergoes a similar transformation, as he first rejects, then accepts the company of a motley crew of people, whose lives center on a Brooklyn cigar store (this film will make you want to buy Schimmelpinincks and use a rusty old typewriter, as well as have your best friends around for dinner.) Spike Lee's *Crooklyn* is set in a similar place but deals with the issues that face a cool black family that shows up *The Cosby Show* for the ivory tower (no pun intended) it was. There are no ivory towers in *Yi-Yi*, Edward Yang's glorious film from Taiwan about a family trying to stay together in the midst of trauma. Its central character is a little kid who will both break your heart and give you one of those big, beaming smiles that come all too rarely. Lots of smiles in the Coen Brothers' *Raising Arizona*, one of the funniest films ever made about family life. The desperation that leads a man to steal a kid because the parents have five others may not seem like a ripe subject for slapstick, but this film manages to make it work, while underlining the very best of "family values" among people more real than we often let ourselves be. The *Antz* are a bit like that, too; the anthropomorphism of putting psycho-babble into the mouths of insects who find it hard to be themselves in a crowd is a stroke of genius. It's the lighter side of communism in a kids' film, revealing the need for the pack to "pull together" for the sake of the weakest member. *Buena Vista Social Club* is simply a joyful record of how some old guys (and one woman) formed a musical community to lift the rest of our souls to salsa heaven.

Of course, there are as many (or perhaps even more) films about the breakdown of community. *Affliction* is another of Paul Schrader's films about darkness and the sins of the fathers and about how families can destroy each other. *Blue Velvet* is just as dark, lifting up the rock of suburban America, discovering as much pain and horror behind the white picket fence as you would expect on Elm Street. Suburban life is also the focus of Woody Allen's *Husbands and Wives*—where divorce and affairs and marriage are put under the microscope. You get more of the same in an amazing film from Ang Lee, *The Ice Storm*, based on Rick Moody's novel. This is what *American Beauty* would have been, without the redemption.

Families are strange, of course, but none more so than the brothers in David Cronenberg's *Dead Ringers*, twin brothers joined at the soul, rather than the hip, who cannot break free from each other. *The Fabulous Baker Boys* doesn't deal in such gruesome terms, but this is still a thoughtful meditation on sibling rivalry (with great jazz, too). But maybe the most dysfunctional family in the movies comes from a long time ago; thank goodness Luke and Leia were adopted, otherwise *The Empire Strikes Back* would have ended on a much darker note …

And it gets worse, because some films don't just analyze broken communities, but show how they sometimes disappear into themselves. Abel Ferrara's *The Funeral* and *The Godfather* are two of the best. Both tell the story of how people—in this case, gangsters—lose their humanity when they prefer their own wants above the needs of others. I think that *The Godfather* trilogy may try to put too clean a gloss on the activities of mafia families; they may get to look sharp, eat good food, and have great parties, but they are full of themselves and have no time for anyone else. In Coppola's films, the consequence of this is that, as the Gospels would say, "they have their reward"; in Ferrara's, the only possible end for those who base their existence on the destruction of others is death. And the best mafia films show how this death begins in not recognizing the common humanity of those around us. *Kids*, by Larry Clark and Harmony Korine, is nothing less than the most disturbing film I've ever seen. Its misanthropic worldview is perfectly suited to the tale of disaffected youth in urban America, but it made me feel complicit in their pain as I watched. And the shock value of the film wears off the second time around. However, when, in the last shot, a character looks straight into camera and says, "Jesus Christ, what happened?" you feel he's addressing this angst-ridden question to God as much as taking this name in vain.

In *Adaptation*, Charlie Kaufman and Spike Jonze's brilliantly complex film about just how difficult it is to write a film (they should try writing a *book on film*), Nicolas Cage's screenwriter angrily declares that he hates films with car chases, sex scenes, and people surmounting obstacles in order to learn the truths of spiritual growth. Oh dear. He wouldn't like *any* of the following: *Alice Doesn't Live Here Anymore* takes us on a journey through divorce and into finding community between mother and child. The same journey is pursued in Mike Leigh's *Secrets and Lies*, a darkly humorous and painfully redemptive story of broken families—just like *All About My Mother* and *Boogie Nights*, where broken people find a sense of family in the unlikeliest of places. Jake and Elwood, *The Blues Brothers*, never had a problem with expressing their anger, but they show that the family that plays together, stays together. Kaufman and Jonze might permit John Sayles' *Limbo* into their screening room, because it's such a serious, lyrically shot, beautifully written film about people finding they need each other whether they love each other or not. It's a perfectly realized story about story-telling itself, and it manages to pull off a reversal of pace in the middle that will leave you reeling. *Sunshine State* and *Passion Fish* are two more of Sayles' films about community—one set in a Florida town ripe for redevelopment (and destruction of the community ties), the other about two woman who find they need each other in unexpected ways.

There are many other fine films about community, too numerous to mention in detail, so let me simply encourage you to see some of these: *Dark Days*, an incredible documentary about people living in New York's subway tunnels, finding their way in the darkness together. *Kolya* is about an older man who, while living with a roof over his head, is spiritually homeless; he "inherits" a son in post-Communist Czech Republic and finds his way back to being childlike. *Eat Drink Man Woman* is another colorful film about food and foreigners and fun and love between families, but also about how beauty can mask coldness, as an Asian father attempts to show love for his daughters by preparing extravagant meals, without ever talking to them meaningfully. There may not be a great deal of meaningful conversation, either, in the communities that form in *Midnight Run* and *O Brother Where Art Thou?* They consist of men running from something, but also finding themselves along the way. And they're both hysterically funny.

Finally, I give you, Krysztof Kieslowski's *Three Colours Trilogy*. These might just be the best films of the '90s, based on the motifs associated with the French flag (freedom, equality, brotherhood—these three masterpieces find a way to *embody* community, liberation, love, friendship, and power). Kieslowski died young, and his collaborators often say that he created the same kind of spirit of community on set that he strove to depict or critique in his films. That is truly incarnational filmmaking.

THE WRAP

Mike Riddell, the New Zealand-based theologian and writer, tells the true story of a church that met in the end terrace of a row of houses. A young girl who lived in the unit next door attended the church. One Sunday morning during the service, the parishioners heard the clear sounds of the girl's father beating her mother. So the worship leader played his music louder. And all was well in the ivory tower. While that story isn't, of course, representative of all churches, I think we may agree that what we experience in the technophiliac West falls far short of the spiritual community envisioned by Jesus. We relate through computers like the one I'm writing this on, we anaesthetize ourselves against honesty by always answering the same way when someone asks us how we're doing, we get married and stay home, maybe inviting a friend over for a short dinner once in a while. Douglas Coupland could have been talking about so many of us when he said that he realized that people he knew ceased being able to make new friends when they bought their first expensive piece of furniture. And in the midst of this bleakness, there appears shoots of hope; people may be recognizing that spirituality cannot be adequately mediated through a sermon or worship performance. That at the very least, smaller groups of people seeking to take God and each other seriously can be the only hope for the future of humanity.

Is it possible that we might, in this generation, understand that our biological families need the help of the spiritual community to survive? That our single people are not freaks who require to be mopped up and married off to each other so we don't have to deal with the fact of their existence? That sometimes marriages end for good reasons, and that the people involved need to be helped to put things back together without the stigma of everybody knowing the intimate details of why and where and who did what to whom? That we may be called to be mothers and fathers and sisters and brothers to more than just the people who once drank the sticky liquid in our mother's womb? That God has not ordained a post-war Western mode of being as the only proper way to live?

How do we re-build a sense of community? Eating is one of a few things we do every day (unless we're very spiritual and are fasting, of course), but I think we have lost the meaning of eating. The most important ritual of the Christian Church revolves around a shared meal, but millennia of tradition and schism have turned even that mystical experience into a bone of contention and dry/dusty exercise. When all is said and done, the thing that I enjoy most is a meal with friends and some good conversation. All the better if we take time to prepare the meal together. And if we see eating together as obedience to Jesus' last supper command, then it may just become a transcendent moment to share, to give thanks for what has gone before, to truly live. Our generation has been McDonaldized into forgetting what shared meals should be like. It's up to us to help restore this most important sacrament.

It has been said that if we were to approach strangers on the street and say, "They know—run for it!" nine out of ten people would run away, because we all have secrets that we're terrified of being exposed. But what seems like the path of least resistance—to hide our true selves in case we appear weak—is actually a more difficult task than being honest about the challenges we face, the mistakes we've made, and the pain we feel. There is great freedom in being honest about who you really are. And sometimes your willingness to be vulnerable with others is a gift that will heal them. No matter what your pain or vulnerability, chances are, someone you know needs it. Please don't withhold that gift.

CHAPTER SEVEN

FEAR
THINGS THAT GO BUMP IN THE NIGHT

"Perfect love casts out fear." —St. John

"This is happening to make us despair of the possibility that God could ever love us." —Father Merrin, *The Exorcist*

YOU'VE ALREADY MET MY DAD IN THESE PAGES— you know, the guy who used to pretend we weren't going to the cinema and kept it a surprise from my brother and I until we were at the box office. He had even greater influence on my film-going than that, though. When I was about ten years old, I asked him to tell me the narrative of the Antichrist film, *The Omen*. So he did. *As a bedtime story.* I knew the actor Patrick Troughton from re-runs of *Doctor Who*, and so I recognized his name when Dad told me of his role in this movie. He's a priest who gets impaled by a collapsed church steeple. David Warner—another one of those great actors who never gets decent parts—plays a photographer who gets his comeuppance in a rather nasty little scene involving photographic plates. Dad told the story so evocatively that I had trouble sleeping for the next month; images of Doctor Who pinned to the ground by a massive church building filled my frame of vision as soon as I closed my eyes. I vowed to never watch this film or its sequels.

So, of course, I watched the whole trilogy about five years later.[1] I saw that Troughton's death was less gruesome than I had thought, but the manner of Leo McKern's (Rumpole of the Bailey!) dispatch was enough to keep me away from sandpits for a good while. Later I watched a pirated copy of *The Exorcist* from behind a sofa with my friend Neill, both of us pretending that the other was more scared.

No discussion of fear in cinema is complete without reference to *The Exorcist* (1973, William Friedkin, William Peter Blatty). I used to think that all that needs to be said is that if you haven't seen it yet, go and rent it, but be prepared to think about it for the next three months and not sleep very well. But I suspect most of you who haven't seen it are unlikely to do that, so, out of the immense kindness that I often find in my soul, here are some thoughts:

This is not a film I would recommend to everyone, but in another sense, it's a film that I think everyone should see. This is not a horror film; it's the triumph of good over evil, and therefore begs to be seen in an optimistic light. It *is* scary, but Kipper ties and flared trousers—perhaps the worst aspect of the 1970s—may outweigh your sense of fear at the demonic activity on display. This film can't hurt you unless you let it—remember that Jesus said it's not what goes *into* a person that makes them evil; but I won't pretend that watching it is an easily forgotten ordeal. In a strange twist of cinematic fate, the movie opens on an archaeological dig in Iraq, the place we love to hate, but

---

[1] Yes, I know there is an *Omen IV*, but it was made for television, so it doesn't count.

would do well to remember was the world's first true artistic and educational culture. Here we find the wise and craggy Father Merrin (whose appearance raises at least two questions: How *do* you get to be a priest and an archaeologist at the same time? Has Max von Sydow *always* looked this old?) confronted by the coming of a demon that he fought before. He's working near Nineveh, the place Jonah refused to travel to because he felt its people to be unworthy of God's message, which is ambiguously related to the theme of this film. It's based on an allegedly true story from the 1940s and is written by a committed Catholic, William Peter Blatty, but I can leave the reliability of the source to the side. This film is more about the mythic battle between good and evil than whether or not real exorcisms happen in real life. The fact that we don't know what's going on at the start is a lovely device; the fact that the story takes place in suburban America even more so. At one level, it's quite funny; I mean, just seeing a stone gargoyle is hardly the kind of portent of doom that should cause a heart attack … But Father Merrin is clearly meant as a kind of "God's lonely man" figure, stumbling through the dusty Iraqi village as the terror to come begins to dawn on him.

So we quickly move to Georgetown (which I have found to be great place for a summer evening coffee) and find that the university area is the location for the satanic engagement (this should be no surprise to any parent who has sent a child to college!). Ellen Burstyn (my favorite actress, as you will no doubt remember) plays an actress, and we see a film-within-a-film being made. Her character is shown addressing a student rally, telling them that they can't accomplish anything unless they do it within the system, a philosophy that will have major relevance later in the film. She walks home and overhears one priest telling a counselor, "There's not a day in my life when I don't feel like a fraud." The central character is the aforementioned counsellor

Father Karras (not the little girl named Regan whom we all know gets possessed), who is also losing his faith in God because he sees too much pain. We discover that his elderly mother has nothing in this world but the radio and a visit from her son, and he is ridden with guilt. When she is finally committed to an asylum, shortly before her death, Karras is distressed by the condition of the inmates, which Friedkin calls "an example of God's having deserted the world, and having deserted him as well."

The actress' daughter is having trouble sleeping (so might you after watching this, but it doesn't have to be that way), and it's not long before all hell breaks loose. In every sense of the term. She hears voices, and things shake, and she shakes, and her face develops sores, and she says some very nasty things, and we're definitely not in Kansas anymore. After a battery of (very hard to watch) medical tests fails to resolve matters (science has its limits), and Regan *really* starts doing damage to herself, the agnostic mother calls in the doubting priest. He is initially skeptical (and unfocused, dealing with the recent death of his manipulative mother), but when he sees the sheer horror of Regan's condition, he realizes that only the power of God can possibly make things right. The voices in her head, spewing obscenity from her mouth, are screaming, "I am no one I am no one." And it seems that the monster that has somehow come to inhabit her will simply consume her. Even her face becomes so dreadful that it is difficult to look at; but in a disturbing sign that God is not letting Regan be tested beyond what she can bear, the words "Help Me" appear burned onto her stomach. So, in spite of his crisis of faith, Karras realizes he needs to help because the girl's needs are too great. So he contacts Father Merrin, and the stage is set.

The old priest, resigned to one more battle with his spiritual enemy, travels to Georgetown. On his arrival, there is a short, kind scene in which he sips a drink with the mother, calming her fears with his very presence, in the way only old people who lead a life of prayer do. When Regan sees things like the snarling demons who occupy her mind (and I do mean occupy—as in military occupation), it may seem totally alien to everyday experience. But for anyone who has been seriously depressed, it's a bit like hearing the voices that undermine your sense of self. We all have "voices" in our heads. Whether audible or simply "sensed," their character is the same—an "adult" voice that reflects and makes decisions and grows and looks after us; a "child" voice that loves and enjoys and hopes and likes going on roller coasters and sometimes gets scared; and a "critical" voice that seeks to destroy us with its bile. All of us should be able to identify with this. Mental and spiritual health are found in allowing the adult and child to find balance with each other, and ignoring the critic. This is not to say that we should not reflect on our actions or critique the way we are, but the adult voice is sufficient for this. The critic is only there to undermine and destroy. Perhaps it is the residue of the titanic battles of childhood, perhaps it is more complex than that. Wherever it comes from, you don't have to be its slave. (See the section later in this book on *The Wizard of Oz* for more on how to disarm the critical voice.) Regan's experience of demonic possession is tantamount to being overwhelmed by the critical voice: "I am no one I am no one I am no one." She has been almost totally subsumed under the power of this monumental terror, and, like the rest of us, she needs others to help her be free. And the demon even attacks Karras' fears, using tricks and obscenities, the most memorable of which is when Regan says in a snarling bark: "Your mother's in here with us; would you like to send her a message? I'll see that she gets it."

The priests begin the exorcism, breaking bread together; they repeat the following mantra: "The power of Christ compels you" and the repetition makes you want to shout, "Amen!" Regan levitates and things get a bit crazy, and Karras needs to rest. Merrin suggests he take a break, as his rampant doubts are making the exorcism impossible. Karras is ashamed, but the older man shows deep love to him, touching him on the shoulder and telling him it's all right. What happens next may scare you out of the room, if you haven't already left, so I'll leave it for you to find out. But I do need to tell you how it finally ends. In an ultimate act of despair—and indeed anger—at God for letting this happen, Karras screams at the demon to "take me." The demon consents, flying out of Regan and into him; with the semblance of humanity that he has left, he throws himself out of the window, destroying the demon by his death.

The demon is constantly trying to test their faith, and the cosmic struggle that plays out in this suburban location is still incredibly disturbing, thirty years after the film was made. Perhaps this is because the unsuspecting terror is happening to an innocent child; we feel that this shouldn't be happening. We often look for reasons why bad things happen and have invented complex theologies to explain the darkness of this world. We have even constructed the notion that Satan only attacks "because God wants to use you"—but what about whole people groups who suffer: Are they *all* good Christians? I think it's more likely that bad things happen all the time and are often impossible to explain. We look for a reason why, and Father Merrin answers us by saying, "I think the point is to make us despair, to see ourselves as animal and ugly, to reject the possibility that God could love us."

This is the struggle for our own souls, the voices we all hear—the threat that God might not love us, that human beings are nothing but garbage and life has no meaning, that we might be depraved, that we might be hateful in the extreme. In *The Exorcist*, this is the consequence of satanic possession, but

I suspect that in real life, our experience of self-despair may actually be part of the legacy of "bad Calvinism," which seems to prescribe self-loathing as the first step on the road to a heaven that actually sounds more boring than hell.

It's a perfectly controlled film—there is no dead weight here, no extra flesh. Everything is developed to achieve maximum effect with the audience, but it doesn't feel manipulative, just incredibly accomplished at doing its job. It's technically brilliant—for a simple example, just consider the use of the camera, which is always looking down on Regan, while watching Karras rise from below; the point is subtle, but seems so clever on reflection. The Reverend Billy Graham once said something like, "There is a genuine power of evil in this film," but I always wondered why a piece of celluloid could hurt people. With due respect to Graham, I think he missed the point. For me, this film is a God-saturated reflection on faith and self-doubt and parents and ministry and evil and good and sacrifice. Its director refers to "this is my body, this is my blood" as "the most beautiful words in any language," and he clearly understands something of the nature of sacrificial love. It's about how fear can trap the mind, and how the moment of least faith may be the moment of most power. Father Karras' character arc should make us sit up and think about how we often place unworkable expectations on spiritual leaders without thinking of how *they* might be feeling. It's also sage on the issue of what demons actually are; there may be both less and more to Regan's predicament than we first imagine. Her father doesn't call on her birthday, and although she and her mother are close, Burstyn's character is not entirely blameless when it comes to Regan's experience of rage. This theme is interestingly built— the mother's use of obscenity, the broken relationship with the father, the media's attention to the mother, not to the daughter … It's a salutary lesson in how the demonic is sometimes just a name given to an experience we don't understand. The film doesn't spell things out for us, and it feels good to be respected in this way; if I were to try to sum it up in a sentence, I'd say *The Exorcist* is about the fact that you can't control the world around you, but you can respond with love.

There's an apocryphal story about the English evangelist Charles Spurgeon, famous for long sermons, stern wisdom, and being a heavy smoker. He is said to have been awakened one night by a strange noise. He went downstairs, only to be confronted by Satan himself, sitting in Spurgeon's favorite armchair, smoking Spurgeon's favorite pipe. The devil looked up and inhaled to speak, but Spurgeon interrupted before he could squeeze a word out. "Make sure you turn the lights off when you leave," he said, and walked quietly (and confidently) back to bed. On one level this is a silly story, and if we believe it to be literally true we may be losing our grip on reality. But it reveals something of the nature of the triumph of good over evil. Non-violent, non-confrontational absorption of the darkness is the way of the cross. There comes a point during the exorcism when Merrin realizes that he's going to die if he stays in the room, but he continues regardless. Isn't this the point of being a Christian? Dietrich Bonhoeffer once said, "When Christ calls someone, he bids them come and die." This is not indulgent morbidity, or the cinematic version of a martyr complex; it's simply a reflection on the seriousness of a life of faith. It's also the way Karras saves Regan, by putting himself in her place. His sacrificial death makes her life possible. That's the metaphor, anyway.

As for "real" exorcisms, well, sometimes what has come to be known as "deliverance ministry" is about as serious—and complex—as this film makes it look. I've all too often seen people suspect demons where the problem is more clearly psychological. And while I believe everyone has something to contribute to the ongoing ministry of Christ, allowing non-specialists, or at least untrained people loose on vulnerable people to test the newest theory of demonization may be pastorally catastrophic. If you don't understand that the *only way to fight fire is with water*, and that sometimes the thing that frightens you most needs you to befriend it so that it can be at peace, then you should realize you're not yet ready to engage in this kind of practice. Only when Karras offers *himself* do things change; the healing of the broken is not a spectacular task. It is often messy, and almost as painful for the healer as the survivor. Henri Nouwen's wonderful theory of the "wounded healer" offers a path a million miles away from militant Christian triumphalism. I have no doubt that *The Exorcist* is about the triumph of good over evil through the self-giving love of a servant of God. It is *not* blasphemous. What is blasphemy anyway? Merely saying particular words, or affirming certain ways of being? On the second count, the commercialized Gospel, the get-rich-quick charms of prosperity teaching, and the domination of oppressive leadership systems are sacrilegious indeed. Meanwhile, *The Exorcist*, with its affirmation of the love of God, of the power of the Christian community to be agents of healing, and of the amazing mystery of faith is closer to a Psalm of praise.

How do we keep faith when we confront evil? How do we keep from destroying each other? If you believe in the power of good over evil, that is what you will take from this film; if you don't, then you may find your pessimism is reinforced. But I hope you will watch it and face the unfolding of reality. It has a reputation for being a dark film, but it ends with a man of God saving a child's life through sacrificial death; I'm not sure how much more sacramental you can get. Like anything that reminds us of the existence of a benevolent God, and of the ultimate absorption of evil by good, *The Exorcist* cannot be seen as anything other than an optimistic film.

A PRIMER IN FEAR

I don't like "horror" films—there's enough darkness in other movies and the real world without my causing myself to be terrified—and having to pay for the privilege. And supernatural gore, or dark arts, often seems like a cheap way of manipulating an audience. That's why I have not dwelt on traditional horror movies in this section. There's enough fear out there already. But there are films around—I like to think of them as "horror with integrity," that have a certain quality which makes them as worthwhile as any; so here, for what *they're* worth, are my reflections on seven guaranteed to keep you up at night.

The Shining is Stanley Kubrick's mad film of Stephen King's epic tale of supernatural forces and family life. King later wrote that he eventually realized it was a book about his own alcoholism, while Kubrick told Jack Nicholson that—like *The Exorcist*—it was an optimistic film, because "any film that suggests there is life after death must be optimistic." If you're a writer, you will identify with the horror of the process of putting *yourself* down on paper, but hopefully it will bring a wry smile to your face, too. You won't necessarily feel very optimistic after seeing it, and it doesn't bear huge relation to the novel, but for an exercise in how to scare an audience stupid, *The Shining* might just be the best artefact on the ghost train.

Signs is the third of M. Night Shyamalan's series of films about coping with death (of the body or the past) which reverse our expectations of heavyweight stars like Bruce Willis and Mel Gibson, as they have to confront their own vulnerabilities in the face of great danger. *Signs* has brilliant Hitchcockian flair, beautiful cinematography and lifelike performances, and most of the story is wonderfully located in an isolated farmhouse. Gibson plays a Lutheran pastor struggling with his lost faith after the death of his wife; just to complicate (or indeed, redeem) things, aliens turn up in his cornfield. They scare the hell out of us, and the heaven into him. There's one great scene in which he tries to calm his frightened brother by explaining that there are two kinds of people in the world—those who believe that we are not alone, and those who believe that we are. He says that the fact that the first kind of person exists should be comfort enough for us in these dark times, and I suppose this is one definition of bearing each other's burdens. Even when we doubt or experience disbelief, the fact that others believe might be adequate to keep us afloat.

There's more fear of what's in the most mundane of places in Hitchcock's *The Birds*, which addresses the anxiety that nature will one day have its revenge on us and gives new meaning to the term "hen-pecked husband." *Rosemary's Baby* is a black comedy horror about a woman who gives birth to the devil. This may just be a metaphor for postnatal depression or the struggle of pregnancy itself, but it does its job in getting us to think about the darkness of everyday life when people are forced to bend to the will of others.

The devil himself makes another appearance in *Angel Heart*, a violent, nasty film about selling your soul. I don't really think this film is a metaphor for anything, and there's absolutely no redemption in it whatsoever, so I'd only recommend it if you want to see de Niro hamming it up as Lucifer, and Mickey Rourke providing tragic evidence that he could have had one of the best careers in Hollywood cinema, if only he'd allowed it to happen. A more nuanced view of evil can be found in *Nosferatu* (I prefer Werner Herzog's 1979 version to Murnau's 1920s silent classic), which has the distinction of making us feel sorry for the eponymous vampire, who, ultimately, does what he does for love's sake. So many horror films are about the tragedy of being an outsider; this is as much about Dracula's own sense of love and loss as it is about his unusual way of showing affection.

There's more sadness than fear also in *The Devil's Backbone*, about a Spanish Civil War-era orphanage where the kids have to grow up very quickly, and the dead cannot be at peace until their murders have been avenged. Of course, for sheer edge-of-your-seat terror, I still think *Jaws* is the leader of the flotilla. Even though the mechanical shark is less technologically accomplished than my toothbrush, I still hide behind the sofa before the head appears and jump out of my skin several times more as the film progresses.

THE WRAP

Fear seems to be the guiding force in so many people's lives; I grew up in fear of the violence that my home society was plunged into in the late 1960s, and later developed a terror that God might never use me if I was not perfect. Sometimes that fear returns, and I don't sleep too well; other times I am filled with a sense of safety and love, and my heart wells up with life as if it's about to break. Perhaps the adrenaline rush that we get from scary movies does us good in the long run—it reminds us that we're still alive, and there's no harm in an escapist thrill rush once in a while. I remember sitting on a beachside cliff top in New Zealand and reflecting on my own life and sense of brokenness. Listening to the thunder of the waves represented to me the presence of a benevolent force, whose will was toward me, and for my good and good alone. Moments like that come along every once in a while, and you should treasure them, because sometimes their memory—what Van Morrison calls "the beauty of the days gone by"—is the only thing that will carry you through fear and struggle in the future.

I used to wonder if I would ever have a moment that was completely free from fear. People around me seemed to be so confident, so self-assured, so secure in their faith, so ready for anything. But as I got older and got to know people better, I realized that this was either wishful thinking on my part, or self-deceit on theirs. Frankly, I now believe that everyone tends to live in fear. There are no "spiritual giants." We all sweat with anxiety at times. Sometimes the fear is reasonable, sometimes not. But unless we learn to deal with our fear, we are doomed to live what has been called "a life of quiet desperation," making ends meet from moment to moment, but living in the constant fear that it all might be snatched away. In fact, it may well be true that the things we fear the most have already happened to us. We are simply trapped in the repetition of old nightmares. It seems to me that there is only one way to deal with your fear—that is to face it for what it is. I'll say more about this later, when I talk about *The Wizard of Oz*, but for now, let me suggest that your life is your own before God. It does not belong to whatever terror seizes you in the night, unless you permit that. Whatever fear traps you—whether real or imagined—can be resolved through facing it. This requires an honest assessment of why you are afraid and of just how real the fear is, but what you need most is to learn to love yourself in all your glorious expressions.

I was terrified of *The Exorcist* when I was younger and believed the world was against me. Now, having begun the journey away from such paranoia and insecurity, I watch it, and it brings me hope. Perhaps movies about fear can serve as healing agents, because they cause us to confront the things that go bump in the night; the shock of the fearful film may lead to a kind of "death" on the part of the viewer, which in the paradox of God-breathed existence, might actually give us more life. I'm not sure that I can prescribe what any of us need to do to journey in this direction, and it's not that I've got the whole thing sewn up. No, I still find myself getting scared—about the future, about the past, about today. I simply observe so much fear in this world, perhaps especially among Christians, and we need to allow ourselves to heal, or we'll never be the kind of creature God made us to be.

CHAPTER EIGHT

GOD

KOYAANISQATSI
(GODFREY REGGIO, 1983)

THERE ARE THINGS THAT EXISTED BEFORE WE did and will be here after we leave. *Koyaanisqatsi* (from the Hopi language, meaning "life out of balance") is perhaps the most powerful film about nature ever[1]; endlessly imitated, never equalled, it could serve both as a prophetic warning and an aid to worship, as we are overwhelmed by the beauty of the earth and the destructiveness of humankind. It has the power to make you see everything with new eyes—like Neo's early experience of the Matrix—to feel like you're looking at the world around you for the first time. I saw it performed "live" once, with Philip Glass playing alongside the projected print—maybe the best experience I've ever had in a cinema. It's dangerously

---

[1] *Koyaanisqatsi* is part of a trilogy—the others are *Powaqqatsi* and *Nagoyqatsi*.

exhilarating to watch, perhaps especially because you have the sneaking suspicion that you're seeing *yourself* on the screen. What has been called "the illusory nature of created things" is one thing, but sometimes those created things are pretty good at damaging other created things—and this is not an illusion. Aboriginal cultures believe that nobody owns the land, and I suppose this is not a million miles away from "the earth is the Lord's, and everything in it." This film will make you awestruck at God's creation, and (hopefully) weep for what we're doing to it. Godfrey Reggio, its director, is a former Catholic monk, and the composer of its remarkable score, Mr. Glass, is a Buddhist—if you think knowing something about the authorship of a work of art is irrelevant to how you understand or appreciate it, think again. These guys are clearly devoted to their own spirituality and want to draw us in, too. They are amply supported by the cinematographer, Ron Fricke; there is no adequate way to describe the photography. The movie has no dialogue; it is simply a journey from unpopulated parts of the planet to the mega-conurbations of the West.

While there is little sign of where human beings have dealt well with what we've been given, Reggio wants to show us what went right, what is chaotic and magnificent about the earth before what went wrong. In the opening scenes, he manages to make us see the earth like we've never gazed on it before—desert spaces evoking Martian landscapes. One of the biblical writers said that the stones would rise up and worship God if we people do not; and it looks like that's just what they're doing in these early sequences. We see sand dunes looking like corrugated cardboard and cloud formations like tidal waves or explosions—convulsions of white light that look like they pose a danger to us—followed by fields of surreally colored flowers that consume our own field of vision. These scenes are reminiscent of the amazing "Rite of Spring" sequence in Disney's *Fantasia* (which from me is high praise indeed), but before we get too comfortable with the images of beautiful nature, we are brought down to the level of the human with a whimper.

We see sunbathers overshadowed by power stations, mechanical diggers looking like mythical monsters, and in a sequence where Fricke manages to actually photograph *heat*, planes seemingly waltzing with each other on the highway, as thousands of cars (looking like tanks) take cover. It's funny seeing the old cars (the movie's twenty years old), but the metaphor has more meaning than ever. And people rush on with their existences. And they destroy things—apartment blocks collapse like sandcastles, pork is fed into a processor from which is ejected an excuse for food (you may never eat a sausage again after you see how they get made on production line), and rockets explode on take off. Bombs are photographed as if they're sex objects (which, of course, for some people, they seem to be); the fetishization of violence is simply portrayed, with the audience free to make its own judgment (see Cronenberg's *Crash* for another thoughtful reflection on old cars and fetishized violence).

The rest of the film focuses on you and me, as we follow people, often with intrusive close ups, through city life. The people are running around like members of a particularly neurotic ant colony, but somehow less than the sum of its parts; those shown in close up look like they're made out of plastic, as if they are on display to be laughed at; the film seems to be asking what is left of their humanity. The violence of food court behavior seems to indicate Reggio's plea that we might once again engage in the *sacrament* of eating together, taking time with each other, instead of working soulless jobs to make just enough money to buy things we don't need. Indeed, it makes me want to scream, "Shouldn't the Church be creating soulful jobs rather than enriching itself on the back of humanoid machines on minimum wage? Can we not just slow down?"

And so it goes, and so it goes, and so it goes … Why do people want to live like this? Why do we accept it? It seems that it's not enough to destroy nature by what we build, but we don't even build the right things, or the things we need; and when we've built them, we destroy them also. Some elements of the Christian Church must bear their share of responsibility for the dangerous instant throwaway culture we've inherited. There are plenty of unhealthy theories about the return of Christ that imply it's okay to let the world go to seed because it's all eventually going to end anyway. But can this really be what Jesus really meant? What if the first commandment that God gave—"subdue," or look after the earth—is still the prime directive for humankind? What if our core task is not to prepare the way for some kind of spectacular second coming (which tends to frighten and confuse people more than it brings hope; and, although some might find this hard to believe, the theory of the rapture proclaimed in recent populist Christian fiction is just that—*fiction*, with little or no relation to a rigorous, well-informed reading of Scripture and church history) but rather to become more human, and in that becoming, make way for Jesus, the Son of Man, or quintessential human to be born in all our lives? To put it another way, we don't have to be Luddites or Amish to be Christians, but that doesn't mean that we don't have to ask ourselves exactly what *would* Jesus drive?

Does *Koyaanisqatsi* reflect anything of the *goodness* of humankind? Maybe not, but that is the point of the film; Reggio is prophesying to us that our failure as a race to be good stewards of the earth has left us in dire straits, and unless we do something about it, we will have nothing left to steward. We are a broken race (and you already know what I think about *that*), people so often living in fear—we see a man by his window, a woman stepping over a fire hose, people getting into an elevator, relentless television evangelists pronouncing violent rhetoric, an old woman's hand reaching out for a touch, and a homeless man counting coppers in his palm, with an unexplained bruise on his forehead, while a choir laments on the soundtrack. When the people get into the elevator, you want to cry out to them to stop, but you feel that it's too late; this reminds me of Ezekiel's words about the need to warn our human brothers and sisters of the enemy's approach, or their blood will be on our hands. There are some examples of how human beings can get it *right*—a heroic firefighter, people smiling, enjoying each other's company, kids playing games together; but, on the whole, this is not a film about the lighter side of life. For me, the most striking image is the close-up of the man with the saddest face I've ever seen—he looks like Max von Sydow on a *really* bad day. You want to reach out and touch him, to take him by the hand and tell him that it's going to be alright, that whatever catastrophe of broken relationships or illness or mental dysfunction that has been visited upon him, you will take responsibility to help heal.

Koyaanisqatsi could be the content of a reflective worship service, an attempt at restoration of the Church's lost tradition of lament. It's so beautiful—as its creator says, a terrible beauty, an awesome beauty, the beauty of the beast—it could make the heart break. Its most shocking aspect is the acknowledgement that Westerners are prima facie guilty of idolatry—that the horrific truth that faces us is the possibility that what we most value is a monster that eats the earth. It's more like a symphony than a narrative film, and we should be left in no doubt of its message—that there is always a limit to human endeavor, and we need something bigger than our best ideas of God to rescue us. We end with a vision of Hopi cave paintings and the disturbing prophecy of a future "Day of Purification" on which the world will be purged of those who seek to destroy it. Those who were here before us have left their mark of epochal wisdom. *Koyaanisqatsi* is a word that has no English equivalent, but can be loosely translated as "life out of balance; a way of life that calls for another way of being." How much more resonance with the Gospel do you want? Reggio says that the Hopi words help him because "Our language is in a state of vast humiliation"—it is no longer adequate to describe the horror of the underbelly of our existence. Everything that we consider sane was a mark of insanity for Aboriginal people. Like the foolishness of God being wiser than the wisdom of humans, we need to consider if our "normal" ways are actually distortions of what's best. We need to find new ways of being, but perhaps we will only be able to do so when we have found the courage to simply *talk* about what we are becoming.

It is likely that you may go away from this film with a sense of despair (it might not be the film to watch last thing at night; although the most frightening thing about it is the clothes people liked to wear in the '80s). But, after you have let it rest in you for a while, you may recognize its prophetic spirit. You may remember the lonely people and realize that these are those whom we are called to serve, to love, to welcome. Human beings, one to another, are gifted with the power to heal the broken, to bind up wounds, to mend divided communities, and to participate in the redemption of the earth. The camera seems to look into the souls of its subjects, which is a necessary step if we are to heal each other.

Reggio has said that, having entered a monastery at age fourteen, he grew up in effect in the middle ages, which was bad and good at the same time, and gave him a special preparation for life, a life of humility and service and prayer. I think it gave him a special preparation for *film*, too; perhaps all directors should spend time in spiritual contemplation before they attempt to portray what it is to be human; in fact, I suspect

most of the best do just that. At the end of *Koyaanisqatsi*, we will
have been exhilarated and challenged; our field of vision will
have been consumed by terrible beauty, our ears will have been
honored by music that seems to come from another world, our
very senses will have been possessed by something that we have
not seen before. And this is all good. But the question is, when
we try to recall the human ant colony we just saw on screen, do
we even recognize their faces? Those who have ears to hear, let
them hear …

THE LAST TEMPTATION OF CHRIST
(MARTIN SCORSESE, PAUL SCHRADER, 1988)

*Jesus' rage did not abate. "I say one thing, you write another, and
those who read you understand still something else! I say: cross, death,
kingdom of heaven, God … and what do you understand? Each of you
attaches his own suffering, interests and desires to each of these sacred
words, and words disappear, my soul is lost. I can't stand it anymore!"*
—Nikos Kazantzakis, *The Last Temptation of Christ*

There are many ways of looking at films. Checking out
the photography, or the acting, or the music, or the story,
or something like that. The truth is, I can only speak about
Scorsese's *Last Temptation* in terms of my own life experience.
There was a time in the early '90s when I decided to try to see
all of Scorsese's films; they weren't all available on video, and
DVD hadn't arrived yet (the cinema's prehistoric era!), so it was
a good day when I read in the *Radio Times* that Britain's Channel
4 was devoting a season to his films. *Last Temptation* is sadly well
known because some Christians couldn't handle it. This may be
no bad thing, as it led to it being seen by far more people than
would otherwise, making a healthy profit for Universal in 1988.

But it says something about the broad Christian community that in 2000 years of church history, the idea of Jesus as a truly human being still cannot find resonance among any but those on the fringes of the institutional church.

We have trivialized the pain of this boy and man, who must have agonized over His destiny, by inventing a theology for Him that we don't apply to anyone else—the idea that He had no choice about His life, and that He responded to the temptations He suffered by reciting Scripture, automaton-like, to someone He *knew* was the devil. We have enervated the crucifixion in our contemporary art, from Zeffirelli's doe-eyed *Jesus of Nazareth* to the commercialization of "What would Jesus do?"—a brand now owned by Hallmark cards! We have even tidied away the meaning of His death and resurrection, turning it into a formula whereby paying mental assent to the substitutionary theory of the atonement gets you instant access to eternal life, without any need to recourse to all that complicated stuff about feeding hungry people and clothing the naked. And we have up-ended His leadership pattern, by making spiritual authority contingent on academic credentials, or gender, or race, or sexual orientation. I would like to suggest that, even many years after its first release, *The Last Temptation of Christ* may yet serve as a prophetic antidote to such heresy. At the risk of over-stating the case, let those who have ears to hear ….

The Christ of *The Last Temptation* is first shown writhing on dusty ground, mentally tortured by His conflicting desires— to serve God or to have a "normal life," with the family He desperately wants. He has obviously been aware of the voices that say He might be Messiah for as long as He can remember, but He fears this more than anything else. Not unreasonable behavior, I suspect. Haven't we all had moments where we encounter something that is either transcendent, or the sickness of our own minds, or both, and not been sure what to do about it? Willem Dafoe's Jesus knows the pain of His people, but also the struggle that awaits He who would be their rescuer. The beauty of this film is that it shows a human Jesus, who, rather than proving Himself in the desert, continues to fight with doubt and confusion over the manner in which His purpose is to be outworked. He knows that He has a mission, but isn't exactly sure what that is. Some have criticized the film for apparently implying that Jesus was weak—but it is a dangerous thing to confuse genuine humanity and the honest search for God with weakness. I would follow this guy, as He cries out for justice, incarnates mercy for outcasts, cleanses His Father's house of the corruption of Roman gods and Jewish elitism, and brings healing and the restoration of community to the broken-bodied, shattered-spirits, and even the dead.

Bringing life where there was none is a messy business, and so is the prophetic incarnation of the kingdom of God. I find it strange that the portrayals of Jesus in visual art and literature that meet with the broader church's approval are the ones that have Him wearing the cleanest robes. The Jesus in Kazantzakis' novel and Scorsese's film of *The Last Temptation* flies in the face of such fluffy-cloud imagery. This is a Jesus who sucks the marrow out of life, eating and drinking, and dancing and crying, and hurting, and being broken apart by giving Himself to the higher calling. He is not a Jesus who manipulates, wrongly intimidates, or elicits guilt from His followers. He is a Jesus who reveals Himself to be the quintessential man and shows the path to truth by giving Himself up. It is not unusual for me to find spiritual nourishment in film, but it is unusual to find a portrayal of Jesus that teaches me more than a dozen unenlightened readings of the Gospels. I can think of no higher praise for *The Last Temptation of Christ* than to assert that, in short, this is a Jesus I could believe in.

FIELD OF DREAMS
(PHIL ALDEN ROBINSON, 1989)

So, here we are. By this stage, I guess you may have made up your mind about me. You will know if you and I speak the same language, or if we live on different planets. You may be able to guess if we like the same kind of ice cream, or indeed if we are, ourselves, the same flavor as each other. Diversity's great, so don't worry if we don't see eye to eye—I mean, I'm not even sure that I agree with myself all the time. Anyway, like I said at the start, the film we're about to discuss means a lot to me. I believe I went as far as saying that I might not be able to love anyone who didn't love it. On reflection, that's going a bit too far. I'll still love ya, but I may not invite you for dinner as much as you'd want.

So, where should I start? At the beginning, I guess. We see the famous UNIVERSAL logo—you know, the one with the planet that seems to always stop rotating when it gets to America—and the film begins. And a universal film it is, too, because when everything is said and done (and dreamed), *Field of Dreams* has a message that's about as universal as it gets. We all need each other, we've all made mistakes, what we do for others has an unusual way of doing good to *us*. The sci-fi logo is appropriate for another reason, for this film feels like it comes from another time, another place, when people had time for each other, and read books, for a start. For any of you who don't know, the movie's just your everyday story about a farmer, weighed down by the guilt of rejecting his father, who hears a voice telling him to plough under his crops and build a baseball diamond there so that Shoeless Joe Jackson can come back from the dead and hit a few strikes. So he builds the field, and his wife tells him she thinks he's cool because he's willing to do crazy things, and Shoeless Joe appears, and he hears the voice again and kidnaps a reclusive writer and travels back in time and meets a kindly old doctor, and the doctor becomes a young man again, and they all go back to the field, and the writer agrees to write again, and the doctor gets his dream of playing ball, and the farmer wonders what's in it for him, and he meets his dead dad and reconciles with him, and everybody cries, and about a thousand people turn up at the field so they can be healed, too. Roll credits.

Don't be angry with me if you think I've just ruined the film for ya—knowing the outcome isn't that important; it's the *experience* of watching that will melt your soul. (Trust me, it's my Dad's favorite film, and he's not one to cry at the drop of a hat; but when we watch it together, I feel my chest tighten from about halfway through and have to suppress the tears that I know will flow from us both by the end.) The farmer—Kevin Costner as Ray Kinsella (a good Irish name, to be sure—all the best things have an Irish root, of course)—seems to build the field in about five minutes, but then it's ages before anything happens. Like Noah, he obeys the voice with little reason to do so other than his own conviction and his family's support; he doesn't know where he's going, and he has to begin to wonder if he's made a monumental mistake before the dream begins to come true. Building the field was a matter of faith, and, like most matters of faith, he needs to be brought to the point of no return—to truly let go—before he is vindicated. We sometimes need to be prepared to give up what's most dear to us before we find what is truly valuable. After the initial euphoria of Shoeless Joe's appearance, things die down, until Ray hears the voice again, telling him to "ease his pain." This seems even more obscure than the instruction to build the field, and Ray argues with the voice, which reminds me of the Psalmist's anger at God and underlines the fact that it's not only okay to be angry or confused, but you must express what's in you if you are to be truly human, or have any hope of a real relationship with the divine.

And so, things move on. Ray and his wife Annie go to a PTA meeting and "halt the spread of neo-Fascism in America" by arguing against banning books that liberate the mind. *Field of Dreams* reveals itself as a subversive fantasy from the mind of a child of the '60s by standing up for freedom of thought and conscience. Ray kidnaps the writer of one of these subversive books (based on J.D. Salinger, and played by Darth Vader himself, James Earl Jones). He's the stereotype of the creative genius and an example of how sometimes a little wisdom can be a corrosive thing, unless you find a way to make sense of yourself in community. Coincidence builds on faith and leads them further down the path the voice has for them. Ray finds himself back in 1972 and meets an elderly physician (a beautiful acting opportunity that Burt Lancaster seized with grace), who tells him that it has always been his dream to play ball in the Major League. There is no concession to our sense of disbelief—like the weird things that have happened to each of us, this story is just *unfolding*—and we're invited to let go of our skepticism and find our place in the story. And so it goes, and so it goes, and we follow on, and it ends (or begins?) with a miracle, as father and son reconcile over the most American of past-times: throwing a ball to and fro.

As an Irishman, I found it hard to understand baseball until I went to a few games—it seemed crazy that people would spend so long watching a few well-heeled, ridiculously wealthy guys hit a ball with a stick and run around in circles. This ritual has been going on for centuries all over the world, but when I finally saw the Braves take on the Blue Jays it began to make sense. I saw that the game gave the crowd a sense of context, of something bigger than the sum of its parts; but you can both lose and find yourself in a baseball crowd. I'm still troubled by the commercialization of sport—Shoeless Joe says that the lights make it hard to see the ball, but Ray replies that it makes more money for the owners for people to go at night, and the hotdogs are far too expensive—but for an experience of the diversity of the human race, of breezy summer nights, of the thrill of a hit, and of the absurdity of the Mexican wave, I can see why this game towers over the rest. In *Field of Dreams*, baseball is a metaphor, of course, but I can't imagine this film being about croquet or poker. The writer has his great speech at the end and waxes lyrical about the glory of baseball as the "one constant in American life." It's testimony to the quality of this film that we're not laughing.

So, what does it matter? I think that we all have the opportunity to live like Ray, if only we would grasp it. He is a man who says "yes" in the face of everything else saying "no." He gives himself to a dream that seems to be for the sake of others. He goes it alone when the chips are stacked against him. And when he eventually asks, "What's in it for me?" he discovers that it was all for him in the first place. We often think we know what's going on in our lives, but we rarely realize that when we do good unto others, good returns to us. What you think you're doing for others, you're doing for yourself, whether you intend good or evil. This is a law of the universe, and it can't be changed. But perhaps only the uncynical can see that—maybe that's why we need to develop childlikeness if we want to enter the kingdom of heaven on earth. The film reminds us to be attentive to our world, because we don't often recognize the most important moments of our lives while they're happening.

How do we make the power of this film real in our own lives? We could start by giving space for our "inner dreamer." If you think this is too far removed from your own reality, maybe you've gotten old too soon; open yourself to the dream, and maybe you'll be young again. Perhaps, in these days of thought control, the movie should serve as a corrective to the wave of fear running through American life. Like Ray, I do crazy things sometimes, but I am the least crazy person that I know. There have been times when I wanted to come home, but I didn't know how, and I needed to be honest about my feelings. *Field of Dreams* reminds us how it's possible to make a mess of things, and then find yourself through doing something for someone else. I've seen it more than any other film, and it never fails to work its magic. It might not be historically accurate (Shoeless Joe was a left-handed hitter, but that's hardly the biggest implausibility), and the story may be wrapped up too neatly, but it dares to suggest that there might be more to life than "What's in it for me?" and ends with the hope that we might all come together one day. The end of this movie is a prophecy of the future healing of humankind—the miracle of redemption, the coming of the kingdom of God, the restoration of all things. It's a brilliantly subversive little film about the nature of work and vision and mid-life, most certainly *not* the cheesy sentimental chocolate cake some people consider it to be. I checked out some web reviews of the movie when I was writing this, and found one that said it was a well-acted film "in the service of one of the silliest, most meaningless plots ever conceived." In a sense that's right, because sometimes I think being human is pretty absurd, too. But that criticism clearly comes from someone who isn't listening for the voice.

THE APOSTLE
(ROBERT DUVALL, 1997)

Robert Duvall has missed his calling. He's a fine actor, but on the evidence of this film, he should have been a preacher. It's a one-man show that he wrote, directed, produced, and—for all I know—made the tea as well. The idea of a prayer meeting with Hollywood people might strike you as about as scary as they come, but this film makes you want to get up and shout "Hallelujah!" It's about as close to a worship experience as you might find in a cinema, and also just about as disturbing as that might indicate. It's about a southern pastor who preaches with the best of them, but isn't that much in control of his personal life. He makes a big mistake and kills a man, and leaves town to escape his past. He does the only thing he knows how, and builds a church in an attempt at atoning for his sin.

The Apostle is a powerful testimony to the courage of a man of conviction; watching it feels like a spiritual experience. The writer-director respects the audience and takes it for granted that we believe in God, the crickets sound so alive they might as well be in the cinema with us, and Duvall is so much invested in the character (called "Sonny") that you expect him to fly out of the screen when his preaching takes over. It's surprisingly compassionate toward a deeply flawed man. (When David Letterman interviewed Duvall, he asked him if the character is a charlatan or a sincere believer; Duvall defined the grace of God when he said he felt that Sonny was able to be both at the same time.) But the film is about more than one man's struggle. For me, it manages to deal, in one fell swoop, with everything that's wrong, and everything that could be right, about the institutional church as we experience it today. You might want to watch it before reading further. Let me list its treasures:

◆ Sonny is shown to have been preaching since he was about eight years old; there are disturbing elements to the way he mimics the old preacher of his childhood. I believe that human beings of all ages have something to contribute to the kingdom of God. But there is a difference between listening to children and abusing them by giving them too much responsibility too early—and, frankly, not allowing them to *be* children. Sonny is a case in point; because of his childhood, he has become unable to speak any language other than "Gospel-speak." This is inadequate to his sense of personal crisis. Only taking responsibility for his actions can solve his predicament. And he can only do that once he has found safety in community again.

◆ He is a travelling evangelist as well as having what is referred to as "his own" church. I know this might be an unpopular thing to say, but I don't think you can do both. You're either responsible for your people, or you're an itinerant preacher. Too many "professional Christians" seem to think they're so important that they need to be all over the place preaching (when I'm sure there are local people who could do the job just as well) while they appear scared to give up their own leadership roles in local congregations. I don't think local pastoral ministry is compatible with being "on the road" as frequently as many preachers seem to be. It's all too easy to leave principle behind when you get on a plane; as the tragic tales of broken marriages resulting from men thinking that they are somehow indispensable to churches on the other side of the country prove. Speaking of planes, I recently read an appeal for an American evangelist to raise nearly $20 million to buy a private jet so that he could fly to anywhere in the world at any time in order to "fulfill the Great Commission." Well, sorry if this offends anyone, but nobody is that important. The human race is big enough for God to call the people who are already *there* to do what's necessary; or at least to send people long term. The delusions of grandeur associated with such appeals are breathtaking. Sonny does not seem as interested in money as some of the more deluded examples of broken humanity who have set up ministries which seem to be based on the totally unbiblical notion that one individual can be more important than others; but his job (which he of course would call a "ministry," but I'm not too sure about that) has led to the breakdown of his family, and he is shown to be unable to care for his mother (who herself seems quite adept at manipulating him; oh, the joys of Christian families) because he has to travel all the time. For some people, amassing thousands of frequent flyer miles in the service of "the Gospel" would be a badge of honor. But if it makes you think you're better than you are, or causes more than a little tension at home, I'm pretty sure God would want you to rethink your life.

◆ Evangelicalism is a *culture* as well as a *worldview*. I've never seen it portrayed as accurately as in this film. All the best and worst—the absurdity and the profundity of that culture—are here:

  • The way religious language can distort the truth—through, for example, the absurdity of shouting "Jesus!" repeatedly, like it's some kind of powerful mantra that will keep demons at bay. (Why have you never heard a sermon on the following words of Jesus: "Do not worship me, but the one who sent me?")

  • People who know what they believe, but have never thought about why they believe it.

  • People who use the phrase "it was God's will" as a

means of divesting themselves of responsibility for their choices.

- People who are unable to describe or explain anything in terms that anyone outside the evangelical set can understand.

- The commercialization of Christianity (huge buildings that lie unused during the week; the fact that Sonny gives a hundred dollar bill to his wife's lover as a means of insulting him; the relentlessness of gold jewelry on evangelical wrists).

- Schism seen as a positive thing—if you disagree with someone, just start another church. We see an example of this when someone says, "I have a holiness background," referring to the "branch" of the church he grew up in, but shouldn't he really have a holiness *foreground*?

- The belief that "big," flashy events are the best way to "win people for Christ." Isn't this a potential distortion of who Jesus claimed to be—a king on a donkey?

- Church as business, church as circus, church unable to deal with its own crises, church a little too interested in money.

- The unprofessionalism of the clergy ("I can set up churches like this in my sleep") and the unrealistic expectations of church members—the old preacher who befriends Sonny says he retired from the ministry after having two heart attacks in six months. At least he had the humility to realize his job wasn't important enough to die for. And church people are often so used to being told what to believe that they can't decide for themselves what to *do*.

• Salvation as a formula—just say the right words, or pay mental assent to the right doctrines, and all will go well. I'm young, but I've been around long enough to see that this kind of clichéd religion does not work and often has very little to do with the path of the cross.

• And, last but not least, my personal bugbear: fear of the devil and how that destroys. I know people who think when they get a cold that it's a satanic attack. Forgive me, but my understanding is that colds come from airborn germs, not demons. And if Satan only attacks people who are supposedly "important" in the kingdom of God, then I guess the people of famine-torn sub-Saharan Africa, or indeed the citizens of Iraq, must have a pretty high calling. People who live in fear of Satan are *not* living as God intended.

But the "good news" is in *The Apostle* too; evangelical faith is portrayed in a balanced way:

◆ The direct relationship between Sonny and God. He is shown praying his heart out, bringing all his concerns and weakness and joy and strength to the table. He has a genuinely conversational relationship with God; what

Brother Lawrence called "practicing the presence of God," and when the walls begin to fall around him, he does not blame the divine. This was helpful to me, and may be for you, too. Perhaps if the Church has become part of the problem for you, you need to engage God in the absence of the institution, without the preconceptions and misconceptions that go hand in hand with formal religion. God does not always answer Sonny's questions, and he has to find out the answer by pursuing a new path, which is another way of showing the truth that sometimes the absence of God may actually be a sign of God's presence.

◆ Sonny has a friend who says, "If you hadn't led me to the Lord, who knows what jail I'd be in." There is a clear belief in the power of God to forgive instantly, and the multi-racial church that Sonny builds is not a sop to political correctness, but a true example of how the Christian impetus of the evangelical worldview can truly transform the world. Everyone is welcome in this community, even those who have not yet "made a decision for Christ."

◆ Sonny has a childlike faith, which at times borders on *childish*, but his old preacher friend is portrayed with the right balance of wonder and wisdom. Childlikeness is a quality not often found in our world; again, the foolishness of God is wiser than our wisdom, and it's another mark of *The Apostle's* greatness as a film that it tells the truth about the difference between child-like awe and immaturity.

◆ Sonny's enthusiasm for setting up the church reminds us of how people really want to make a difference in people's lives. Evangelicalism at its best offers a genuinely transformative experience, giving birth to a community of the broken, for the broken.

♦ One character says, "Always be ready to make God welcome." The film encourages us to create space for God in our lives, and that when we find it, the space will be just the right size.

♦ Being part of a faith-based community helps Sonny to accept his fate, and the church accepts his failure; grace is everywhere. This is also shown in the scene where Sonny baptizes himself—the cleansing of the waters gave me chills.

♦ Finally, the vibrancy and sheer laughability of the human-ness of the Church is found throughout the film. There is nothing as *alive* as a church when it's working. An old man badly blows his trumpet in church; this was a sign of the genuine humor of church, and perhaps this ability to laugh at ourselves is what I value most about the Christian community.

Sometimes I think everyone should be exposed to the American evangelical movement, but maybe the safest introduction would be through this film. It's as if they filmed real worship services as a documentary, and in a sense they did. The final scene, where Sonny declares his faith to a revival service, is a tour-de-force, and you might find yourself wanting to touch the screen to get some kind of blessing, such is the power of the film. It reminded me of my own experience of making a faith commitment, when the hairs on the back of my neck stood up at a Billy Graham crusade. But it also underlines the need to take things further than an altar call; Sonny's life can only find meaning in community, and only when he finds community can he take responsibility for his actions and face the past. He made a mistake, which started with him allowing his principles to be eroded, believing that "Thou shalt not kill, but thou canst throw a baseball through a window," but he found a way back to being human when he gave something good to others and admitted his brokenness. In the meantime, he has given some dignity back to lonely people, and in building the church has built community where there was none.

The Apostle is a rare thing—a film that forgives a killer and takes Christians seriously. Some of my closest friends hate this movie, and I guess I can see why—we like our heroes clean cut, don't we? You watch it and feel terrible for him—I have conflicting emotions in that I want him to be free, even though I know he's done an awful thing. And I don't blame him when he runs away. I mean, don't we all want to disappear at times? I never know how to deal with the biblical verse that says, "your sin will find you out"—it seems too threatening to come from a gracious God. But perhaps this film explains what it really means. We are not *threatened* by the possibility that we'll be exposed; but when we give space to our conscience and to God's grace, and live in community, then maybe we can face our own inner darkness with confidence. How can a man like Sonny be a servant of God? The same way you and I can. *The Apostle*, although set in the recent past, seems to take place in a world both far away—and strangely near—to me. Its community both attracts and repels. I want to be *with* people, but I want to avoid pietism. I want to *believe* with certainty like Sonny does, but I don't want to sacrifice my mind. I want to know God, but sometimes I'm afraid that I may just be speaking to a voice in my own head. The movie's publicity tagline was "The hardest soul to save was his own"; you may feel the same way, but if you feel you need catharsis and healing from your own experience of the Church (and who doesn't?), then this film may be just the medicine you need.

SUPERMAN
(RICHARD DONNER, MARIO PUZO, DAVID NEWMAN, LESLIE NEWMAN, ROBERT BENTON, 1978)

It's twenty-five years old and means more today than ever. One of the best-crafted blockbusters of all time, *Superman* is a much deeper film than you may remember. A Christ metaphor that actually *works* without being either cheesy or too literalist, the movie illustrates the inexplicable biblical adage that "In weakness is strength made perfect." Superman's father has a great speech that is worth remembering, when he says of the human race: "They can be a great people, they need to be, they only need the light to show the way—for this reason, above all, their capacity for good, I have sent them you, my only son." The film also underlines something of the nature of being both human and divine when it says that Superman will be "near invincible, but vulnerable." Cheesy, perhaps, but very true. Let's briefly reflect on the wealth of spiritual metaphor in this film:

- Superman learns his destiny in solitude where he discusses with his father the nature of things; like the rest of us, his first and most important question is "Who am I?"

- He is told to live among humans "to discover where your strength is needed."

- He doesn't always use his strength, but enables others to make right decisions.

◆ He is reminded that we humans "will call upon you for help, even when they don't need you; it is their habit to abuse their resources in this way."

◆ And at one point a character says, "I've never been able to make sense of violence in any form."

◆ He is more like Jesus than many of us think. His strength is made perfect in weakness. I used to respond to this film primarily as an example of fantasy wish-fulfilment. I mean, if *I* could take a girl for a night flight over Manhattan, I'd have no trouble getting dates ... But when I watched it as part of my research for this book, I saw much more than that. When Superman finally reverses the earth's orbit to save the one he loves, he is turning back time. Redeeming time, if you will. This invokes the cross of Christ, as a moment unequalled in human history, where the past, present, and future were all cosmically resolved in an instant. This interpretation of Superman may have developed in my mind because I have lost all sense of objectivity and have begun to see Christ metaphors around every corner. Perhaps, but I think I'll take my Kryptonite Christ metaphors over superficial super-heroism any day.

A PRIMER IN GOD

I've said before that sometimes I agree with Scorsese in that I find it difficult to tell the difference between going to the cinema and going to church. Obviously, I don't *really* mean that; I mean, I know which is which, but I also know which I prefer, most of the time. What I meant was that going to the cinema can be a spiritual experience akin to worship, which can inspire and convict as well as any sermon. So, let's remind ourselves of a few of cinema's worshipers. St. Francis of Assisi is my favorite saint (if you're allowed to rank them). For some unknown reason, in 1972, Franco Zeffirelli decided to make a Francis biopic, *Brother Sun, Sister Moon*, and I'm glad that he did. While the film is clearly bound in the 1970s—it fit the culture of hippiedom and free love—Francis is portrayed for what he was: a single minded lover of God, servant of the poor, and steward of nature. The scene where he announces his conversion to his rich father and all the people of his town by stripping naked in the square is a wonderful example of how God uses the foolish things to shame the wise. Would we recognize the deep spirituality of such madness, or would we react as Francis' father did, with humiliated self-protection, if it were to happen today?

Ben-Hur had more of a sense of decorum, but that film's respect for Christ is honorable. We never see Christ's face, and although he is a little de-humanized, the film encourages an appropriate sense of awe. (Useless trivia: Leslie Nielson from *The Naked Gun* auditioned for the role of Judah Ben-Hur's best friend, the Roman soldier Messala. Oh, how things could have been so different …) Andrei Tarkovsky was one of cinema's greatest poets. His Russian films don't appeal to the kind of audience that wants its information *FAST*, but his was a true mystic cinema. The experience of God that enfolds us in his films is unmatched elsewhere. I recommend you start with *Andrei Rublev*, about an icon artist in the middle ages. Words cannot begin to describe the power of this film; it is almost a religious icon in itself. (There will be more Tarkovsky later, you lucky people.) *Signs* made an appearance in the chapter on fear, but it fits here as well, because its story is more about the healing of broken faith in God as it is about scary little aliens in the backyard. Its ending is a little too neat for me, and its answers too tight, but I cannot deny that it helped my faith at a low point. Perhaps it will do the same for you.

You might also find spiritual solace in films about the grace of God. *Chocolat* is quite similar to *Babette's Feast* in that it's about a stranger coming to an isolated village and bringing strange foodstuffs. But it takes on the power of legalistic religion more directly, and perhaps is the weaker for it. It's still a wonderful film, and there is one moment—when the weak priest finally summons the strength to say what he really believes—when you might want to applaud aloud. He cautions his people against judging others, saying: "Don't let your goodness be defined by what you don't do; or your community by who you exclude, but by what and whom you embrace." There is a hilarious, beautiful, and deeply moving example of this, when the Pharisaic mayor gorges himself on chocolate. He lies like a baby on a mound of sweet heaven—a better metaphor for what it feels like to be forgiven would be hard to define. There is a glaring flaw, however, because the people of this village ultimately exclude one of their number—an abusive husband. He is not allowed to return. Now, perhaps this is simply a sign that the people have not yet fully understood the implications of grace; they may learn in the future that he should be welcomed back. But, regretfully, I suspect this was an example of political correctness on the part of the filmmakers; forgiveness and grace can only go so far in Hollywood cinema.

Of course, forgiveness and grace go the distance in *It's a Wonderful Life*; this film's appeal seems to be much greater in the U.S.A. than elsewhere, so as a foreigner I won't risk saying too much about it. You've all seen it about twenty times anyway. But it's always worth a repeat visit. *Life is Beautiful* is a more recent parable of grace, where Roberto Benigni protects his son from the trauma of Nazism by inventing a world of safety and games. Some Holocaust survivors have ridiculed this film, saying that concentration camp conditions were so extraordinarily sub-human that nobody would have been able to play along with Benigni's game. Somebody would at least have tried to win favor with the guards by revealing the hidden child. That may be true, and I am not in a place to argue with it. But *Life is Beautiful* is still a magnificent metaphor for good parenting, and for the fact that there may sometimes be a moral imperative to lie.

The key film on grace is based on Victor Hugo's amazing tome *Les Miserables*, which is much more than the reason why the theatre at the top of London's Shaftesbury Avenue is still open. It is too massive a story to be summed up by one theme, but for our purposes, this book is about the Christian community at its best. You all know the story—Valjean, a thief, stays the night at a bishop's house and steals some expensive cutlery before sneaking out in the middle of the night. He is caught and returned to the bishop's house by soldiers, now under the threat of death for his crime. The bishop, instead of agreeing to press charges, greets Valjean with open arms and tear-filled eyes, saying: I'm so glad you returned. You forgot something! Then he gives Valjean his silver candlesticks and insists that the soldiers let him be on his way. And he quietly advises Valjean to use this grace for others. This is nothing less than a sacramental gift of life from the Church, a truly Christian act (if by "Christian" we mean the imitation of Christ, which I'm not sure the Church always understands these days). We are, all of us, in need of such grace. And we all, I am sure, are confronted by situations that need our grace. *Les Miserables* reminds us that there is a better way. (There are several film versions, but I most highly recommend the 1995 French version *Les Miserables du Vingtieme Siecle*, which interweaves the story with the Holocaust.)

Grace is often the characteristic most fully embodied by cinematic Christ figures, and they seem to be a dime a dozen these days. So let's just admit that we've all seen *The Matrix* and it inspired us and made us think of the need for a Messiah, etc. etc. etc. We'll come to that film later. For now, let me encourage you to look beyond the most obvious or well known God-figures in the movies, and sample some of the following:

A less serious, but not less thought-provoking film is *Monty Python's Life of Brian*, another example of where the religious thought police put their foot squarely in their mouths. This movie was denounced as blasphemous by the very people who needed to see it. It's hilarious, and that's its main purpose, I suppose, but it also has some very trenchant things to say about the seeming inability of Christians to get on with each other. The final crucifixion scene is troubling, as rows of the condemned sing "Always look on the bright side of life," and I still haven't resolved what I think of this. It may be that the writers were satirizing the tendency of some Christians to turn the pain of the cross into something almost happy—passing over (excuse the pun) the horror and lamentation of Good Friday to rush headlong into the joys of Easter Sunday. Or it may be that they simply created one of the most offensive scenes in art history. You decide. But for goodness' sake allow yourself to see it and make your decision an informed one.

Maybe the funniest film with a Christ figure at its center is *The Big Lebowski*. I can hear eyebrows raising all over the place now. Has Higgins finally gone mad? I hope not. On first viewing, I just thought this Coen Brothers film was a delightful comedy about nothing much in particular. But then a good friend opened my eyes. The central character is called the Dude, and does very little except hang out, drink copious White Russians, and go to see his friends do performance art. He doesn't work, he doesn't struggle with existentialism, he doesn't get up at a reasonable hour. He just is. As a metaphor for what the Sabbath should really be like, for what the Sabbath is really *for*, the Dude can't be beat, man.

The self-sacrifice of Christ is turned into metaphor in some of the greatest films I know. I find it difficult to convey anything meaningful about these films in mere words, so I won't say very much. *Gandhi* is an obvious choice—a film about the man who imitated the pattern of Jesus, preached regularly from the sermon on the Mount, and, before dying for his cause, said (and I paraphrase): The only people who don't believe that Jesus advocated non-violence are Christians themselves. I would follow Christ if it weren't for the Christians.

Watching *The Prince of Egypt* was the first time I realized that the biblical story of Moses requires him to give up everything—privilege, security, family—before he can be led by God into the desert that will cause him to devote his life to his people. And *The Mission* also leads its characters into a kind of desert—as evangelists in the jungle—where they shall die alongside the original inhabitants at the behest of the corrupt marriage between church and state.

Scorsese created another religious story in *Kundun*, the story of the Dalai Lama's early life before China invaded and he was led into exile. The self-giving of one boy, Tenzin Gyatso, as he accepts his destiny, and learns to lead while developing a deep love for his people may lead to a sense of deep inadequacy on the part of Western Christians. Like Gandhi, the Dalai Lama appears to know things about being human that many of us seriously lack.

Of course, God as *creator* is found at the movies. I only want to mention two films that evoke our sense of awe at the imagination behind the universe. Luc Bessons' *Atlantis* is a magnificent documentary about life on two-thirds of the earth's surface; there are creatures here that never see the light of day, and Besson does us a service by letting us snoop on their world. Another magisterial piece on the nature of nature is *2001: A Space Odyssey*. Some readers may think this is a strange choice for this chapter on God, as it is usually acclaimed as the greatest humanist tract that cinema has produced. But I think differently (and you would expect me to, wouldn't you?). This film ends with a declaration that there is something "out there" bigger than ourselves; it doesn't make explicit just what that something is, but for me, it has to be divine revelation. The nice thing is, Kubrick always said that he did not want to prescribe for people what his film meant. And he certainly wasn't about to declare a belief in God; so I can say what I like about this one. And, I guess, so can you.

As for the shadow side of religion, controversy, legalism, despair, abuse, and the intolerance of religious institutions come under the cinematic microscope in surprisingly few films. *The Truman Show* imagines the darker implications of Psalm 139 (when it is claimed that God watches our every move) as the main character realizes he is a pawn in a mammoth game, watched over by one man, whose distorted "love" for the character has led him to keep him prisoner. This is what life would be like if God hated us (although I do wish Peter Weir had chosen to end the film on a less acclamatory note). Graham Greene's *The End of the Affair* has been filmed twice; I prefer Neil Jordan's 1999 version, and not just because he's Irish. The story discusses how faith and love are sometimes incompatible, the impossible choice between faith in a God who controls and love for the person that God rejects. It's a powerful piece of cinema that should have been more widely discussed than it was.

There's more "bad religion" in *Priest*, where issues of sexuality, integrity, honesty, and grace are examined in painful detail. How the Church so often seems to fail to deal graciously with reality was exemplified when this film was almost denied a U.S. release because of protests from Christians. Don't people realize that they need to face these issues rather than brush them away like flies? Unfortunately, these issues will not be dead in the winter; they are with us all year round and cannot be gotten rid of with insect repellent.

Finally, and appropriately, I bring you the "end-times," and here we need a note on terminology. "Apocalypse" *does not mean the end of the world*. It means "revelation." Francis Coppola has made some wonderful contributions to popular culture, but he, probably more than anyone, has helped us misunderstand that term. Apocalypse is a word used to refer to the revealing of something that could not be seen before. It is a misnomer to apply it to the end-times. Now we've got that out of the way, let's get down to the doom of the end. There's a lot of doom in *The Rapture*, a little-seen film from the mid-'90s, illustrating pre-millennial tension among the middle class. One of the characters doesn't get what she prayed for and becomes terribly angry toward God. The anger seeps into her soul to the extent where she refuses to enter heaven when she dies. It's a shocking evocation of how rage can destroy us. And it's both more honest, and an infinitely better work than the psychologically suspect, scripturally ambiguous run of end-times films and books that have recently colonized the North American popular Christian consciousness. Some of the end-times anxiety I've encountered among Christians is borderline cultic, and we might do well to look at Jane Campion's *Holy Smoke* for a lesson. It's a splendidly witty story about a "cult de-programmer" who gets seduced by one of his subjects in the desert. Like so many of us, he simply does not know what he's doing. Thankfully, Tarkovsky knew what *he* was doing when he made *The Sacrifice*, a surreal spiritual journey on the cusp of the world's end. He was also responsible for the first film of Stanislaw Lem's novel *Solaris*, where a man is visited by the dream of his dead wife and offered the opportunity to stay with the unreal dream, or to return to the sadness of truth. Steven Soderbergh filmed another version of the book, which I actually prefer (sorry, film fans, I have to be wrong sometimes), in which Mr. Clooney got to really act, and we encounter something akin to what heaven might be like. One of the versions has the central character simply waiting, while in the other, he finds what he's looking for. When he asks, "Am I alive or dead?" the answer comes back, "We don't have to think like that anymore." It proposes that there are no answers, only choices. To choose God above all else, when the chips are down, when the evidence is against us, to hope for something bigger than ourselves, to muster faith that what we have believed is real, to recall the times when we actually *did* believe it … The power of these films about God is that, at their best, they transport us into a Presence we don't understand, but that we know we need. It's not quite the same thing as a transcendent moment in a cathedral, as the pipe organ swells, the incense intoxicates our senses, and the congregation experiences a moment of oneness unparalleled elsewhere. But it's not totally different either.

CHAPTER NINE

JUSTICE
WE MAY BE THROUGH WITH THE PAST, BUT THE PAST AIN'T THROUGH WITH US

"Cut the baby in two." —King Solomon

WHEN *POPSTARS*, THE EXPLOITATIVE "WE WILL MAKE you a star and control your lives forever" show (later evolving into *American Idol*) was first broadcast in the U.K., one of the auditions came from Belfast. There was a kid who couldn't really sing (bless him), and, frankly, didn't look like the kind of guy they were going to choose for a scantily-clad sexual trivia roadshow. After he failed his audition, the camera crew followed him down a corridor where he phoned his mum. Close to tears, we heard him exclaim, "There's no justice!" It was amusing to see the "Most Oppressed People Ever (MOPE)" syndrome taken this far. The nefarious Brits, not content to merely colonize Ireland and subject her people to centuries of wickedness, had even gone as far as to rig the *Popstars* contest so a Northern Irish Catholic could be humiliated once more. There really is no justice! (For those readers who may be unfamiliar with British-Irish relations, that was a joke.)

Justice, and the process by which we deal with the past in cinema, is a hard nut to crack; courtroom drama rarely bears much relation to the real thing, and audiences are easily swayed into supporting bad guys if the people they hurt are portrayed as "worse" than they are—see *Hannibal*, for the best recent example. Social justice, too, often suffers from cinematic streamlining; Michelle Pfeiffer and Meryl Streep's gloopy teachers in *Dangerous Minds* and *Music of the Heart* respectively, bringing salvation to the inner city by empathy alone spring to mind. Thankfully, for every hundred of these, there's an *On the Waterfront* or *The Insider*. Honest films about honest struggles by flawed individuals. But the key question for me is, Do they inspire us to greater things, or salve our consciences by letting us live vicariously? I mean, how many of us have stood up for oppressed peoples since we were stirred to the depths of our souls by *Braveheart*, a historically inaccurate but spiritually "true" film, if ever there was one? Are we merely indulging our desire to feel catharsis, or are we *learning* and *changing* through what we watch?

CRIMES AND MISDEMEANORS
(WOODY ALLEN, 1989)

One of the challenges of writing this book has been deciding which Woody Allen films to include. I can come home late at night, exhausted after another day of twentysomething existential angst, ready for nothing but sleep, but if there's a Woody Allen film on TV, I will gladly sacrifice my need for rest to indulge in ninety minutes of elitist Manhattanite neurosis. He makes New York look like we always wished it would be and manages to make the terror of urban life look funny without ever resolving his conflicts. I really would like to tell you about

Hannah and Her Sisters, where he examines three sisters and how they include the whole world, or *Husbands and Wives*, which illustrates just how difficult it is to be monogamous, or *Love and Death*, which is a masterful parody of Russian literature that would have Dostoevsky spinning in his grave (in a melancholy fashion, of course). But those will have to wait for another day. For now, *Crimes and Misdemeanors* is my focus. It's the story of an opthamologist and a documentarian. The eye doctor has a problem, in that his mistress is threatening to tell his wife about their affair; while the filmmaker struggles to find funding for a film on the meaning of life, making ends meet by selling his soul to make bad television.

The opthamologist—a darkly subtle performance from Martin Landau—arranges for his lover to be murdered, and, after some initial pangs of anxiety, finds that he not only gets away with it, but can live with himself. Meanwhile, the filmmaker gets nowhere with his documentary, not least when his subject, a wise old philosopher, seemingly based on Holocaust contemplative Primo Levi, commits suicide. And the woman he loves abandons him for the TV producer who represents everything he considers shallow. This film is Allen's most successful fusion of comedy and tragedy, his most perfectly realized blend of New York wit and Scandinavian pathos. In it, Alan Alda's superficial producer defines comedy as "tragedy plus time," although it's impossible to laugh at the tragedy of the opthamologist's actions. How could we live with ourselves after taking the life of another? In flashbacks, Landau's character— the man who helps others to see—is shown at Jewish family gatherings, hearing that "the *eyes* of God are always upon us," but the God of *Crimes and Misdemeanors* is either vengeful or absent. Meanwhile, the atheistic philosopher proposes that the best we can hope for is that the human race might find ways to free itself from dependence on such a God, so that we celebrate life together, to find something better without destroying each other.

Allen is often criticized for what we know of his private life. I don't know any more about this than you do, but I guess you know me well enough by know to expect me to say that he should be judged primarily on the basis of his art. He makes films every year without concern for whether or not people will go to see them in large numbers, putting his thoughts on the screen to entertain and inform, challenge, and affirm. Whether or not he has his personal life under control is irrelevant to the quality of his films. We don't boycott Tchaikovsky concerts because the composer's sex life may have been a mess, or refuse to read Ernest Hemingway because he had a particular way with women. The lens through which biblical characters are read would seem to imply that they were all morally upright, heroic men who only had eyes for the presence of God. We don't need to read that much about Abraham (liar) and Noah (not known for his sexual propriety) and David (developed a conspiracy to allow someone to be killed so he could sleep with the victim's wife) to see that they would not be likely candidates for church leadership today, but we still hold their stories up as examples. So why should it be different with someone more contemporary?

Allen's themes are well known—family, relationships, fear of death, the insulation of the rich, fertility, singleness, art, pretentiousness, chemical dependency as a means of mitigating pain, bookshops, adultery as a bad idea, God, hypochondria, New York itself. He writes great parts for women, who are as likely to appear as career professionals as homemakers; there is no gender division of labor in his work. His use of music—string quartets, jazz songs, opera—is almost as intelligent as Michael Mann (who turns each of his films, from *The Last of the Mohicans* to *Heat* to *Ali* into something approaching a kind of symphonic cinema).

He understands the misanthropic nature of French existentialism and Russian nineteenth-century literature, which is more than you can say for me. He recognizes the healing potential of the Marx Brothers. And he knows what to do with the cold, sharp light of New York City. He makes New York look like we always hoped it would, but never neglects the genuine darkness of the underbelly of urban life. It is ironic that the existential peace he searches for in his films seems to elude him in real life. He seems to be more like his quintessential neurotic man than he would let on, but we are missing the point if we reduce him to nothing more than an intelligent court jester.

This is not to say that he is perfect. There are clearly flaws, or at least gaps, in Allen's work. For instance, black people rarely appear, except as servants or sex workers (although this may simply be reflective of the kind of white elitist social tier he tends to write about). His insistence on making one film a year leads to overwork and repetition. He rarely seems to grow, to get anywhere, especially in the arcs of the characters he himself plays. His greatest strength is that he manages to make consistent return journeys to the question of how to be good without alienating his audience. But it has become almost too much to hope for that he might come up with some answers.

Crimes and Misdemeanors asks how we could live with ourselves after taking human life. It presents the dark truth that some people get away with murder, but isn't sure how to deal with such people. But its provocative quest applies to all moral choices; you don't have to have pulled a trigger to have dark things on your conscience. The film is not unrealistic in what it hopes for the future of humanity—in *Hannah and Her Sisters*, one of the more philosophically minded characters muses that we're actually in pretty good shape; regarding the "reasons" for the Holocaust, he says, "Given what people are, the real question is why it doesn't happen more often." Allen gives himself the line, however, that declares where most people are at: "How the hell do I know why there were Nazis? I don't even know how the can opener works."

Allen's belief that most people don't take responsibility for asking the "big questions" is a pessimistic view of the world, but I think it might be close to the truth. In *Crimes and Misdemeanors*, the death of God is palpable throughout, until the very last scene, when a blind Rabbi dances with his daughter, while the dead philosopher muses on the soundtrack about the resilience of humanity and its ability to renew itself. The philosopher sees nothing but human responsibility; for him and Woody Allen, there is no bigger cause or power of benevolence at work. Allen is angry at organized religion for its historical complicity in injustice, but he fails to acknowledge the other side of the coin. The consolations of faith, especially the power of forgiveness, are obvious by their absence from his films. I am not one to judge his experience of religion; it may well have been as distorted as it comes. And perhaps this is why we need to listen to him. Neurosis and depression can be a lens through which come a kind of truth that can't be realized elsewhere. It's problematic if we remain stuck in oppressive existential angst, but it's okay to keep asking the questions.

Churches are not always comfortable places in which to ask questions. Simplistic answers are too often the response from sincere people to the kind of deep questions that will never find an adequate resolution in mere words. Allen seems to have settled into a pattern of staying with the questions, without ever finding resolution. To attempt to write answers to these would be to misunderstand the quest. The only answer to the question of how to deal with the past, of how to forgive one another, of how to be *human* is found through getting on with life. So I'll say that while I love his films, I wish he could find some resolution to the angst. But, as there is no true closure but God, for the time being, we may treasure the questions, make choices, love another, pick each other up, and remember always that we are all capable of treating each other with grace or contempt. Those who suffer the slings and arrows of pathological guilt may or may not need to make amends for their actions, but their lives are more than the sum of their mistakes. And God is always bigger than our best (or worst) ideas of the divine.

THE SWEET HEREAFTER
(ATOM EGOYAN, 1997)

"Nothing's wrong with trying to talk to me. The problem is I don't know who I'm talking to right now." —Mitchell Stephens

A child lies in her father's arms, gazing upward, not so much into the camera as through it. She has neo-preternaturally long hair for her age, and her eyes are like oil pools. She is wrapped in white cotton. And an adult hand holds a scalpel by her throat. He may have to cut into her neck soon, for she has been bitten by a poisonous insect, and may need an emergency tracheotomy to save her. The cruelty of adults to children, of children to parents, of the weather and the uncontrollable, and the need to be cruel to be kind are summed up in this, the central image of *The Sweet Hereafter*, a powerful and affecting drama from Canada's second greatest director (after David Cronenberg, but it's close, very close). It's shot like a nature documentary, opens like a thriller, and turns into a horror film where the only acts of violence are psychological. A school bus crash has decimated a small community in the tundra, and an ambulance-chasing lawyer has come to town to "direct their rage" in the suit that seems to have replaced a sense of loss as the primary way to mourn accidental death in North America. *The*

Sweet Hereafter takes its title from the horrific (and analogous) tale of the Pied Piper of Hamelin, who led all but one of the children of a town to their deaths when the powers that be refused to honor his service.

The place where the film is set—cold, harsh, stark, white—hosts a community that at first seems like a throwback to small town Americana. But the film says something about community that isn't naïve; these people are grieving a terrible loss, to be sure, but they aren't "kind innocents." They may be the kind of people who wait for the school bus with their kids, but they share the same brokenness (relationships sliced in two, child abuse, gossip) as the urban spiritually poor, too. This parallel is writ large in the character of the lawyer (a deeply empathetic performance by Ian Holm), who is trying to "help" these people when his strung out daughter needs him—but rejects him—the most. Perhaps they just deal with it differently (and they may have held on to more of the resources for healing).

The sinister music evokes the seriousness of what is happening here—this man is unscrupulous, taking advantage of people's grief, using terms like "to represent the Walkers only in their anger, not their grief"—the kind of meaningless lawspeak that oppresses people. The story flips between time frames—past/present/future rolled into one. There's one serious technical flaw, though: Sarah Polley plays a teenage singer, and there is noticeably bad dubbing of her guitar playing; but perhaps her music is supposed to be trite and this shouldn't bother us. The rest of the music is more appropriate to the film, evoking what a friend calls "the lost tradition of lament"; sometimes it seems that our immediate consumer culture has forgotten that how to truly grieve includes not pretending that it doesn't hurt. The lawyer is trying—and failing—to suppress his terror at the inevitability of losing his daughter. He can't cope because he wants to believe in an ordered universe; he is trying to "ensure moral responsibility in this society," while he is so spiritually bereft that can't even look after himself, and he says that the bus crash would not have happened "if everyone had done their job with integrity." But this isn't true. What makes accidents happen? What control do we have over our lives? In one of the "future" sections of the film, the lawyer acknowledges his own disempowerment and lack of control in one of the most honest speeches in cinema about the potential pain of parenthood: "Enough rage and helplessness and your love turns to something else. What does it turn to? It turns to steaming piss."

This is a truly meaningful expression of anger, and my respect for this film makes me wonder why I'm so preoccupied with films about fathers and families. There's so much more to *The Sweet Hereafter* than I can either process or convey. I could write a whole chapter on the photography, use of light, and the iconoclastic fact that its constant use of uncorrupted white is not representative of purity. That would only scratch the surface. This is a film to be experienced, but perhaps not during one of those melancholic times. It's about how people sometimes use a form of revenge to heal the spirit; about how manipulating others for financial gain seems to be the (dis)order of the universe; about how the wisdom of children can circumvent the malevolence of adults; about weak men and strong men; about the brokenness that lies behind every professional smile.

The film reaches its climax when the surviving child, the Sarah Polley character, gives her testimony in an empty ballroom, where the community must once have enjoyed its own presence. As in the Browning poem, one child was lame and could not dance the whole of the way; but this "curse" saved her life. The film's child empowers herself by telling her truth, and slices through the layers of dishonesty and bile that the older, "wiser" adults worship as idols. And here Egoyan must be highly praised for his poetic skill as director. The reaction shots are cold, afraid, in a state of stasis, fearful, uncomprehending. We are witnesses to a decisive act that will mark the community's break with its past. As with the most traumatic of encounters, nothing shall be the same again. Everything shall be "strange and new," with unspoken rules and regulations for the eggshell dance that will guide people's lives from now on. This is a film about coping with the past that is so redolent with tragedy that it's hard not to feel like you're living through it yourself. To try to wrap it up with some kind of "redemptive" conclusion would be to seriously misunderstand its value as a work of art. Egoyan deals with people who are holding spiritual acid inside; they have been infected by a virus called inoperable grief, and nothing can save them except letting go of the impulse for revenge.

THE WRAP:
A PRIMER IN DEALING WITH THE PAST

The biblical prophecy of the future flowing of "righteousness like a never-ending stream" may not convey to us what was really meant—what exactly is this "righteousness"? "Righteousness" in this context is better translated as "justice." But what is justice? One person's justice is another person's revenge; and for many, peace means simply the absence of violence, rather than the biblical "shalom." Churches often sing about justice—about how we will dance on it, or speak out for those who cannot speak for themselves, or how this is the "year of the Lord's favor"—but it is all too easy to think we have *done* something when all we have done is *sung* something. I spent a week shadowing a lawyer once. I was seventeen and thought that's what I wanted to be when I grew up. Didn't follow through, obviously. Real court was nowhere near as exciting as movie law. Anytime I want to have the thrill of a case, I turn to *And Justice For All*, Norman Jewison's film of Al Pacino shouting at judges a lot; if that doesn't perk me up, then *Batteries Not Included*, the wonderful movie about old people saving their building from unscrupulous developers with the help of aliens—triumph for the little guy. And If I still need to feel that there is justice in the world, I'll put *Brassed Off* on and be moved by the tale of British miners recapturing their dignity when the pit closes, or slot in *The Full Monty*, which is basically the same story about steelworkers. All of these films inspire me to want to make the world a better place. And all of them make it seem possible.

Such possibilities are viewed with a more pessimistic lens in four magnificent American films from the past fifteen years. Sayles' *Eight Men Out* deals with a sports betting scandal and shows how the big guys get away with it; *Dead Man Walking* takes a long hard look at the death penalty and leaves you feeling both helpless and enraged; *Cradle Will Rock* reminds us of an element of American culture that just will not die—censorship and exclusion of those who ask difficult questions about the government; and Nicholas Hytner's film of Arthur Miller's *The Crucible* is not only the greatest screen adaptation of an American play, but powerful enough to make you believe that a man would rather die than lose his name.

Names, reputations, and honor are the crucible of *Waking the Dead*—a superb unknown gem about selfish political ambition and doing things within "the system"—and *The Insider*, where a corporate whistleblower has to agonize over his decision to tell the world the truth. The characters of *In the Bedroom* know the truth—that their son's murderer has gotten away with it—and it's killing them. They haven't found a way to let this truth set them free, so they decide to kill the guy. They have confused revenge with justice, and it's a haunting dissection of how tragedy can erode moral compasses. Similar themes are picked up in *A Simple Plan*, where the notion of "victimless crime" and the love of money (and how it corrodes relationships) are explored with devastating consequences. The moral compasses are on the other side of the legal equation in *In the Name of the Father*, which focuses on miscarriages of justice in the Northern Ireland conflict. The brutality of the police is matched only by the trauma suffered by the victims. And justice is not served.

The poor of Australia's Aborigines are the object of Philip Noyce's *Rabbit-Proof Fence*, a film about injustice without measure, as it follows three girls who walked twelve hundred miles to return to their mothers after being kidnapped by the British Protectorate. Meanwhile, *Papillon* is about one man's relentless insistence that he will not bow to oppression, as Steve McQueen resists the French penal colony regime (this film might just have the most inspirational ending in history). And without *Papillon*, there would be no *Shawshank Redemption*—a more recent stunning film about how liberation needs to happen on the inside before freedom on the outside has any meaning. Orson Welles' *The Trial*, based on Kafka's novel, is the anti-*Shawshank*—a man is arrested and tried without ever being told the charge; it's a nightmare world of social control and a prophecy of what human nature can be like when the powerful fear free thought.

Free thinkers subvert the system and bring a kind of justice in films as varied as *Twelve Angry Men*, *Mississippi Burning*, and *Things Change*. Of course, they don't always get justice—often the good die young and without wickedness getting its just reward. Films on this theme are easy to find, so I'll just mention one that didn't get as much attention on its release as it deserved. *The Widow of St. Pierre* is Patrice Leconte's gritty but lyrical adaptation of the true story of how one man showed grace to another, but because he was welcoming a "deviant" stranger, his community rejected, and ultimately killed him. There may be no better metaphor for what following Jesus may require of us. And the Church holds the key, or at least one of the keys, to change. The embrace of people on the basis of their humanity exemplified by Jesus is the answer to injustice. Clothing the naked, feeding the hungry, visiting those in prison, bringing sight to the blind, healing to the lame, becoming incarnated beacons of justice and peace is an overwhelming task, but one that we're all called to.

CHAPTER TEN

ALL YOU NEED IS LOVE

"Three things remain: faith, hope, and love—but the greatest of these is love." —1 Corinthians 13:13

LOVE, TO ANYONE WHO HAS SUFFERED FROM IT, IS an unquantifiable mystery. How can mere words do justice to the thing that has kept the human race going for so long? To the very essence of God? The challenge is huge, but failing to engage it is dangerous, for our world needs a reappraisal of love. All too often, when people say "I *love* you," what they really mean is "I *need* you." This may not be a sin; it may not even be too great a problem, but if that's the whole story, we're in trouble. The American psychiatrist and theologian M. Scott Peck has perhaps been the victim of his own success. His "Road Less Traveled" series has sold so many copies that we may be inclined not to take it seriously, because what is popular is so frequently of low quality. But Peck is one of the exceptions that proves the rule, and his definition of love is the best I've encountered: "Love is sacrificing for the sake of another's spiritual growth."

The incarnation of Christ is of course the ultimate act of love—the meta compromise that God made for the sake of us humans. But in a sense, all love, when truly realized, whether romantic or sexual or platonic, or of a cause, is about sacrifice for the sake of another. It should be clear to readers by now that I believe that film and social mores have a recursive relationship— that is, they reflect each other. There is no chicken and egg. What we see on screen may remind us of ourselves while at the same time teaching us or leading us astray. This chapter seeks to draw some love lessons from our cinematic counterparts. In the midst of the cheap sex, need-based relationships, and unrealistic, unhelpful "magic" of screen romance, there are a few pearls of great price.

MONSTER'S BALL
(MARC FOSTER, 2001)

You may remember this as the film that lost Halle Berry half her body weight in tears when she picked up one of those little golden statuettes for what is, quite frankly, an outstanding performance. That wasn't bad, because I hope it meant that more people saw it—it's one of those films that nobody sees because it doesn't have the juggernaut of a Burger King tie-in to bring the punters in. You really should see more films like this; and more companies like Lion's Gate should be prepared to take risks. Okay, art-politics lecture over; let's get to the film:

We're lured in by the gentle darkness of the music and opening; we see Billy Bob Thornton in bed, not resting or really sleeping, lost in some dark reverie that we don't yet understand. The music and images gently pull you in—we're watching something you think you're going to see but aren't sure. Like the hero of Paul Golding's amazing novel *The Abomination*, he's a man who wakes up at night and goes to the same café/cage every day, where they know what to bring him. He orders chocolate ice cream, which might be a little too cheesy, but reveals his childlike side. Anyway, he's a death row prison officer, with Puff Daddy on his watch. Ms. Berry's the wife. Thornton's character's son is an officer too, and they both live with Grandpa (Peter Boyle—the darkest portrayal I've ever seen of the potential of old age to corrode). Father and son regularly (and separately) visit the same sex worker. They have untidy, unhappy, broken sex, with a woman whose face we don't even see. They both want her to stay—he just wants to talk.

The wife and kid visit their dying man, and the boy asks why he's being executed; he answers, "Because I'm a bad man. But I want you to know something. You ain't me. You're everything that's good about me. This man sitting here today, you ain't." This film joins *Dead Man Walking* and an honorable list of others dedicated to exposing the myth of the "moral value" of the death penalty. You don't have to see the pain etched on a child's face as he realizes his father is about to be executed to think that judicial killing is not a good idea. I mean, if we don't even trust the government to raise the right kind of taxes, how can we trust them to kill the right people? More to the point, how can followers of Christ support the death penalty? Sorry, people, but the onus is on you to defend your idea to me if you think Jesus likes the idea of the state taking people's lives. They execute the prisoner, and the horror is expertly conveyed with cutting between the electric chair and the boy's chocolate bar. Later, the boy dies in a car accident. Thornton's character's son commits suicide, too, after the inarticulate rage of a father against his son leaves him in the certain knowledge that his dad despises him. At the funeral, when the minister asks Thornton's character if he wants to say a few words, this is the response: "All I wanna hear is that dirt hitting that box."

Grandpa is the epitome of broken old age. He is percolated in bitterness; all he can say of his dead grandson is, "He was weak," and of his late wife: "That woman failed me." Such brokenness is almost too much to bear. His character makes me want to rephrase T.S. Eliot—rather than the world closing with not a bang, but a whimper, *this* is how the universe ends: a man reduced to sitting alone watching television.

Thornton's and Berry's characters meet through the death of her son, even though he knew her before when she served him in the diner. (But then we rarely recognize the humanity of those who serve us, do we?) He drives her home one night, and she cries on his shoulder, pleading for him to "help make me feel good." Thus begins one of the most honest sex scenes in cinema. This is wild, lonely, animalistic sex. They find a way to communicate through sex, when he can't even understand what she's saying; it's a risky, beautifully observed scene of brokenness between two people. It reveals what sex can mean; and, for me, it screams aloud the need for a wider discussion about sex in the Church. I don't want to tell you about the rest of the film, because it's worth experiencing for yourself, but there are themes I can discuss without giving the game away.

The love between these two characters is alive with reality. They teeter on the brink of destruction—she doesn't know who he is, he doesn't know how to make it work, grandpa does his worst to destroy things. Thornton's character's transformation from spiritually dead racist to a man of grace has been criticized by some who say it happens too quickly. But I'm not too sure about that. His transformation is not suspect for me—he is a man who reveals little at the start when he's screwed up, and his healing is evidenced by his revealing gradually more as the story develops. When his father makes the remark about his mother being a failure, when his son kills himself, he clearly begins to reflect on what kind of man he has become. The re-awakening of the potential for love within him, and with the "wrong" kind of person, happens by accident. When he wakes up with her, the damage—or healing—has already been done. He can't go back. And his humanity is further revealed in the very sweet touch of having him ask the names of the kids he has previously shot at for intruding on "his" land.

Berry's character doesn't have any friends, and neither does he; his relationship with the sex worker is a case in point, but not a million miles away from how most of us relate to each other much of the time—using people for what they can give us. It's about as far away from the logic of "do unto others" as you can get without coming back in the other direction. I know I labor this point, but the breakdown of community is at the root of all human problems—if people would only love each other ... And *Monster's Ball* shows us the vast, unlimited landscape that is the place where love runs free. You can't get "out" from inside yourself. The epochal questions that your own spiritual imprisonment forces you to ask will not be answered by a philosophy, but by a person, or people, who will love you for yourself. But until you let that person in, you'll be trapped within yourself. We need each other, but we can't meet that need unless it's opened to us. The two say to each other: "I wanna take care of you. Good, cause I really need to be taken care of." And when we see that we need each other, we are more likely to ask for their forgiveness. That's what this movie's about, pure—very pure—and simple.

So by the middle of the film, we've already had enough tragedy to last a lifetime. But this film is not a tragedy. It is about the capacity of human beings to heal themselves through loving each other. It's a love story, it's about racial integration, it's about fatherhood, it's about the death penalty, it's about the breakdown of community, it's about the poor, it's about why people feel they can't take gifts from each other, it's about finding redemption, it's about loneliness and grief, it's about marriage, it's about the ability to leave the past behind, it's about what you can convey with a look or glance or a tub of ice cream. There are no significant speeches, no grandstanding, no philosophy, just real people talking the way real people talk. But does a wrenching experience a great film make? No—shock or pain are not themselves marks of quality, but *Monster's Ball* has got what it takes.

It's one of those films whose atmosphere makes you feel things nothing else can. It's suffused with both death and love and grants mercy to its protagonists just as we would if we knew them. At the end, when the loose ends are still untied, we want the closure of knowing that they stay together, but the film is honest enough to show that real life isn't like that. Technically, the film is highly accomplished: There's some really beautiful camera work and nicely bleached color to the images that heighten the reality, and the music is beautifully tuned to the story. But its value is not primarily in its photography or editing or sound design, wonderful as these are. It asks the questions that I ask myself all the time: What does it feel like to be a man? How can love exist between people who should hate each other? How do we deal with the past?

The characters in this film are about as broken as you'll find. But they're not there for us to pity them—but maybe we need someone so tragic to awaken us to the possibility of grace. How much horror can one person take? Thankfully, *Monster's Ball* is honest about this, what the Bible calls God not letting you be tested beyond what you can bear. In one strange moment, we see a man holding a sign; it's a fleeting image, but if we look closely, we'll see that the sign says, "It's gotta be somebody's fault." But the film, like grace, says that the way to deal with "fault" is to forgive. We cannot bring back the past, but we can maybe move on in a better way than before. The final, highly dramatic, but very quiet scenes are so gripping that they may make you forget to breathe. You watch the two protagonists try to resolve their pain; you want to be in that room with them, you want to be nowhere else, and yet you feel as if you're trespassing on a private moment. You and I may think we will never have such evocative private moments, but I suspect most of us will. Things like love and death and pain and redemption happen all the time. So why not to us? Love stories are usually funnier, more obviously redemptive, and more "fluffy" than this. But are they more honest?

EYES WIDE SHUT
(STANLEY KUBRICK,
FREDERIC RAPHAEL, 1999)

"The dominant tendency of our age is the breaking of faith and the making of divisions among things that once were joined. This story obviously must be told by somebody. Perhaps, in one form or another, it must be told (because it must be experienced) by everybody. The story can be told in a way that clarifies, that makes imaginable and compassionable, the suffering and the costs; or it can be told in a way that seems to grant an easy permission and absolution to adultery and divorce. Can [art], for example, be [made] according to standards that are not merely [artistic]? Obviously it can. And it had better be."— Wendell Berry, *Life is a Miracle*

"This is what you get for making house calls."—Tom Cruise, *Eyes Wide Shut*

For someone who has loved Stanley Kubrick's films since I was a teenager, *Eyes Wide Shut*, his first film for twelve years, was a prospect over which to salivate. I had followed the tortuous

production—the longest continuous film shoot in history—
from reports in the early 1990s that the greatest filmmaker ever
was about to make something new, and I was looking forward
immensely to what would be an extraordinary piece of cinema.
Then, in March 1999, three months before it was due to be
released, tragedy struck: Kubrick was dead from a heart attack at
seventy years old.

I remember coming in late at night on a Sunday and
seeing the news; I freely confess that my initial response was
to worry if *EWS* would ever be released and to feel sad that
his long-cherished sci-fi epic *A.I.* (later made quite brilliantly
by Spielberg) would definitely never make it to the big screen.
However, all was not lost, and I got to see *Eyes Wide Shut* later
that summer. And here's what I think. This is a fascinating,
flawed film, a huge conservative canvas, which is destined to be
misunderstood by those members of the thought police who
cannot tell the difference between portrayal and advocacy. It is
a deceptively simple story about the value of marriage and the
lengths to which some men go to destroy it. It is, quite frankly,
a horror movie about marital infidelity, and you can't get much
riskier than that.

After Kubrick's traditional opening credit sequence—
exactly the same as most of his other films (Woody Allen
does this, too; there's something comforting about seeing the
consistency of tone and music over his credits; it feels like going
home)—like most of his oeuvre, we're immediately thrust into
the story; there's nothing left to chance, no dead weight or
flab here. We see an unfeasibly rich beautiful couple, Dr. Bill
and Alice Hartford, played by the most unfeasibly rich and
beautiful, if no longer real, Hollywood couple Tom and Nicole,
preparing to attend a Christmas party hosted by the powerful
Mr. Ziegler (played by Sydney Pollack, who should really act
more than direct). This evokes the first of the film's themes—

the emptiness of opulence, and Kubrick's antipathy toward the rich and powerful (see *Strangelove, Spartacus, Clockwork Orange,* and especially *Barry Lyndon* for other examples). We follow some smoky tracking shots into a ballroom, which is highly reminiscent of *The Shining*, where possibly ghostly presences compete for the Hartford's attention. At this point, if you haven't seen the film, I would highly recommend it, for you won't understand a word of what I'm about to say otherwise, and you certainly won't be able to disagree with it.

Dr. Bill goes off on a little adventure after being freaked out by Alice's confession of once being attracted to another man. He is propositioned by the daughter of one of his patients, gets not very far with a sex worker, and meets an old friend who leads him to a place where the dream of every man comes true—commitment-free sex, all night long, and no one has to see your face. This weird, totally unerotic orgy scene "climaxes" with Dr. Bill being—almost literally—exposed by the powerful men encircling him. (In fact, one of the keys to the movie is that everybody else has more power than Bill does, from Mr. Ziegler to the orderly he meets later at the morgue.) He escapes only when a woman whom he previously "saved" offers to "die" in his place. This leads to a guilt trip, much anguished pounding of New York's streets, and a terrifying little scene when he goes home to find Alice has "unmasked" him, too. All very unusual; some have said it's even downright silly, but I beg to differ:

Here's my overriding thought about *EWS*—it is almost all a dream; every section of the film where Dr. Bill is separated from Alice takes place in an alternative reality, where the dream logic of adolescence prevails. He asks the two models who flirt outrageously with him at the Christmas party where they are taking him. They tell him that "We're going where the rainbow ends," but he is plunged into something more reminiscent of a nightmare. Some evidence for the dream:

◆ There's a very strange quality to the light and the film stock—the movie looks the way dreams sometimes do.

◆ It's Christmas—a time of dreams, when people forget their moral responsibilities.

◆ Bill is seduced by a woman with a dead body in the room—if only Freud were around to interpret this film.

◆ A young girl hides behind him for protection—this is clearly his power fantasy.

◆ Throughout the entire story, Bill can't manage to have any illicit sex, as in dreams associated with impotency.

◆ The costumers where Bill rents his mask and cape is called "Under the Rainbow."

◆ If this is a dream, then it resolves such things as timing problems with Bill's friend Nightingale and how he gets from his gig to the orgy—"Every time it's in a different place."

◆ Remember that Bill is stoned when his adventure begins.

This "dream story" (adapted from Schnitzler's "Traumnovelle"), far from being the sexually explicit titillater that its hype suggested, appears in fact to be a conservative reflection on the nature of love and marital commitment. I do ask whether or not it says that extra-marital sex is bad for good reasons (Alice says that Bill only doesn't have sex with other women because he is married, but does the film believe that sex within the commitment of marriage is qualitatively better?). And I certainly don't agree with the Machiavellian count at the dance when he says, "Don't you think that one of the charms of marriage is that it makes deception a necessity for both partners?" But as for the orgy scene: Is this scene really a very conservative reflection on the horror of what men really want to do to women? Interestingly, when Bill is found out, it's like a school fear or a neurotic dream of public nakedness, with which most men should be able to identify.

Eyes Wide Shut is nicely framed and beautifully shot, as we would expect, but, all told, it's a very clever film: It's an amusement, made up of many neat symmetrical pairs—Bill and the piano player both went to medical school but took different paths; Bill "saves" one woman at the party but fails to save the costumer's daughter; there are two Eastern European male characters of dubious sexual ethics—the count and the costumer. It manages to touch on cinematic themes such as horror films, *The Wizard of Oz*, Satanism, thrillers, and romance, and, ironically, the movie takes forever getting where it wants to go—perhaps mirroring impotence. It's noteworthy that the sex worker is called Domino and is the first woman he meets whom he allows to be the catalyst for his infidelity journey. In the café he listens to Mozart's "Requiem," while the cover of his paper says "Lucky to be Alive."

Possibly only Kubrick could make such stuff not look silly, although sometimes it comes very close; the dream logic is really quite imaginative and makes for a fascinating discussion over some good red wine and cheese. My only disappointment is that Domino the sex worker is a *sociology student*, thus becoming yet another in the long line of movie characters with similarities to myself who end up dead. One lives in hope of a romantic action movie with a hero called Gareth!

There are perhaps three key lines in the movie, which I

quote here without comment, for the benefit of those about to have an argument with loved ones about whether this film is an intelligent masterpiece or a load of rubbish:

- ◆ "When a promise has been made here (in the dream world) there is no turning back."

- ◆ "We should be grateful that we have managed to have survived through all of our adventures, whether they were real, or only a dream."

- ◆ "The reality of one night can never be the whole truth, and no dream is ever just a dream."

The film exerts a strange pull and power to provoke. It leaves me unable to imagine Kubrick having much sympathy for men who commit adultery; he was known to have had one of the most enduring marriages, and his wife has pronounced herself to be "the best entertained woman in the world." Watching *Eyes Wide Shut* with the benefit of hindsight, now that Kubrick's death has become part of the fabric of film history, and Tom Cruise and Nicole Kidman are divorced, it is striking that we may feel complicit in the break-up of the marriage—now *that's* an example of where the lines between art and life are dangerously blurred.

A PRIMER IN LOVE

Avoid J.Lo. I know that will make me unpopular with many, but it will increase my respect with others, so I'm on safe ground. Otherwise, if you wanna know movie love, try these for size:

The Abyss—Heroism in a bottle when a guy realizes he just has to get his woman back, even though she's dead.

The African Queen—The romantic affair between two of the most unlikely lovers, Bogart as the epitome of machismo, Hepburn as the ultimate in politeness.

The Age of Innocence—One of those films that leaves you conflicted; the hero is married to the wrong woman and chooses to give up the one he really loves. What might be morally best is often the most difficult decision to take.

Amores Perros—The title of this amazing Mexican film translates as "Love's a B----," and that's just what it's about— how love is so often confused with need, how people often feel they cannot be themselves unless they are in someone else's arms, but also how love for another can redeem even the most broken person. There is a scene of repentance toward the end of this movie that will etch itself on your memory.

Annie Hall—Woody Allen's masterful assessment of yuppy-puppy love in the '70s was originally titled *Anhedonia*—the inability to enjoy yourself—which is just about the most inappropriate title you could give it. It's about the way we don't say what we really feel when we're attracted to someone, the tension leading to a first kiss, the entertainment of lobster-anxiety, and the fantasy that a leading academic might just appear to defend you from intellectual attack in a movie theater line. I have yearned for this, but alas, it has never happened.

Casablanca—The fundamental things apply.

Crouching Tiger, Hidden Dragon—The sacrificial love shown by one for another, giving her life to bring back a man she hardly knew was lost on many people who seem to think of this film as a simple chopsocky kick 'em up. But it's really about the atonement.

The Crying Game—This is now an old film—many of us seem to have forgotten its portrayal of love across boundaries, but it's well worth rediscovering.

Days of Heaven—One of the most self-consciously beautiful films ever made. With director Terrence Malick only filming for an hour a day during the "magic" time, perhaps never has more been accomplished through so much effort. The light in this film breathes; the action (if you can call it that) can only be described as the physical incarnation of poetry. It gives two of my favorite actors, Sam Shepard and Brooke Adams, a chance to suck the marrow out of their characters, and Richard Gere proves why he still deserves to be on the screen.

Deep Impact—Yeah, I know, nobody takes this film seriously except me, and it's hardly an accurate attempt at what the end of the world would look like (London's *Time Out* said that the director's "idea of social breakdown begins and ends with a traffic jam"). But it holds within itself one of the most moving portrayals of sacrificial love in mainstream cinema, when the crew of the aptly named "Messiah" space shuttle decide to give their lives for the human race. As Spock would say, the needs of the many outweigh the needs of the few.

Much Ado About Nothing—Branagh's wonderful Shakespeare adaptation trims all the fat and presents a simply hilarious, joyful experience of star-crossed (and merely cross) lovers in Tuscany. Great music from Patrick Doyle, too.

The Remains of the Day—A film about the risk of not making yourself vulnerable to the one you love; Anthony Hopkins' butler simply cannot bring himself to open up to the object of his affection, played by Emma Thompson. It's testament to the film's strength and quality that it doesn't seek to resolve itself with a pat happy ending.

Talk to Her—How can you make a film about rape and comas and death and still make the characters sympathetic? Ask Pedro Almodovar. He is the master of teasing out the glory of God in the lives of the broken.

The War of the Roses—Where love gets nasty; a misanthropic marriage disaster flick from Danny deVito, of all people. Michael Douglas and Kathleen Turner act like Tracy and Hepburn on a really bad day. If ever there was a film about the need to as for help as soon as you realize something's going wrong, this is it.

When Harry Met Sally—And finally, a film that really tells (some of) the truth about relationships; how we meet and pretend and amuse ourselves and get scared and laugh and always seem to use other people as a way of finding out what we ourselves think. Having said that, *When Harry Met Sally*, like most love stories, doesn't have the wisdom required to get on with love in this world. Meg Ryan, wonderful as she seems on screen, will not satisfy all our desires. If we're looking for "the answer" to our existential questions, we won't find it in another human being, but only be learning to love ourselves and lead an ethical life.

A friend told me that after 40 years of marriage, he realized that he did not love his wife when he made his wedding vows. He *lusted* after her, but he had not yet realized anything of the meaning of love as sacrificing for the sake of another's spiritual growth. Love is the antidote to brokenness. I've already mentioned the metaphor of the three voices—adult, child, critic—we all identify with these, don't we? Well, if you want to learn to silence the critic, put yourself in a place where your "adult" can be nurtured, and take the space to love yourself. Real love cannot be restricted or bound by time and space. In this case, perhaps *Dracula* is the best story about love there is—a man who doesn't even let his own death stand in the way of his love.

CHAPTER ELEVEN

1968–1975, AMERICA

THE BOOK OF GENESIS DESCRIBES A PERIOD IN THE life of Israel when there were seven years of feasting, followed by seven years of famine. While I do not think there was necessarily any divine strategy at work, it is clear that the same principle— or at least the first half of it—was in place from 1968-1975. This, for my money (and although I don't have a lot of that, it must count for something), was the golden age of American film. No period before or since has even come close to equalling the quality, imagination, and sheer in-your-face vision of this time. Just look at the titles of only twenty-four of this period's gems:

Planet of the Apes
The Wild Bunch
2001: A Space Odyssey
Bonnie and Clyde
Easy Rider
Five Easy Pieces
Once Upon a Time in the West

The Godfather

Chinatown

Mean Streets

The Exorcist

The Godfather, Part II

The Conversation

Catch-22

The Producers

Papillon

Patton

Easy Rider

Alice Doesn't Live Here Anymore

Jaws

Nashville

Silent Running

Young Frankenstein

M*A*S*H

Looking at this list conjures up a bittersweet virtual nostalgia for me (it cannot constitute *actual* nostalgia, because I wasn't even born before any of these films was made). These films not only were made by American men of different generations and political persuasions (Dennis Hopper's a Republican, Franklin Schaffner was no spring chicken) and financed by a dying studio system not known for its aesthetic flair, but they also managed to pull in significant audiences. People actually wanted to *see* these movies and actively sought them out. I do not believe that this means that today's cinema-going public is less intelligent than its 1970s forebears (although cultural intelligence is at an all-time low); I just feel that in a capitalistic monopoly, in which accountants and lawyers decide on the nature of what art to produce, choice will be limited, and people will consume whatever is fed them. Whether of a high, medium, or low quality, people will go to see whatever they have easiest access to and whatever is most publicized. Hence, *American Beauty* can be a huge hit and win best picture one year, and *Gladiator* can do the same the next. One is approaching a work of art with serious things to say about the postmodern male, and the other offers nothing but nicely staged operatic battle sequences and a grunting sex symbol. Accountants and lawyers ran Hollywood thirty years ago, so what was it that made 1968-1975 seven years of feasting? I'm not entirely sure; perhaps it had something to do with the student activism of the then recent past, hopefulness, freedom, the fact that these filmmakers were the first generation raised to take the movies seriously, the popular acceptance of simply *thinking* as a credible pastime ... Who knows? I, for one, am grateful that the witness of these years is available and more accessible to us than ever before. This weekend, you could do yourself a big favor by renting any three of the films on the list above. If I were you, I'd start with *The Wild Bunch, The Conversation,* and *Papillon,* but—hey!—this is a democracy, so knock yourself out.

CHAPTER TWELVE

QUEST
THE JOURNEY IS THE DESTINATION

"Seek and you shall find." —Jesus Christ

"There are no answers anymore, only choices." —Stanislaw Lem, *Solaris*

THE JOURNEY IS THE MOST FREQUENTLY USED metaphor for Christian discipleship, or indeed any kind of spirituality these days. An ancient Zen tale explains that if you think you have met the Buddha on the road, you need to kill him (or at least leave him behind; I mean, we don't want to get too violent) because he is not the true Buddha, but merely an expression of your longing. This story has a more explicitly Christian counterpart in the story of the man who, with his dying breath, clenched his fist to gather some of the earth of his beloved homeland of Tuscany to bring with him to the afterlife. He was insistent that nothing would separate him from his beloved country. But when he arrived on the near side of heaven, the angel told him that no one can bring anything in except themselves. The man stubbornly refused, and millennia passed before the angel once more invited him in. He was still determined to keep his fist closed, so the angel reluctantly retreated behind the pearly gates. More millennia passed, and the angel returned, this time in the form of an old drinking buddy who the man instantly recognized. "We miss you in heaven, old friend," he said. "Won't you come in, and leave the earth behind?" The old man was touched by the love his friend had for him, and extended his arms to embrace him. In so doing, he accidentally opened his hand, and the earth fell as dust into the wind. With tear-stained eyes, the two men walked slowly, but with anticipation toward the gates. And to the old man's surprise, the first thing he saw on the other side was the land where he would spend eternity. And it looked strangely like the hill country of Tuscany. That's just another way of saying that the answer to life is sometimes elusive, and it is easy to be deceived or, more likely, to deceive ourselves. Meanwhile, our true treasure is so often right in front of us. Whether our hope is for a brain/a heart/courage/to get home before midnight or fulfilling our destiny as "the one" to make a difference, it's weird and cool and useful that so much in cinema reflects the thing that Christians call "pilgrimage," the journey deeper within. You don't have to leave your chair to go on that journey, though. Just follow the cinematic yellow brick road ...

THE WIZARD OF OZ
(1939)

Christmas wouldn't be the same without it. Childhood wouldn't be the same without it. Come to think of it, David Lynch wouldn't be the same without it. What I remember most about *The Wizard of Oz* was how scary the monkeys were when

I first saw it at nine years old in rehearsals for my greatest ever stage performance, as the cowardly lion. Believe me, standing in front of five hundred adults wearing a costume that appears to made from brown towel and oven gloves and having to sing "If I only had the nerve" in a pseudo-Southern American accent, while affecting a camp demeanor, will mark you for life. But I'm glad to report that there's more to the yellow brick road than that. No more and no less, this is the meaning of life—at the end of the rainbow (which is a bit rich, considering you can't ever find the end of a rainbow). This is a film that reminds us that it's the simplest things that may be the truest; as the opening scroll itself tells us of the story: "Time has been powerless to put its kindly philosophy out of fashion."

But what is that kindly philosophy? I think it can be reduced to a couple of simple but profound ideas, and I know of no better way to put them than to paraphrase Thomas Merton and T.S. Eliot: All of us live—to some degree—in fear of losing what's most dear to us; true spirituality consists in recognizing the illusory nature of created things, that the journey is the destination, and that at the end of all our searchings, we will end where we begin, and know ourselves for the first time.

Now, there's more to the film than that—it is a critique of imperialism and the philosophy that "money makes the world go round," for a start—but I want to concentrate on what it says about human nature and spiritual pilgrimage. It's worth remembering that *The Wizard of Oz* was released the same year Hitler invaded Poland and sparked off the Second World War. Meanwhile, in the midst of such darkness, American audiences were overawed as sepia-tinted Dorothy was being tornado-swept into "a place where there isn't any trouble," having followed the typical conventions of myth by being "rejected" (or at least not protected) by her family, bringing a companion on a dangerous journey, and meeting a wizened character along the way. We all know what happens next—lots of noise and bad weather, and a flying house that crushes an evil witch (although, unfortunately not the very annoying Glinda, the Good Witch of the North, who is so twee that I kinda wish the house had landed on her, too). Dorothy emerges from the house surprisingly unscathed and into magnificent production design and loud warbling from Technicolor small people. (If my entrance to the afterlife is going to be greeted by these kind of sing-songs, I don't want to die for a long time). Anyway, then, as we know, she heads off on the road and makes three weird friends (didn't anyone ever tell her not to talk to strangers?). They all need something, or at least they believe that they need it, and have to negotiate various obstacles along the way, not least of which is the scariest movie villain of my childhood—the Wicked Witch of the West. As a revisionist, though, it occurs to me that there should actually have been a chance for redemption for the wicked witch; let's face it, a house just fell on her sister, and she has just realized Liza Minnelli's going to inherit her groovy shoes in a couple of decades, so maybe we should be more sympathetic.

Despite some dodgy near-homophobia regarding the lion and a very unusual deployment of hallucinogenic substances (for a kids' film) when our heroes cross through a poppy field, they finally get to the Emerald City and meet some men with big moustaches who won't let them in. Some monkey-bashing and one dissolved witch later, and they're back to see the Great Oz, whom they believe will solve all their worldly and existential problems (a bit like Depeche Mode's "Personal Jesus"). And then comes one of the most profound scenes in American cinema. The Great Oz declares his true humility, saying "I'm a very good man, just a very bad wizard," and invites the lion, the scarecrow, Dorothy, and the tin man to recognize their real condition—that the voice they were so afraid of was just an old man behind a curtain, and that their journeys are their own responsibility. The lion, for instance, is not weak-willed, but merely a "victim of disorganized thinking" who "confuses courage with wisdom." The four are presented with medals, testimonials, and diplomas, which, in my view, represent symbols of self-recognition through the love of God. And Dorothy always had the power to get back to Kansas, but she had to learn this for herself. Once she sees this—truly sees it—she is there in a flash.

And I am beginning to think that the same might be true of our lives on this planet. The fear that so often paralyzes us, perhaps especially the fear that God might be angry with us, is just an old man behind a curtain. It only has the authority we give it. It is easy—and sometimes reasonable—to blame God for seemingly making us incomplete, but true friendship may give us the wisdom to see that we have everything we need, if only we would take it. I feel safe in this film because, in spite of the monkey-anxiety, it reminds me of the happy parts of childhood and of the hope that I am still invited to be childlike. It also reminds me that sometimes the tornados of our lives are given us so that we might rest and be healed, and, even though it might hurt us, the tornado may even kill some of our demons. While I wouldn't necessarily agree that the back yard is always the best place to find your destiny, I think it is true that, as the wizard says, hearts will never be practical until they can be made unbreakable. But who needs an unbreakable heart?

VANILLA SKY
(CAMERON CROWE, 2001)

"Not all rich kids are souless and not all psychiatrists care about dreams." —Kurt Russell, *Vanilla Sky*

Another film with a weird title that declares that the

answer is within you is Cameron Crowe's woefully underrated *Vanilla Sky*, which takes a great deal of risk by acid-melting the most famous face in the world and inviting us to open our eyes to what's really going on. (And, unusually enough, has more mythic resonance than the film it remakes—*Abre los Ojos*). Tom Cruise plays a spiritually dormant magazine publisher who takes little or no interest in taking responsibility for his life. We first see him waking up in an empty city, in a scene evocative of the old fear of facing the rapture alone—the neurosis of choice held by many Christians. We're not immediately certain whether this represents his greatest fear or greatest hope; he answers for us by running away in fear, but we soon realize that, even though he is surrounded by people, he is alone anyway. We learn that he is about to turn thirty-three (the Christ metaphors in this film aren't always very subtle), and that he almost believes he could "be the one person in the history of man who would live forever." And, although he's sleeping with Cameron Diaz, he doesn't seem to have learned much about responsibility in relationships: He speaks of his "intricate systems" to get them to do what he wants them to. Unusual for a Hollywood movie, his immaturity in relationships is portrayed as a bad thing, which leads ultimately to both his downfall and resurrection.

The relationship with Diaz's character is a textbook example of how expectations in relationships are key to their success. He feels that she is someone there for him to have sex with when they both fancy some of it, while she underlines the depth of the meaning of sex, saying that he doesn't realize "the consequences of the promises you made." She is presented as a sad woman who takes only slightly more responsibility for her life than he does; but the point is still there: Sex is something too important to be treated as lightly as most people seem to treat it, and many relationships between adults never make it past the adolescent stage. Anyway, Tom's shallow character journeys between Diaz's and Penelope Cruz's and begins to discover what a real love can do to you. This film is so good that I don't want to spoil it for you, and it's so complicated I probably couldn't explain it if I tried. Suffice to say, it will make you think about how we use the myths of childhood to sustain life in a difficult world, how "there's nothing bigger than the little things," and how nobody and no time is beyond redemption. Until you experience a kind of "death," you will never find the key to life. Until you learn gratitude for the gifts from God and other people, you will never be able to relate to what you've got. Unless you experience the troughs of life's challenges, you will not understand the glories—as one character says, "The sweet is never as sweet without the sour." Ultimately, this is a film about memory and future and truth and being and breathing and life and fear and love and peace and forgiveness and guilt and music—great music—and laughter and tears, and the dark but liberating fact that if you're not centered, you'll end up killing yourself or someone else.

GROUNDHOG DAY
(HAROLD RAMIS, DANNY RUBIN, 1993)

"Do not worry about your life, what you will eat or drink; or about your body, what you will wear." —Matthew 6:25

There's a moment in *The Rocky Horror Picture Show* when the narrator Charles Gray (my favorite Blofeld, by the way) invokes a portent of doom, saying: "There were daaaaaark storm clouds gathering that night ..." Seasoned RHPS audiences will, at this point, shout out: "Describe your balls!" And the eminent Mr. Gray will blithely assert: "Heavy, black, and pendulous."

So we could be forgiven the expectation that *Groundhog*

Day, with its opening scenes of dark storm clouds, may be the natural heir to RHPS's crazy mantle. It's much more profound than that pansexual festival of bawdy humor and screeching music. Storm clouds don't always have to be tragic, and *Groundhog Day*'s version of the cyclonic portent is not only hilarious, but profound in its analysis of the nature of time and personal responsibility. The comedy weatherman is a phenomenon that Irish people don't understand—ours are very serious folk; so is the fact of Groundhog Day itself, so it's useful to point out to non-U.S. readers that Groundhog Day is the annual moment in Punxsatawney, Pennsylvania, when a strange little creature emerges from its hole and indicates the time that spring comes. Or something like that. Perhaps this is a beautiful ritual, a fusion of man and nature, a declaration of the glory of tradition, and the majesty of creation; or perhaps it reflects the fact that America's view of history is so narrow that they have to invent these things to make it look like they have roots that preceded the destruction of the Natives. Anyway, Bill Murray (sometimes my favorite actor) and Andie Macdowall (she of the worst hairdo and best smile in modern cinema) spark off each other as Murray's character, named Phil (shock! so is the groundhog!) is forced to re-live the same day over and over, for what seems like about a year, in a search for himself and the meaning of life. And, simply, apart from that horrible and often terribly intrusive phenomenon of using pop songs written just to sell the soundtrack, this might just be my favorite comedy, full of spiritual resonance and answers to the questions that preoccupy us all.

Bill's character Phil is a guy who eats alone, only focused on the potential for further success. He refers to himself as "the world's most famous weatherman," which is a bit like calling the U.S. baseball championships the "world series" (oops, there I go again with my skeptical views of America) … He's a selfish guy who looks like he likes himself too much—but like everyone in love with themselves, he doesn't like himself at all. Although he gets to live in Pittsburgh, one of my favorite cities, the place where I first heard Billy Joel's "Scenes from an Italian Restaurant" and ate at the Grandview Café. The Beehive cinema's pretty cool, too. But that's straying too much from *Groundhog Day*. We all know what happens when he gets cursed to re-live the same day. It's a movie Merton would love—what we would be like if we could see life coming at us, how we would learn to experience the sacrament of the present moment. Phil's condition reminds me of the unpleasant proverb about a dog returning to its own vomit—sometimes we need to re-live certain things until they are redeemed. This is not salvation by works, though—it's not that we are saved by the good things we do, just that we will never become fully realized human beings until we make peace with the past.

At first Phil loves his curse, using his newfound knowledge to seduce women; but eventually he realizes that knowing you're always going to win is a terrible thing. Living without moral consequences is fun for a while, but it deadens the soul. Soon Phil comes to regret what it is to be "a god"—he has "killed himself so many times he feels like he doesn't even exist anymore." He decides to start telling the truth in the hope that it will set him free, but finds that you cannot "use" morality to get what you want. Only when he is motivated by love rather than self-interest can his life start again.

Groundhog Day is not a perfect film—the old homeless man whom Phil first ignores, then helps, then regrets being unable to save is symbolic of injustice; but as usual with Hollywood, there is no critique of the system that put him the gutter in the first place. It is, however, one of the most beautifully structured comedy scripts I've ever seen—it doesn't end when you think it's going to, and it's the best kind of comedy—one that tells the truth about the human drama—and it asks the question, "If you only had one day to live, what would you do?" Some of us may answer, like one of the characters, "I'd just want to know where to put the camera," but maybe the more attentive will find what Jesus really meant when he told us not to be worried about anything anymore, ever. It forces us to ask ourselves what it would mean to invest every moment in treating others as we would want to be treated, doing the things you've always wanted, giving love to others, not worrying about tomorrow. It recognizes that you can't change everything—but, as with *Schindler's List*, whoever saves one life saves the entire world. People who do good things are flawed too, but a human being fully alive is the glory of God; and to be fully alive means to be able to do what is necessary at the right time. And of course time, and our ability to choose what to do with it, is all we have.

THE STRAIGHT STORY
(DAVID LYNCH, MARY SWEENEY, JOHN ROACH 1999)

David Lynch is not best known for his appreciation of sweetness and light. His films are usually into the dark underbelly of Americana, but *The Straight Story* proves that he hasn't totally given up on the human spirit. This is a Disney production of a Lynch film, lest we forget; this is appropriate, for the characters are like cartoons—slightly removed from what we might think of as "real life." Lynch's lurking camera sneaks up on the people and somehow manages to show us their souls. This movie is based on the true story of Alvin Straight, an elderly man who drove his ride-on lawnmower several hundred miles to reconcile with his ailing brother. It strikes just the right note between comic-book buffoonery and melancholia.

Alvin is introduced lying on the floor of his kitchen after a fall—and old men really do make a thud when they fall; then we see his buddies, the kind of old guys who spend every day in their local bar, the kind of place where everybody knows your name, but you would never see *Cheers* on the TV screen. These guys are eccentrically inflexible and amusingly inaccessible; this characteristic had tragic resonance when the lead actor, Richard Farnsworth, took his own life before it took him, shortly after the film was released.

Alvin's relationship with his brother has broken down: "We said some unforgivable things the last time we met, but I'm trying to put those things right. I just hope I'm not too late." And isn't this what we all feel? He is making the journey that we all eventually need to make—to make peace with all aspects of the past, to rediscover our childhood, to find peace with God. Not for nothing does Alvin meet a priest and make a kind of confession before he sees his brother. While Alvin wants to stay connected to the local, he realizes that he needs to travel beyond to find himself: "Imagining the great yonder making our trials seem smaller." When he meets a woman who keeps killing deer with her car because she has to drive an eighty-mile round trip to get to work, Lynch is at his most evocative of Kieslowski. In *The Decalogue* and the *Three Colours Trilogy*, the Polish master was at pains to portray his belief that bad things can be avoided by strengthening community. In *A Short Film About Killing*, the young boy about to be executed tearfully tells his lawyer that he knows he would not have murdered anyone if he had not left his family's farm because of a tragic accident. Now, of course, it is easy to make an idol of rural existence, as if there were such things as "the good old days." But just as there is no smoke without fire, the myth of close-knit communities has a ring of truth to it as well. There is nothing wrong with people finding a sense of identity with group membership. The rot begins to set in when membership of that group depends on excluding others.

The Straight Story is one of those movies that has to be experienced—to call it "beautiful" is to diminish it with inadequate adjectives. But the Midwest has never looked so edible (credit to Freddie Francis' amazing photography), and watching the movie will touch us even if we don't like the story: the longueurs, the music, the photography, the lulling to rest that we find within it. It's about the pleasure of a barbecued hot dog under the stars, how forgiving others brings healing to us, how regret for the past is a waste of spirit, but most of all how "a brother's a brother." It's about how we need each other, and there's no point staying angry for very long. Alvin comes from a place where it still takes two months to get a decent grabber on order, where the pace of life might actually be good for the soul, where people have never doubted that the journey is the destination. At first, he seems to be going nowhere fast on his lawnmower, and he even has one false start before the journey actually begins. (His is not the tragic-comedic motto of so many: If at first you don't succeed, then erase all evidence that you ever tried.) Unlike me, when Alvin travels, he doesn't bring any reading material, just his smokes, his heart, and his memories.

I could go on, but I think I've already said earlier why this film is important. A fragmented society is easily broken, but when people are tied together, connected to one another, there is less chance of breaking. This may sound cheesy, but I haven't found a better alternative. At one point, Alvin encourages some guys to recognize that the worst part about being old is remembering when you was young; enjoy the days of thy youth, for they shall not return. His journey is daunting—it's noisy and scary and none too quiet; his unhappy daughter has been failed by the system—but he persists, because he knows that to try to find healing and fail is infinitely better than never trying at all. We learn something about generosity—how it requires a fair degree of fearlessness to make hospitality work. True hospitality means clothing the naked stranger, not just having your friends around for dinner. If we were to meet Alvin and his brother Lyle, they might appear to us like naked strangers. But there is the presence of God behind every human face. When Lyle realizes what his brother has done to find him, he looks up, as if to thank heaven; at the end of *The Straight Story*, you may do the same.

THE WRAP

My pilgrim's progress often feels like it's moving in the wrong direction. Three steps forward, six back, along the twisting roads of hope and pain. I have returned so often to T.S. Eliot's metaphor for self-discovery and becoming human—that we end where we begin—because I don't think anyone has put it better. But there is a problem if we feel we must wander in circles without ever going anywhere. The journey requires us to take responsibility for our own movements; to travel light— with a sense of place and a sense of humor; and to welcome companions on the way, some of whom are way ahead of us, some of whom need our help just to stand up straight.

I recommend that, alongside Woody Allen's self-deprecation and Maximus' strong shoes, we might wish to follow the lead of a few of cinema's wanderers.

Richard Dreyfuss' character, in *Close Encounters of the Third Kind*—which recaptures a sense of wonder too often lost in our world, reminding us that "he is no fool who gives up what he cannot keep to gain what he cannot lose"—responds to a crazy call to do a crazy thing, like Abraham. This suburban prophet with a sunburnt face makes a single-minded pursuit of an unknown goal, and becomes a child again in the process. This kind of character is also in the forefront of Terry Gilliam and Richard La Gravenese's masterpiece *The Fisher King*, where Robin Williams' and Jeff Bridges' characters—two men with a tragic past—chase the Holy Grail around New York and end up finding themselves. The same tone of travelling darkness is achieved in *Being John Malkovich*, which is also in a sense about wanting to go back into the womb. Malkovich pops up again in Antonioni & Wenders' *Beyond the Clouds*, which is notable for Van Morrison's music and not being about much other than wandering purposelessly through Europe. The doctor in John Sayles' *Men With Guns* travels more purposefully—into the jungle to find the students he trained to care for the poor of his unnamed Latin American country. He has tried to salve his conscience by teaching them, without standing against the unjust military regime, and realizes the consequences of his actions when it is only too late. His conversation with a radical priest is one of the most strikingly honest examples of sacramental talk in cinema. Sacrament abounds, but in a much less serious film, in *The Lion King*, which has always held a strange fascination for me. I'm not an Elton John fan, and Whoopi Goldberg does not do it for me, but the story of a little guy who wanders in the jungle while his people suffer before he "remembers who he is" manages to both be an entertaining kids' film and leave me with a few questions about just what on earth it is I'm doing with my life. *Unbreakable*, *Scrooged*, and *Jerry Maguire* would make a great triple bill in my house—in spite of the difference in tone. Each is about a man in mid-life who finds within himself the power to change. They each begin with the sentiment expressed by Jerry Maguire: "I'm thirty-five years old and I hate my place in the world."

And each of them ends with a new beginning. In Scrooge's

case, the whole world has changed—or at least he thinks it has, when actually it's just his way of looking at it. *Unbreakable* is a little darker, with one guy waking up to the true weight of his calling (I wish I had a whole book to write on this one— maybe next time). He has a single quest—to heroically help others—which, when you think about it, is your calling, too. But he needs to be awakened from his slumber before he starts living his life. Weird, isn't it, how we feel that we need to hear a loud voice from heaven and see the sky open before we make ethical decisions? I have a friend who works among the urban poor of North America; he often tells me that he didn't hear a call—he just opened his eyes to the needs around him. Perhaps movies like *Unbreakable* have an unhelpful view of the world, but at least their protagonists do something in response to their circumstances.

The single-minded quest of such characters is taken to extremes by guys like Klaus Kinski's *Fitzcarraldo*, about an entrepreneur who carried a steamboat over a mountain in order to build an opera house in the jungle. As you do, of course. Or Spencer Tracy's magnificent and salty interpretation of Hemingway's *The Old Man and the Sea*, who nearly dies while catching the biggest fish of his life and is satisfied with the fact of victory, even though the fish has been eaten by others by his return to shore. Single-minded seafaring is also the theme of the underrated Columbus film *1492: Conquest of Paradise*, which is at least honest enough to portray the rape and massacre of indigenous people, but paints Columbus himself as a wild-eyed man of destiny, one who is prepared to sacrifice his family life for what he sees as his higher purpose. Postmodern church leaders, take note. You can travel to the ends of the earth and still be going nowhere, like John Wayne's character in *The Searchers*, who tracks down the kidnappers of his niece but destroys his soul in the process; or the five taxi drivers in Jim Jarmusch's wonderful *Night on Earth*, who are satisfied with too little and might as well be driving in circles.

I can't write a chapter on "quest" films without mentioning *The Lord of the Rings*. I never read it when I should have, which may well mean that I will never read it at all. And, for the record, I preferred the first of the trilogy. I saw a hilarious interview with Tolkien once in which the upper crust BBC-type kept asking him, "So what does the Ring of Power represent?" Tolkien just puffed on his pipe and answered with, "What do you think?"

CHAPTER THIRTEEN

OUTSIDERS
I REALLY DO HAVE TO LOVE TO GIVE, I JUST DON'T KNOW WHERE TO PUT IT

"I really do have love to give—I just don't know where to put it."
—Quiz Kid Donnie Smith, *Magnolia*

"I've gotta hold onto my angst. It's what keeps me sharp, where I got to be." —Vincent Hanna, *Heat*

MY MUM USED TO SAY THAT IF JESUS TURNED UP at our house, He could take us as He found us; He'd be welcome in for tea, but she wouldn't necessarily get the vacuum out. That made me wonder about my mum's sense of decorum at first, but now I realize she was teaching me something about Jesus that I needed to know. He's an outsider. He's not like the rest of them. He doesn't need the dust removed before He'll come to your place. When I ask myself what it is that makes me identify with Him, the thing that makes me weep for Him when I think about his life, that makes me smile to myself as I consider His persona, it seems like it's His outsider status that has most meaning. All we know about His childhood is His wandering—as a baby into Egypt, as a kid into the temple, as a man into the desert. He is so often alone that you could be forgiven for thinking He preferred the hermit life (if He didn't have those disciple-guys around Him all the time). He wasn't a hermit, but He managed to integrate solitude with community, melancholic reflection with partying, tending to a sacred space within himself with a rage against the machine. It's clear that He felt isolated at times—not "of this world," but certainly in it. It's also clear that—by social standards—He was an abject failure. His world-changing movement did not. His subversion of the Roman Empire resulted in Him dying alone, watched by only His best friend and two women. Ultimately, what people expected of Him did not come to pass. His failure is yet another example of his outsider status, keeping Him distant from those who don't want to catch the virus of things not working.

And the most interesting people in his life and stories are outsiders, too. The Samaritan who does the only compassionate thing is a sworn enemy of the audience who must have been listening to that particular parable. The tax collector who casts himself on the mercy of God in the temple while the Pharisee's gaze burns through the back of his neck is a self-aggrandizing abuser of people, unlikely to have too many friends. (Just consider Zaccheus' surprise when Jesus says He's coming around for dinner—the poor guy may well be so used to TV dinners that he has forgotten how to cook.) The sex worker who anoints His feet is not merely an outsider but an outcast—thrown upon the societal scrap heap because people need a scapegoat to take away the creeping sense of guilt and fear that keeps us all awake sometimes. The centurion who seeks healing for his servant is perhaps the most far removed of all—ethnic and political boundaries hold him at arm's length from Jesus, and yet he has the kind of faith Christ said He hadn't seen anywhere else.

The redeemable outsider is not an exclusively biblical

construct—so many of the key figures in history lived on the fringes and worked their own special magic there. Abraham Lincoln failed to get elected so many times that he must have given up hope; it would have been difficult for him to feel a part of things. And yet he eventually made America's greatest President. Dorothy Day founded the Catholic Worker Movement only after early tragedy had squeezed her out of the trendy journo set in New York and onto the edges of what was considered "normal." The New Zealand poet James K. Baxter attempted to incarnate something of a prophetic community where the broken could be loved, but landed himself the opprobrium of "decent people" for his trouble, and ended his days wondering if any of it had mattered at all. When I think of outsiders in movies, George McFly in *Back to the Future*—the film I loved most as a kid—springs to mind. A stumbling, anxious man who believes in aliens and tries to do his best, but never imagines anyone could love him. Or John Merrick, *The Elephant Man*—magnificently played by John Hurt—whose profound beauty and deep humanity have been subsumed under years of rejection because he looks different. And the angels in *Wings of Desire*, who are cursed with the ability to know everything but feel nothing.

The outsider can be difficult to accommodate. They may be the life and soul of the party, but can also get up your nose. And outsiders are never really alone—Woody Allen could no more be separated from his neurosis than Chuck Jones could lose a cartoon rabbit. But it's worth the effort to learn to speak the language of the outsider. And, let's face it, there's an outsider lurking *inside* us all. What good thing comes out of Nazareth? asks someone in the Gospels (or maybe just in one of those movies they show at Easter). What good thing comes out of Belfast? Or Watts? Or a Bombay slum? Or a Sao Paulo corrugated hut? I'll tell you what: the seeds of the healing of the world.

BLADE RUNNER
(RIDLEY SCOTT, HAMPTON FANCHER, 1982)

"I've seen things you people wouldn't believe." –Roy Batty

Philip K. Dick wrote unfinished tales. There's a sense when we read him that he often had a great source idea, but was so desperate for money that he rattled out so many stories in his all too brief career but never fully developed what he was trying to say. (A bit like that sentence!) "Do Androids Dream of Electric Sheep?" like *Minority Report*, is that rare thing, a story which gains something deeper in transference to the screen. *Blade Runner*, one of those films that took some time after its initial release to become what its director intended, is a masterpiece of literary adaptation, but that is not its greatest strength. Like all good science fiction, it speaks to a universal human condition, while ostensibly imagining an implausible future. It's such a well known film that it's hardly worth rehearsing what happens. Suffice to say, there are androids running around in Los Angeles 2019, and our hero has to track them down and terminate them, or "air 'em out," as one character says.

So there are lots of chases and gunfights and one of the best man-to-man combat scenes in film history. The production design is as astonishing as we should expect from an art student, and the performances have just a slight degree of unreality. The spiritual resonance of *Blade Runner* is most clearly found in its main characters—the replicants who have come to earth in search of their maker. These guys are superhuman but have a built-in four-year lifespan. Not a problem I'd like to be faced with. But that's the lot of the Nexus 6. There is a magnificent scene in which Roy, the compassionate leader of the replicants who has "done questionable things" in controlled desperation, goes to see Tyrell, the replicant inventor. Tyrell is in an opulent white dressing gown, surrounded by candles in a throne-like bedroom, and the metaphoric resonance is not lost on us. He's God, living high above the clouds, playing chess with a stranger over the phone. No real contact with humans, spending his days manipulating the creatures he's made and his nights trading stocks when he certainly has no need of more money. Roy has come to ask his maker if his lifespan can be extended (a little bit like reverse evangelism—I mean, isn't that what we're all asking for when we seek salvation?). He tries three different questions, desperate to exhaust the possibilities of hope. "It's not an easy thing to meet your Maker. But can the Maker repair what he makes?" And when the maker tells him that "the brightest lights shine the shortest," he knows his destiny is out of his hands. He resolves himself to his fate and does what any of us might do— allows his anger to take hold and, after kissing God, kills him by crushing his head. There is an enormous lesson here.

The anti-heroic characters of the Old Testament—like Abraham, Joseph, Ezekiel, Jeremiah—are marked by their arrogance. None of them felt insecure about shouting at God— remember Jeremiah's cursing of the day he was conceived, Elijah's flight from Jezebel, and Abraham's deceit of the Egyptians. These guys seemed to realize something about God—that God is not insecure about what we feel—indeed, that God *prefers* our honest struggling to our pretending that all is well. *Blade Runner* says something about outsiders, those of us (all of us?) who sometimes feel nobody, not even we, understand the terrain of our souls. It says that it's okay, in fact that it's sometimes the only thing we *can* do, to rage against God. God is always bigger than our best thoughts. But no matter what we think of God at the best of times, sometimes our experience of the divine can lead us to believe that God is less than our worst fears. Life is difficult, and the human need for spiritual affirmation is not met in the dark night of the soul. Faithful people have suffered such dark nights for as long as the human world's been spinning, and those who have made it to the other side of darkness have not been afraid to ask questions of their maker. When Roy the replicant realizes that he is soon to die, and that all his being will be "lost, like tears in rain," he is speaking for all of us, who fear nothingness like we need oxygen. Unlike the replicants, we will not kill God, but sometimes we need to let go of images of God that we once held dear so that they might mature into something new. And it may be a tough process to get us there. We should not be afraid of this. It's called spiritual growth.

RATCATCHER
(LYNNE RAMSAY, 1999)

This might just be the most beautiful film ever made, and, like most things of profound beauty, hardly anyone has seen it. But you must. The word "mesmeric" could have been invented for this film. Seeing it was like awakening from a nightmare in which all British films were either about "mockney" gangsters or kitchen sinks. *Ratcatcher* has its share of both violence and kitchens, but it's closer in tone, and indeed quality, to the most evocative hybrid of Robert Bresson and Mike Leigh imaginable. It's about a wee kid in Glasgow in the '70s, living on a tenement estate during the garbage strike. Rats crawl the streets, and kids play in a muggy canal. Women sacrifice to buy shoes for their children and men lie about in a drunken stupor, suffering the drip-feed shell shock of life not delivering anything like what they were promised at school. And into this communitarian mess comes a kid, played in one of those once in a lifetime performances by a non-professional (what is professionalism anyway?) actor, William Eadie. He's got a fragile body and soul, which is not a good recipe for where he lives. He plays on his own and wonders about just what the hell life is. And one day, in one of those irrevocable moments of tragedy so many of us have encountered, he sees his wee friend drown after they have pushed each other in the canal.

So his life becomes consumed by guilt and fear, and he never recovers. He can't tell anyone what he has done—who is there to tell? What would they say anyway? He can't make any sense of his world. All he can do is scuff his shoes in order to forget. He takes a bus ride to the countryside and spends a sunny afternoon in a cornfield. In the hands of others, this scene might be mawkish and sentimentalized, but Ramsay is so hugely accomplished and mature that she manages to let the pathos be writ large and speak for itself. It is heartbreaking to watch him explore a nearly built house and imagine what his life could be like if he were to live there—with an inside toilet and a tiny, but living garden. His rage at the hand life has dealt him should penetrate your soul. *Ratcatcher* is about little, broken people trying to make sense of a big broken world; about how the wonder and cruelty of children makes them our most precious resource, most in need of protection; about trying to fit in—about letting bullies steal your pet rat and fly him to the moon because it might just mean they won't beat you up. It is worth taking the time to really watch. Like the lost tradition of lament, it's closer to a sacrament than most and will wreck your emotions for a day or two. And that's the reason why it deserves your attention. *Ratcatcher* is not an easy film at all; but in its dark beauty, its tragic narrative, its melancholic disposition, it manages to ask the most important question we'll ever face: "Could there, finally, be forgiveness in this world?"

THE FILMS OF JOEL AND ETHAN COEN
(1983–A LONG TIME IN THE FUTURE, I HOPE)

It's difficult to write about the Coen Brothers. They're so clever, I fear that they might read this book and think I'm totally missing the point. They famously wrote their masterpiece—or at least one of their masterpieces—*Barton Fink*, a film about a guy with writer's block as their own means of dealing with the writer's block that occupied them while trying to carve *Miller's Crossing* out of the past. There is a certain irony, then, that I find myself hardly able to write anything meaningful about their work and have left this short section to near the end of the book because I can't bring myself out of the fog of writer's block that has consumed me over the past few weeks. All of their films are about outsiders—the fringe lovers in *Blood Simple,* the white trash glory of *Raising Arizona*, the anti-heroic gangster rebels of *Miller's Crossing, Barton Fink's* serious playwright swimming as a fish out of water in Hollywood, the "little guy" hero of *The Hudsucker Proxy*, the majestic Sabbath-personification of the Dude, who apparently makes no contribution to "normal" society in *The Big Lebowski*, the sacramental escapees of *O Brother, Where Art Thou?*, and the numbed soul of *The Man Who Wasn't There.*

You wonder if the Coens consider themselves to be outsiders, or if it just looks that way. Their films are the definition of "nothing being what it seems." One of their films opens like a cartoon with a spinning barber pole, while melancholy classical music tells us to expect something else. Characters escape from a 1930s chain gang and find God along the way. Men write a seventy-five dollar check to pay for a liter of milk in a late night convenience store. A baby is kidnapped because he has five brothers, and therefore his parents won't miss one. A simple guy comes up with an invention that will radically change the experience of children the world over, but can only describe it by drawing a circle. And the man who wasn't there sums up his world by saying: "I worked in a barber shop, but I never considered myself a barber."

Billy Bob Thornton's character in this mystical film is the anti-hero as one of us; he doesn't mind his wife having an affair because it's a "free country" and is one of the billions of people defined by their jobs. Which reminds me of a story: When one of my favorite people in the world left his job as a theology professor "by mutual agreement," which is another way of saying the college was too small for his brain, he found himself unemployed for a few months. Anytime he met someone new, they would invariably ask, "So what do you do?" In a sign that he was much more mature than me, he said, "Sometimes I take my dog for a walk on the beach." Like the Dude and so many other of the Coen's celluloid children, he had learned the difference between what he does and who he *is*. There is infinitely more to their work than these short paragraphs can convey, but that's okay. My words can never do for you what watching their films can.

THE WRAP

I'm wondering as I try to finish this chapter just what it is that draws me to the outsider. And it may just be as simple as the fact that feeling "outside" things is something most of us seem to share. Aren't we all outsiders? Maybe the sense of seeing something in a film that no one else understands is the point. Ironically, if you're one of those people who strongly identifies with the outsider, then you're probably already spending your days in darkened theatres watching the same films as me, so this primer won't do you much good.

My favorite "outsider" movie is *A.I.: Artificial Intelligence*, and you can't get much more outside "normal" than being a robot. And I know that I've just lost half the readership of this book because you probably hated it like everyone else I know (apart from my friends Ewan and Trevor, two men of exceptional taste, who *know* how to enjoy end credit sequences). This film was derided on its release for being sentimental, as if Spielberg felt he knew better than Kubrick and Brian Aldiss' original ideas. But the story of a robot trying to become a real boy while suffering the slings and arrows of people's rejection is so dark, and ends on such a bleak note, that I can only suggest that those who hate it simply didn't get it. It's a magical film, but its magic is tragic. If the only thing we can look forward to when we finally understand ourselves is permanent night, then this is not an optimistic film.

It would make an ironic double bill with *E.T., The Extra Terrestrial*, another dark Spielberg film about lost childhood and alien (outsiders) beings. Neither *E.T.* nor *A.I.* should leave us feeling like everything's going to be okay, unlike *Being There*, a wondrous achievement, with Peter Sellers giving what I think might just be my favorite performance on film. It's about a man-child whose entire knowledge of the world comes from television; and I suppose if all we ever did was watch *Sesame Street* and eat with each other, the world would be a better place. But *Being There* is more than a story of a man who exemplified grace; it's a satire on how cynical people are often still able to be stirred in the depths of their souls by true humanity. And, when you think about it, a kid in an adult body is a good metaphor for spiritual growth. I hope *Being There* will be seen by a few more people after they read this; if you think *Big*'s the whole story, think again. *Being There* also has some of the most beautiful music used on film—especially some of Janacek's delicate piano. The same piece is used in the more recent but thematically similar *About Schmidt*, which gives Jack Nicholson another chance to "not be Jack" and become a man who has no sense of place or purpose left after retirement and the death of his wife. But everything he needs for a meaningful life is staring him in the face, if only he would stare back.

One of the characters in *The Elephant Man* asks the audience, "All life is a circus, is it not?" It's about the horror of being different, the fear of going out in public, the terror of realizing that we will never be like "the others." The outsider is Lynch's key theme, wrapped up in ugliness and fear, and he doesn't shirk from showing horrible things ("Abominable things these machines, because you can't reason with them"). It's a truly beautiful, deeply moving, and powerful film; and I really must mention the photography. It's easy to praise monochrome just because it is monochrome, but this is truly amazing.

Great black and white photography is a quality it shares with another great outsider film, *The Hunchback of Notre Dame* (not the Disney one). You need to seek out the Charles Laughton version from the 1930s; it's a masterpiece that fits into the category I have come to call "films with unusual people that are better than (or as good as) *Rain Man*." There's something of the spirit of Dustin Hoffman's Raymond Babbit in *Donnie Darko*, a far profounder film, with so many layers of meaning and provocation and complex pleasure in the story and visuals and use of music. But it's mostly a stand out because of Jake Gylennhaal's performance as the teenager who may be schizophrenic or prophetic or both, who is at first terrified, and then determined to do something about the impending end of the world. He has a sister in the movie, but if Donnie lived in *my* fantasy world, he'd be the flip side of joyous, vulnerable, classy, wide-eyed *Amelie*, whose French love story manages to be both lyrical and sweet and dark and tragic.

There's a strain in North American outsider movies that

could be called "grunge cinema"—which basically means anything in which the protagonists don't use deodorant and sweat too much. David Mamet's *American Buffalo* gives Dustin Hoffman and Dennis Franz a chance to dwell in the murky post-*Death of a Salesman* world of trinket shops and guys who think they can make it if they could only just ... The little-known and underrated *Cutter's Way* covers much of the same territory, with Jeff Bridges and John Heard doing their thing with cigarettes and alcohol and existential conversation and a whole lotta death. More recently, Michael Douglas gave himself a buzz cut and went a little over the edge in *Falling Down*. His reaction to not being served breakfast in a fast food restaurant did go a little too far, but as a populist analysis of workplace stress and the breakdown of community, this film is right on the button.

The protagonist of *Falling Down* (we never know his name) is only trying to do what's right, or at least to get other people to do what's right. He's a tortured do-gooder and therefore can join the hall of fame that includes *Batman, Edward Scissorhands*, and even Woody's *Broadway Danny Rose*. It's probably facetious for me to include *Hamlet* in here, but this book hasn't gotten this far without being facetious, so there he is (compare Ethan Hawke with Kenneth Branagh—if you can stay awake that long; two very different interpretations of the same divided guy). Decisiveness is Hamlet's problem; if only he could make any decision, but he is constrained by the curse of "damned if I do, damned if I don't."

Films about artists fascinate me—art about art is a weird proposition, don't you think? If the artist is the quintessential outsider, then artists who make art about art should be pretty far away from the rest of us mere mortals. That's the impression you get, anyway, in films like the outrageous and dreamlike *Basquiat*, itself directed by a self-conscious New York painter,

Julian Schnabel; or *Shine*, about how art—in this case a piano concerto—can get under the skin and remove the artist from what might be called "normal" life (see Jack in *Five Easy Pieces* for more piano pain); or *Deconstructing Harry*, where Woody Allen's nasty writer finds himself a character in one of his own isolating stories; and of course *Wilde*, the story of Oscar Wilde, an artist who was in the gutter much of the time but was always "looking at the stars." *Ali* is another film about an artistic outsider, and in spite of my resistance to boxing, Muhammed Ali is nothing if not an artist, and Michael Mann's film captures his outsider status without laying it on too thick.

Perhaps the outsider who we can most easily identify with is the one who lives inside us—the parts of ourselves that seem alien, a little distant, not at peace, the parts that we will invest our whole lives integrating. Perhaps this is what *Beauty and the Beast* is really about—a guy who needs to let go of his ego before he can be who he really is. As with the hunchback, don't rely on Disney to tell you this story—Jean Cocteau's magnificent *La Belle et La Bete* is in a different league altogether.

Forest Whitaker plays the title character in Jim Jarmusch's *Ghost Dog—The Way of the Samurai* like he's already dead, a hitman who exists in near-comatose silence, way, way out on the fringes. The movie doesn't explicitly criticize the lifestyle choices of the assassin, but it's clear that Jarmusch would prefer that Ghost Dog cold just invest his time in his friendship with a Haitian ice cream seller who doesn't understand a word he says, but knows him deeper than anyone else.

CHAPTER FOURTEEN

POWER

REAL POWER CANNOT BE GIVEN; IT MUST BE TAKEN

THE TAGLINE FOR THE *GODFATHER, PART III* WAS, "Real power cannot be given; it must be taken." But what about giving it away? It never ceases to amaze me (well it does, actually; I ceased being amazed by religious institutions a long time ago) that Christian tradition, as the inheritor of the belief that God gave up everything to become human and die, seems unable to let go of its power. Surely the incarnation is the supreme act of compromise? But compromise has become a dirty word in many church circles. We are told to "stand up" for truth; discipleship is blindly compared to a military conflict, without considering the possibility that this might reinforce prejudice against our neighbors; we invent a non-existent "culture war" because we somehow think Jesus needs protecting from liberal journalists and Hollywood; we call our home groups "cells," without seeing the irony that prison is what we are in.

I find it fascinating that so much of cinema understands that too much power ain't good for the soul. It has been said that the glory of God is a human being fully alive—not the destruction of others. So, in the first instance, the name of God cannot be invoked in the purpose of the exercise of power over others. The "wonder-working power" of Jesus is not there to make us feel big and clever, but to serve. Jesus in Scripture did not use His power to overthrow cultures or tear down structures. He non-violently subverted from within. Why, then, do we think God wants us to do otherwise?

THE GODFATHER, PART II
(FRANCIS FORD COPPOLA, 1974)

Francis Ford Coppola's *The Godfather, Part II* is possibly the richest film of the past fifty years; it's a tragic piece about a man who loses his own soul by giving up the power of choice, blindly following mafia tradition in order to dominate those around him. Fealty to the Don, out of fear, is the basis of relationships in this film. Everyone loves Al Pacino's Michael for who he is—a monster who can destroy them at the drop of a hat. In the end, he is actually less powerful than before, for he has traded his humanity for power, which is actually no power at all. When, in the first *Godfather* Michael is introduced as a war hero, he is more powerful than at any time in the trilogy. He has some independence, he is making choices not predetermined by his socialization, and there is some hope that he might be different from his family. The temptations of power and loyalty to his father lead him down a different path. In embracing fear as a means of controlling others, he loses his very self.

BULWORTH
(WARREN BEATTY, JEREMY PIVEN, 1998)

Although it stars and was co-written, produced, and directed by Hollywood icon Warren Beatty, *Bulworth* is not your average star vehicle. Sex and violence, when they appear, are pretty unconventional. There's only one gun, and it only goes off once. There's a car chase, but it's not very exciting. The music is by Ennio Morricone, he of *The Good, the Bad and the Ugly* fame, and Dr. Dre, among others. It should therefore come as no surprise that *Bulworth* is a peculiar film … just your run-of-the-mill story of a white U.S. Senator who has a nervous breakdown, takes out a contract on his own life, falls in love with an African-American hitwoman, and raps his new campaign strategy using more mutha-f---ers than you'd find at Snoop Dogg's poker table.

The real-life Beatty has impeccable left-wing credentials. The film reminds us of this in the opening shots of Senator Bulworth's office, with close-ups of photos of the young WB with such luminaries of '60s liberalism as Bobby Kennedy. There was a time, although it's hard to believe now, when Hollywood's A-list were counted among the credible political voices of the day. We had "Hanoi" Jane Fonda denouncing the Vietnam War, Vanessa Redgrave famously highlighting the PLO struggle in an award acceptance speech, and Marlon Brando quickly following suit by sending an actress who claimed Native American descent to collect his Oscar for *The Godfather* with a speech railing against the injustices perpetrated against "her" people. Beatty, who in the mid-'60s was the kind of star Leonardo di Caprio is today, was one of many in the entertainment business who seemed genuinely committed to the struggle for a more equitable society. His suspicion of "big government," belief in freedom of speech, and commitment to liberal democracy was born out in his work on screen, from *The Parallax View* (1974) to *Reds* (1981), and most recently in *Bulworth*.

The film is a sharp black comedy that drives the point home that politicians who rely on the rich to finance their campaigns are less and less likely to favor their poorer constituents. The film's clear targets are racism in general and the corruption of campaign financing, about which there is seemingly never-ending discussion and no action. The divide between rich and poor evidently causes Beatty great concern, and he has taken a considerable risk to show it. In the film's most memorable and shocking scene, he dresses gangsta style and raps an interview, waxing lyrical on the traps of the working class and the ignorance of the rest of us.

He is asked why he uses such "obscenity" in his sloganeering. His response should cut to the heart of middle class "stiff upper lip" sensibilities—"Obscenity!? I'll tell you what's obscene—the fact that there are people in this city who can't afford to buy enough food to survive." Do you get it? Bulworth makes the salient point that poor white people and poor black people have more in common with each other than with rich people. There's a lesson in this for those of us in this society committed to seeking the transformation of our divided communities into communities united by our common humanity. It may be a simplistic notion, but it has yet to be fleshed out: The disenfranchised of my society—the underclass, the homeless, other minorities—have more in common with each other, Protestant/unionist, Catholic/nationalist, than they do with their rich counterparts who happen to be part of the same sectarian group. The hidden common ground between Catholic and Protestant students, nationalist and unionist working class families, Protestant and Catholic artists, Catholic and Protestant *whatevers* must be allowed to surface. This is a template for resolving social conflict, whatever its nature.

Some politicians may try to deceive us into thinking that there is more to drive us apart than draw us together, as if sectarian division were divinely ordained, as if harmony between communities would constitute some kind of unimaginable horror. Don't believe the hype. *Bulworth* reminds us that we have reasons to bring our communities together in hope—which far surpass the importance of our respective commitment to such "macro"-issues as the Union/the Republic. It also serves as a significant warning of how our political participation often depends on our economic power. *Bulworth* is a profound, provocative, dark film that will make you laugh—and make you think more about how "to do politics" better.

DEAD POETS SOCIETY
(PETER WEIR, TOM SCHULMAN, 1989)

What does it mean to fulfill the law? *Dead Poets Society* is about the power of words, and we may have much to learn from it. It was one of the key films of my teenage years; everyone saw it, everyone cried, everyone talked about it, everyone thought it had something profound to say about the human condition. I was one of them. It's a beautifully nuanced film that still evokes my teenage years every time I see it. But, nearly fifteen years on, I've changed my mind about its meaning. It is a gloriously shot and perfectly controlled film, but it has deception at its heart. I don't want to hurt anyone's feelings; I mean, I know why so many people love it, and Peter Weir is one of the finest directors in the world, but I can't let it continue to be held up as an inspirational masterpiece without throwing my hat into the ring.

We open with the titles appearing beside a flickering candle: This is the light of knowledge, as we follow a procession into the assembly hall of one of those posh schools in which American cinema loves to locate its titanic metaphoric battles (see *Scent of a Woman* for more of this, if you must). We hear the motto of the school enunciated with military precision by the pupils: Tradition. Honor. Discipline. Excellence. And I guess none of these things is bad in itself, but what do these words mean? The film shows that they are what Jesus called "whitewashed walls," meaningless statements without any heart. Frankly, this is modern Pharisaism. Like so many traditional institutions, this school was established for good reasons, on good principles, but time and the felt need to maintain a reputation in the face of the prying eyes of the public have made it a shadow of its former self. It's therefore reminiscent of so many originally radical phenomena—from Protestantism to American democracy.

The austerity of this institution is reflected in the weather-beaten headmaster, who thinks he has seen it all before and is goose-stepping toward retirement, and the relationship the main character (Robert Sean Leonard) has with his father—he calls his dad "sir." (This always makes me think of Jesus' instruction to "call no man teacher." Can parents really be that important?) His father, coldly played by Kurtwood Smith, is also the kind of man who would force his son to live the kind of life he missed, who will oppress his child by the manipulation of "You know how much this means to your mother." The son is becoming liberated by his time in Robin Williams' classroom, where he is inspired to "seize the day" (quite what he is supposed to do with the day once he has seized it, we are not sure). But the film makes us feel that something inspirational is going on, that there is substance to the teacher's words, even though he doesn't say very much at all.

And this is the problem with *Dead Poets Society*. True, the film has a beautiful way of capturing things like the chaos of the corridors versus the stiffness of the school's public rituals; it evokes the kind of male friendship many guys yearn for when they get older; the script has a lovely turn of phrase (Keating says, "I would go to the beach and people would kick copies of Byron in my face"); when the teacher gets the boys to kick a soccer ball to express their passion, we want to slam it over the net; and its visual style is sometimes quite profound: It illustrates the potential freedom and foreboding of the life journey with birds flying free when they sense a clock's ominous strike. But Williams' character John Keating is held up as a paragon of radical inspiration, when all he actually says is telling the kids they better make something of their lives and that the rules don't have to apply to them. In spite of his brilliant performance—whoever first thought he should be given the chance to do this deserves a medal—I didn't need a movie to tell me that. I need more.

Keating is definitely right about some things. We are indeed food for worms, when all is said and done. And it is more than just a good idea to make decisions based on a desire to change the world. But to simply make a few pithy statements about gathering rosebuds and win the confidence—no, the adulation—of a group of teenagers by having an English class in the—revolutionary—OPEN AIR … Well, it's hardly Socrates, is it? Keating understands that words and ideas can change the world and that the struggle to become human in the face of economic exploitation is "A battle, a war, and the casualties could be your hearts and souls."

He knows that poetry is beyond profundity, that using mathematics to decide the measure of a poem's greatness is about as absurd as it gets (film critics take note!), but his prescription is inane psychobabble. He simply tells the boys that they should make something of their lives. He doesn't analyze "the system," or encourage these kids to subvert it beyond reading poetry in a cave and tearing out the pages of a sacred text. (You should have seen what happened when my friend Pete did this to a Bible when preaching a sermon once; it was interesting to note how many people seemed unable to distinguish between the Word of God and the printed page.) We need to be liberated from such taboos at times (as Keating says, "You're not going to go to hell for this"). God knows we need more of our sacred cows to be roasted. And I'll admit that Keating is certainly trying to light such a barbecue. But he seems unable to follow through with his own provocations, to practice what he preaches. For instance, if he really believes in all this stuff about beauty and truth and freedom and love, why has he chosen to trap himself in such a claustrophobic job, while his girlfriend is in another country? And he only really offers platitudes, rather than practical alternatives; why is he teaching there anyway? Has he seized the day? And yet, he is taking a risk; it's dangerous to encourage people to swim against the tide. Keating should be respected for that at least. But he'd be a better teacher, and a better man, if he helped his boys to find or develop the tools to make sense of their lives, rather than set them up for disappointment.

I guess I better tell you what I like about *Dead Poets Society* before I get too carried away. It's an honest enough film to remind us that things do go wrong in this world, and that we need to open up a space for ourselves outside the "norm" in order to survive or have any chance of changing things. It explicitly states that "love is what we stay alive for" and knows something about the need to be childlike before we can be truly wise. And it knows that we need to change our perspective: "I stand on my desk to remind myself that we must constantly look at things in a different way. Just when you think you know something, you must look at it in another way."

But that's about as far as it goes. Apart from the simplistic words of Mr. Keating, we also have a very disturbing suicide at the heart of *Dead Poets Society*. A key character takes his own life because his father won't let him be an actor. I understand that some people think this was his only option, but on reflection, I think it is a very foolish act. Surely Keating's teaching should have told him he could also subvert this oppression. It's irresponsible of the filmmakers to present it in such a light. He commits beautiful suicide—it is so artfully shot you'd think you were watching a commercial for "shooting yourself the romantic way." And Keating is fired, and the boys confess their involvement, and the headmaster takes over their class. They stand on their desks as a sign of solidarity, of course, but there are no guarantees that these guys will lead the kind of extraordinary lives their teacher hoped for. In that light, the ending of the movie, which for so many people represents Keating's triumph, is actually tragic. Truth can be, as one character says, like a blanket that leaves your feet cold.

And yet, when I saw the film for the first time, and I'll admit, sometimes when I watch it even now, from the jaded perspective of an ancient twenty-eight-year-old, it made me want to change the world. It's up to me—and you—to take that responsibility seriously, to work out for ourselves what that actually means. Maybe that's the point of *Dead Poets Society*. Maybe it's trying to help us take responsibility for our lives, to learn to use our own power in ways that will benefit the world, or at least not kill anyone. I certainly agree with Keating when he says, "We all have a great need for acceptance, but you must trust that your beliefs are your own, even if others think them weird." I want to be the kind of man that John Keating thinks he is. But I wish I didn't feel like I was being generous when I wrote that.

THE WRAP

The British actor and Quaker Paul Eddington gave an interview shortly before he died and was asked, as famous people about to die always are, what he would like on his gravestone. Eddington thought for a moment, and said: "He did very little harm." He explained that he felt that most people go through life like a tornado through the Midwest—causing havoc wherever they went. He felt that life was so difficult to get right that to do good was perhaps too much to hope for; if he could get through it without hurting anyone, then he would be happy. I think he was being a little pessimistic, but his words do show that he understood something profound about how we need to learn to discipline our own sense of power to prevent it from controlling us. We might learn something from

Bob Roberts—Tim Robbins' intelligent satire on what people will do to get ahead in U.S. politics.

The Candidate—Robert Redford as an idealistic activist who finds himself unable to be himself once he casts himself on the mercies of electoral politics. He has to spend so much time and money getting noticed that he begins to forget why he got into the process in the first place. Once he gets elected, his first words to his agent (and the last words of the movie) are: "What are we going to do now?"

Election is another great film about U.S. politics, but this time it's the nefarious double-dealing of high school class presidency. Reese Witherspoon starts out ambitious, self-centered, and obsessed with power, which seems to make her ripe for a career in Congress.

Mulholland Drive is another Hollywood power play; it's David Lynch's crazy masterpiece about the lust for power and the power of lust to destroy. Its focus is the same as Joseph Losey's 1963 Brit-flick *The Servant*, where the tables are turned when a manipulative butler takes up a new appointment with a weak-willed aristocrat. It's a disturbing and poetic look at how people so often want to control each other.

Finally, *The Last Emperor* focuses on those rare people who are born into power. The unreality and inhumanity of arriving on earth in charge of your world is evoked with great power by Bertolucci, and, like the best films about power, the lessons about true meaning coming from within are applicable to all kinds of powerful people, whether they are Chinese royalty, church leaders, homemakers, or college students.

CHAPTER FIFTEEN

WAR
WHAT IS IT GOOD FOR?

"Blessed are the peacemakers for they shall see God." —Jesus

"Charging someone with murder out here is like handing out speeding tickets at the Indy 500." —Captain Willard, *Apocalypse Now*

THE CHURCH TODAY, UNLIKE JESUS, IS WOEFULLY split on the issue of war. I want to follow the guy who said, "Love your neighbor as yourself," and tried to get rid of the old eye for eye, tooth for tooth manifesto which makes everyone blind and makes t-bone steaks obsolete. It amazes me that churches so often easily co-operate with political power when the author and perfecter of our faith was nothing if not non-violently subversive of that same power. Christians who are anti-war are often ridiculed by their own denominations. This is one of the scandals of the contemporary Church. Many Christians don't realize that for three hundred years, the Early Church was fundamentally opposed to the oppressive or violent use of state power. This changed under Emperor Constantine, when in the fourth century he imaginatively decided to put a cross on his army's shields. And the institutional Church has all too often been giving its automatic blessing to war ever since.

The Church's role in Nazi Germany has come under the microscope recently, as controversy rages about the relationship between religious leaders and Hitler's regime. But there was another kind of Christian activism present during the Second World War, known as the "Confessing" Church. One of its proponents was Dietrich Bonhoeffer, a Lutheran pastor who spoke fearlessly against the injustices perpetrated by his government. He finally became involved in a plot to kill Hitler; this conspiracy has often been used by those who support war as a "Christian" defense of the use of violence. But this is a misinterpretation of what Bonhoeffer stood for. He believed that the only way to stop Nazism was to stop Hitler, and the only way to stop Hitler was to kill him. He agonized over this decision and never sought to justify it as a morally right act. He consistently insisted that to kill any other human being was sinful; this was no less true in Hitler's case. Killing Hitler might prevent a greater evil but would still be a sin that Bonhoeffer would have on his conscience, requiring the grace of God and his repentance. This critique of oppressive power without losing sight of the need for a moral vision for the response of the oppressed may be Bonhoeffer's most vital legacy.

Walter Wink has done much to increase our understanding of violence and its mythical hold on the Christian imagination. He suggests that the "fight or flight" syndrome—where we respond to conflict either by violence or escape—is a false choice. For Wink, Jesus was proposing a radical alternative— non-violent resistance. In this interpretation, "turn the other cheek" becomes an act of subversion, shaming the oppressor with the violence of their action; "give your shirt also" confronts the enemy with the humiliating nature of their behavior; and "go the extra mile" is a declaration of independence from the oppressive social norms enacted by the Roman Empire. Of course, these particular responses would not have the same meaning today, so Wink encourages people to translate their "spirit" into contemporary action. Thus a black woman in apartheid-era South Africa returns the spit of a white man not with her fists or by running away, but by inviting the man to spit on her children too (he never does it again). A potential victim of violence defuses the situation not by shooting her attacker or jumping out the window, but by asking him the time and why he has come to her house (he doesn't touch her and leaves peaceably). Gandhi's supporters arrive at the police station where he is in custody demanding that they be arrested too, but in such huge numbers that it overwhelms the police (the non-violent revolution works, and casualties are minimized). And people in Northern Ireland create space for old enemies to drink together, sharing common cause on cultural matters, leaving the politics for another day.

Of course these examples are not the norm, and the patterns of conflict in the world do not lend themselves to simple solutions. However, Wink believes that these principles of non-violent resistance force oppressors to confront the reality of their actions, leading to the possibility of real change and offer a better way than the old debate about just war vs. pacifism; no one can say that they have been proven wrong because they have not been adequately attempted. But there are signs of change. Some movements propose non-violent alternatives to war, ranging from the bolstering of peaceful resistance, to dictatorship, to the development of diplomatic ties, to the comprehensive challenge of human rights abuses. Perhaps we are witnessing the early stages of a fresh movement of Christians who are prepared to put themselves on the line for peace.

The radical priest Daniel Berrigan says that during the

Vietnam War, the American Catholic bishops had nothing to say and said nothing, whereas in their support for the war on terror, they have nothing to say, but now they say it. If we are to be followers of the way of Christ, we need to get to grips with his non-violence. It is not good enough for us to justify violence because the end of *Saving Private Ryan* makes us feel warm inside or because the battle scenes in *Pearl Harbor* take our breath away. And the recent resurgence of "end-times" films made by the "Christian" movie industry gets about as far away as possible from the movement of Christ without coming back the other direction when it portrays the godly remnant as having a divine mandate to kill. This may sound like woolly liberal moralizing, but if there is to be a future for our planet, this generation must face the question of war and the need to respond by offering solutions that reduce violence, rather than prop up the military-industrial-entertainment complex. War in film, like many other "realistic" genres, may not have an honorable reputation with regards to historical accuracy, but the symbolic truth of violence and its meanings is well presented in many films.

SALVADOR
(OLIVER STONE, 1986)

Oliver Stone is the quintessential Hollywood angry man; he makes movies about America gone wrong—loud movies shouting loud things. And often he's the kind of truth-teller capable not merely of hitting the nail on the head, but of smashing the head right open. *JFK* and *Nixon* are his political diptych, about fallen heroes, broken men; *Platoon, Born on the Fourth of July,* and *Heaven and Earth* constitute his Vietnam trilogy, lambasting the myth of American heroism and clean hands in Southeast Asia; *Wall Street* and *Any Given Sunday* are two that focus on his favorite theme—the deconstruction of masculinity. *Salvador* gathers the best elements of Stone's oeuvre, telling the story of America's nefarious dealings in El Salvador, covering politics, flawed men, and American myth-making. *Salvador* is a film about the courage to ask the right questions at the right time in all places, and courage is a precious resource in these dark days.

The dramatic device of telling a Big Story through "one man's eyes" is often clichéd, but *Salvador* manages to avoid this because of a fantastic script and a compelling central performance from James Woods. Woods plays Richard Boyle, a real journalist who covered the revolution in Salvador from a position of "detached engagement," falling in love with the people and supporting their cause, but still taking photographs of dead bodies to sell to *Newsweek*. The film begins with him in dire financial straits, trying to get someone to pay him to go to Salvador—the early very short, fast scenes, which communicate a great deal, should provide painful resonance for any freelance writers who are watching. He's a twister and an endearing con artist, borrowing from Peter to pay Paul (although with no intention of clearing the debt); he relies on his wit and charm to get through the day. Woods plays him with such gusto that, even though he seems like a loser, he immediately holds our interest. He's a profligate liar, although we like him; when he drives straight out of jail where he's been held for driving without a license, we laugh with him, knowing, I suspect, that we might do the same. We want to know what's going to happen to him when he goes to Salvador, which he decides to *drive* to from San Francisco, another endearing eccentricity, although we may be put off by his declaration that he's looking for multiple sexual conquests as well.

When cinema's white North Americans go south, I always get a sinking feeling; they don't have to go far over the gringo border before they run into sweaty men with aviator sunglasses and over-sized moustaches; you can rest assured that at some point, a fruit cart will be toppled over in a car chase wherein the local police pursue the "wrong man"; and, if there's a revolution (there's always a revolution), there will almost certainly be a shot of a little kid standing alone in a frantic crowd, usually clutching a soft toy. *Salvador*, thankfully, manages to avoid most of these latino clichés, although there are a lot of moustaches in this film.

On their journey down, Woods and his friend—the horribly '80s-named Dr. Rock, played by James Belushi, in a reminder of how good he can be given the right material—encounter a road block, with burning bodies as the first sign that something is going very badly wrong in El Salvador. Soon after, they see a student murdered by a soldier for not having identity papers; the military junta is behaving the way military juntas often do, the violent repression of thinking people as the last resort of desperately fearful power. When Woods bids farewell to a Salvadoran child, he says "Via con Dios," but this is met with the child's assertion that "there is no more god." The rest of the film is a docu-drama, highlighting aspects of the oppression and revolution, from the "disappearance" of thousands at the hands of the American-sponsored military, to the assassination of the great Archbishop Romero, to the mainstream American media's complicity in the horror. Stone gives us a bird's-eye view, and, as in all his best films, marshals his resources like a general—this is a "big story," but not so big that it dwarfs a human-interest story at its center. In fact, the storytelling is so realistic that it is easy to momentarily forget that the film is fictionalized.

As for Stone's politics, readers should know by now where this author's sympathies lie. One character says, "The will of the people and the march of history cannot be changed, not even by the North Americans," which led me to consider suing Stone for plagiarizing the fundamentalist liberal dinner-party conversation that regularly occurs chez moi over my undercooked pasta bake.

Salvador is about how America created its "Frankenstein" in Latin America from the 1970s onward and has yet to recognize the terror that this has perpetrated. The film is a little too straightforward—"big" news doesn't ask questions, only "mavericks"; this is probably how Stone sees himself. I also feel that it is irresponsible to play compasino music while the rebels are shooting people, as if it's some kind of celebration of violent revolution. You can be both pro-freedom and anti-violence; Stone should have listened to one of his own characters, who says, "Don't allow yourself to be steamrollered." Despite this, the film is an important document of one of the most under-valued facts of recent history—the terror of America. And in spite of his tendency toward ideologue, Stone is a master at telling us what is wrong with the world.

THREE KINGS
(DAVID O RUSSELL, 1999)

"What is the most important thing in life? Necessity, as in people do what is most necessary to them at any given time." —George Clooney, *Three Kings*

Three Kings is one of those films that was ignored on first release but cries out for our attention more than ever. Watching it as the preparations for war gathered pace, I felt a certain sense of déjà-vu; hadn't we been here before? The answer is, of course, yes, but not only during Gulf War One. Humanity has found itself unable to make peace, not because it has exhausted diplomacy or discovered that non-violent means fail, but because it has decided that the cost of peace in terms of changing our own lifestyles is too high.

This movie is set in the period immediately following the end of the war in 1991; the troops are partying, waiting for the order to return home, so they get a little high, get a lot drunk, and shoot some Iraqis for the hell of it. Don't try to tell me that this kind of thing doesn't go on in our name. We see a bird covered in oil, and a character indicates that this is horrifying, even more so than the war itself. That may be enough for us, actually, for with that incisive line, we have been told what the film is about—that war solves nothing, and we think more highly of ourselves and consumer goods than we do of our fellow human beings. The story's fairly simple—a bit like Clint Eastwood's old film *Kelly's Heroes*, except with a bit of moral conscience—soldiers go after the treasure held by their enemy, but discover the true humanity of the other.

Three Kings is cinematically much more accomplished than the Clint film. Four examples:

◆ There's great use of different color stock—blood flows like treacle on the sand, and lighting effects in the desert sequences heighten the sense of the unreal.

◆ The cinematography is an integral part of the story, too; cloud formations evoke the mythic nature of men killing other men—but the violence in this film is moral, not gratuitous. It's infinitely more responsible than you would expect from Hollywood.

◆ It's brilliantly detailed—we catch a fleeting glimpse of a little girl with the plaster casts on her arms as a reminder of the human costs of war; who else would have thought to put that in?

◆ Nice film in-joke: the Iraqi rebels are almost certainly supposed to look like characters from *Star Wars*.

The soldiers believe that "Everything you stole from Kuwait belongs to us now" (I guess Kuwait doesn't matter anymore …), but when they see the terror visited upon the Iraqi people, and the fact that America is not going to help them, they make the choice to help. "What happened to necessity?" one of them asks, incredulous at the risk they're about to take. "It just changed" is the response, from a wise man who realizes that what is needed right now is something higher than self-gratification.

Three Kings is about much more than the specific politics of the Gulf War(s) (although there's enough of that in here, too; an Iraqi interrogator pours oil down an American's throat in a reminder of what the war was really about, and we're never too far from reminders of some of the media's unethical role in that conflict). It's about war *per se*. It's about how easy it is to forget the men and women who end up as cannon fodder because our governments don't employ the kind of foreign policy that will transform impoverished societies, or, frankly, so we can have cheap gas. What is war if not plunder? Why does it take so much to engender any kind of responsible action from us? Aren't we—the powerful Christians of the West—supposed to forgo our own desires—and even rights—in order to *defend* the weak? I don't believe that warmongers, or "hawks" as they are usually called nowadays, are bad people; I think they just jump to making bad choices without considering radical non-violent alternatives. Anything that causes us to have to consider changing our lifestyles is the ultimate taboo. I mean, we can help with reducing greenhouse gases, but if one American has to pay one cent more for a gallon of gas, then no siree, thanks, we'll take the planet and run. The same seems to be true of foreign and defense policy. We might sing "It's a small world after all," but when it comes down to it, there are certain people we prefer to keep out of our world. Worse than that, there seems to be people who we would rather wipe off the face of the earth. That's about as far from the gospel of grace as it's possible to travel without coming back in the opposite direction. And while I believe in political activism, it seems that the power of the media is so great that to make political points through entertainment may be about the only hope we have left for change in this world. One of the characters in *Three Kings* says, "The war is over and I don't even f---ing know what it was about." If we're honest with ourselves, he may well be speaking for you and me. But when we see these people killed; when we hear what our governments continue to say (on the one hand) and do (on the other); when we know that there is no happy ending or closure for most of the world's experience of daily life; why do we keep at it?

A PRIMER IN WAR

The "best" war films are often acclaimed for their "realistic" depiction of battle. This is strange, I guess, because I don't suppose too many film critics have spent much time on the front line (although Graham Greene was at least in the ball park). There is so much absurdity in war films and the stuff we write about it that I was tempted to simply provide a list of films and invite people to let them speak for themselves. But I'm on a roll, so I can't stop now.

My favorite war film is a guilty pleasure—because it defends all the elements of war that I can't stand. *Patton: Lust for Glory* is valuable, however, for several reasons. It features one of the very best, angriest, all-consuming performances in cinema, from George C. Scott. It has the most striking, grab-you-in-your-seat-and-make-you-sit-up-straight opening scene, as the general addresses his troops—that's us, by the way. It's another opportunity to gaze on Scott's badly aged eyebrows and Karl Malden's magnificent tulip-bulbous nose. It reminds me of my great friend Al, who, like Patton, is a romantic warrior lost in the poetic, glorious past. It's such a high quality film that even though it was released at the height of the Vietnam War protests, it was incredibly popular—perhaps because Patton was himself a rebellious anti-hero. And in this it is evocative of its writer's—Francis Coppola—public image. But most of all, it is gutsy enough to tell the truth about the so-called "glory" of war, as Scott's Patton says, "No b------- ever won a war by dying for his country; he won it by making the other poor b------- die for his country."

War is hell, but it's hell for everyone. Nowhere is this declared with more stamina, skill, artistry, and sincerity as in Coppola's magnificent (but misnamed) *Apocalypse Now* (more on that film later[1]). Coppola's film, like the best war cinema, is not really about Vietnam, anymore than the parable of the sower is about preventing crab grass. The same is true of *Full Metal Jacket*, Kubrick's visceral demolition of the idea that war is honorable, and Terrence Malick's *The Thin Red Line*, which is—I think—the most perfect match of poetic image and dark context I've seen. There is little poetry in *Saving Private Ryan*, and I still don't quite know what to make of it, years after it was acclaimed as The Greatest War Film Ever, but the horror of what men went through in a just cause has never been more starkly portrayed, except perhaps in *Gallipoli*, or *LaReine Margot*, where the blood of the wasted lives of armed conflict soaks the screen.

---

[1] "Apocalypse" doesn't actually mean "catastrophe." It means "revealing" or "revelation." Chalk that one up to the lack of good Greek-English dictionaries in high school (or at least at Francis Coppola's house).

In armed conflict, nobody wants to admit they're wrong. Witness the propaganda that calls the killing of our soldiers as "murder" but our killing of "the 'enemy's' children" as "collateral damage." It has been said that there are always three sides to every story—mine, yours, and the truth. And the truth, of course, is the first casualty of war. Conflict films that attempt to reveal the shades of gray in every war and the humanity of all combatants are few and far between. But Gillo Pontecorvo's documentary-style masterpiece of colonial exit strategy, *The Battle of Algiers*, is one example of a film that attempts to show both the injustice of colonial experience and the brutality of paramilitarism, helped along by one of Ennio Morricone's most thunderous scores. *Das Boot* is a rare film about what it might have been like to be an ordinary German soldier in the Second World War; *Prisoner of the Mountains* tries to show both sides of the outrageous Russian-Chechnyan conflict of more recent times; *The Quiet American* reminds us that the involvement of the United States in Vietnam was partly its own fault; Michael Winterbottom's amazing *Welcome to Sarajevo* serves as a war crimes indictment of the United Nations for its failure to act in time; and *Black Hawk Down* at least attempts to show the human costs of America's too-late interventionism.

The battles in *Black Hawk Down* take place in city streets, but it is not strictly an urban warfare film; unlike *Bowling for Columbine*, Michael Moore's sprawling, powerful, and hilarious indictment of North American gun culture. As with much of Moore's work, he sometimes exaggerates a point to make it, but I think this damages his cause—the truth is bad enough, although maybe we need it to be made to look worse before we will do anything about it. Soderbergh and Gaghan's *Traffic* is about a connected urban war—the supply, trade, and use of illegal drugs—and it is an excellent assessment. You may sit up and nod vigorously when one character reminds us that, for

North American teenagers, drugs are much easier to come by than alcohol. There is no shortage of either in Scorsese's white elephant *Gangs of New York*, which, while badly structured (I'm sure that wasn't his fault), at least has the wisdom to explain that the myth of American pluralism is just that—a myth. "America was born in the streets," went the tagline—but *Gangs* shows that this means it was born in blood and tribulation. Its characters live and die by the sword, and the myth of redemptive violence is brought to life. It is all the more confusing, then, that Scorsese chose to end the film with a view of the Manhattan skyline with the Twin Towers intact, as if a note of triumph could ever be struck here. This has the effect of undermining the critique of American violence that went before; I hope Marty regains his sense of purpose before too long. There's more North American (sub)urban warfare in both *Gremlins* and *Ghostbusters*, but I fear you won't take me seriously if I write about them, so I'll move on to talking about the stiff upper lip in war movies.

The "glory of war" is a theme that I guess only people who haven't held their best friends guts in would contemplate. Maybe this is where war films are most guilty of dishonesty. *The Bridge on the River Kwai* illustrates an illustrious British officer and his honorable relationship with a Japanese POW commandant, but his stiff upper lip is his downfall. *Paths of Glory* is another Kubrick masterpiece about people following rules that destroy them, as an unjust court martial is used by senior officers as a morale-boosting "lesson" to the men who ran away from the battle their superiors refused to go near in the first place. Renoir's *La Grande Illusion* covers similar ground, giving the lie to simple notions of heroism and good vs. evil. And *Glory* reminds us that it is usually poor people and minority groups who end up as cannon fodder.

The most attractive conflict cinema for me is that which is focused on freedom fighters. I come from a place where the "physical force tradition" has not yet fully ended, so I'm somewhat familiar with how these things go. They're not as glorious or as exciting as the movies would have us think. And soldiers with a just cause have as many sleepless nights as those without. But if you want to pretend that violence can be good for the soul, then *Braveheart* will certainly make you feel great. *Con Air* may be a superficial action thriller about the planes used to transport so-called hardened criminals across America, but I find it difficult to watch because one of the few true freedom fighters I know was shackled on it with violent criminals for his non-violent opposition to state terror in the U.S.

And of course there's dear old *Spartacus*, that staple of Christmas holiday TV schedules and dinner party jokes (No, *I'm* Spartacus!) everywhere (in the industrialized West, at least). How easy it is to mock, but it does pack a powerful punch to see oppressed people rise up and stop taking it from the ruling classes.

And as for what happens after war … if indeed war ever ends … *Death and the Maiden* provides a gripping testimony to the temptation to get revenge as a woman traps the man she believes to have been her kidnapper. In *The Deer Hunter* and *Born on the Fourth of July*, a generation of young men fight in Vietnam. Some stay there, some come home, all of them die. And when they die, they are buried in vast military cemeteries—the *Gardens of Stone* that Coppola filmed. The brass lament played over their funerals is the only gold their families may ever see. The honor of the war dead is also a theme of *Schindler's List*, which is somewhat critic-proof due to its subject matter. And I'm grateful that it was made accessible to many people for whom the Holocaust might otherwise have been a historical footnote. But Spielberg had already made one great Second World War picture—*Empire of the Sun*, which manages the difficult feat of showing war through a child's eyes without seeming mawkish.

While the absurdity of total war should speak for itself, I guess we humans still need to be slapped in the face with its barbarity. So I'm grateful for *Fail Safe* and *La Jetee* and *M★A★S★H* and *Planet of the Apes* and *When the Wind Blows*, but most of all for *Dr. Strangelove*, indisputably the finest war film ever made. That's if you don't count Claude Lanzmann's incredible nine-hour documentary of the Holocaust *Shoah*, which needs a better writer than I to assess.

Finally, it may seem unusual to put *Do the Right Thing* in a chapter on war, but I think it fits. This is Spike Lee's classic tale of urban anomie, facing the question of "Who owns the streets?" It slams into being with LOUD Public Enemy's Fight the Power. This is music as combat, and that's the truth, Ruth. It's been accused of incitement, but the last line in the film denies this: "The cash word money is 'chill'"; however, Lee does declare the difference between Martin Luther King and Malcolm X in coda quotations and leaves it to the audience to decide between them. Malcolm said, "I don't even call violence when it's self-defense, I call it intelligence"; but this is troubling to me. As with my own society, disciplined non-violence has not so much failed as never been consistently attempted. Which means I have to ask a question: Is the Christian faith simply not big enough to cope with the patience required for non-violent resistance?

THE WRAP

In *Apocalypse Now*, Marlon Brando reads aloud from his journals: "They train our young men to drop fire on children, but they won't let them write 'f---' on their bombs because they say it's obscene." A friend of my once said that church people tend to be more offended by the use of the "F" word than they are by the death of children by avoidable malnutrition. Maybe we can get the f--- beyond that. But maybe the fact that I can't even quote the f-word in full in this book because some bookshops won't sell it is evidence for my pessimism. Maybe the time has come when we can put aside our preconceptions and prejudices and recognize that peacemaking is always messy, and it may not often deal in moral or philosophical absolutes. The Jewish Christian philosopher, Simone Weil, said, "We possess nothing in this world other than the power to say 'I.'" Personal responsibility to act is all we have, and all we *need* to make a start. For those of us in Northern Ireland, this will mean choosing to behave courageously in ways that sectarianism in a divided society conspires to prevent. For others, it may mean inter-faith dialogue, lobbying politicians to seek a non-violent response to terrorism, or simply condemning the deaths of Afghani civilians in the 2001–2002 "war" with the same resolve as the deaths that occurred in the United States on September 11, 2001. And of course, the Christian faith is about individuals taking risks in community. From a mustard seed of twelve wayward apostles has grown the Church.

The conflict in my home, Northern Ireland, teaches us that the pressing need for societal change is *our problem*. The peoples of Great Britain and the Republic of Ireland also have a responsibility to help us make peace, yet there has been a disturbing tendency of dissociation. Distance merely allows us to think it is nothing to do with us—until a terrorist bomb in a city center reminds us otherwise.

The same is true for the world in the early twenty-first century. Peacemakers believe that we cannot afford to drift away and leave it—the future of the world—to the politicians. Jesus did not call us to an "easy life" but to life in all its fullness. That means great joy mingled with deep, often wounded compassion for the injustices faced by our brothers and sisters across the globe, whether they suffer at the hands of terrorists in New

York, or despotic regimes in Iraq, or under a hail of gunfire from helicopters that our taxes subsidize, or on trial in Egypt for being gay, or without basic medical supplies in Gaza, or victimized by terror in Jerusalem.

As for present fears about the end-times, it is vital that we don't become sidetracked by apocalyptic anxiety. There are many beliefs about the Second Coming and the end of history; Christians have never agreed on what all these things mean—in fact, we don't even interpret the word "apocalypse" correctly. The recent re-emergence of populist millennialism, particularly in the best-selling "Left Behind" books, is only one kind of extraordinarily skewed cultural perspective; it is worth remembering that these books are found in the "fiction" section of the bookstore. Some theologians believe that Jesus may not have been predicting His personal return at all, but declaring something far more profound about the final establishment of the kingdom of God. Whatever the end-times belief, the Church has a 100 percent failure record in predicting what will happen when. This is simply not worth wasting time on. The task of "bringing sight to the blind, healing to the lame, declaring the year of the Lord's favor" by clothing the naked, feeding the hungry, and visiting those in prison is the responsibility of would-be Christians. The end of the world we can leave for another day.

Jesus was not an American, although you could be forgiven for thinking that He grew up blue-eyed and on the college football team in the Midwest of the 1950s, with values to match. And it's not unpatriotic to ask difficult questions of your government when you fear its moral compass has begun to waver. Truth is complex at the best of times, but we live in even more confusing times, uncertain times, anxious times. War, and what the Bible calls "rumors of war," appears to be increasing. And we are all involved. We cannot pretend that we don't have a responsibility to act in international affairs anymore than we can say we have no responsibility for the homeless person begging on the sidewalk outside the place where we live. International conflict may seem too overwhelming to deal with, but you can act to change things by participating with others, and you can at least do something about your own life.

At twenty-eight years old, my memories of growing up in a violent, divided society remind me that peace is not simply the absence of bombs in Western cities; it is about safety, and community, and generosity. If our faith is about the imitation of Christ, then we must be prepared to forgo easy solutions, like the bombing of people on the other side of the world, and take sacrificial steps of love and even forgiveness. This is, of course, a provocative suggestion, for the "powers that be" will always try to co-opt the truth-tellers to a more nefarious agenda; and when they cannot co-opt, they will seek to suppress. But that is simply a constant historical challenge to discipleship, as old as the temptations of the desert. The key question is not, "When is Jesus coming back?" or "How do we get revenge?" or even "How do we stop Saddam?" The key question is, "Will I learn to lead an ethical life?" Perhaps the tragedy of war and terror might lead this generation of Christians to discover again that the call to discipleship does not invite us to worry about the end-times, but asks us to be prepared to be imaginative in how we respond to conflict, perhaps even to take the kind of non-violent action that led Jesus to the cross.

CHAPTER SIXTEEN

THE MATRIX
THE ANSWER WILL FIND YOU

THE MATRIX
(LARRY AND ANDY WACHOWSKI, 1999)

THE MATRIX IS A WORK OF SPIRITUAL DISCERNMENT. Although it's too often talked about as if it's the only film with any kind of spiritual resonance, and it is too easy to refuse to reflect on the violence, I do love the helicopters. And it might just be the most valuable film about taking life seriously that we're likely to see at a multiplex. And it needs to appear in this book, even though I don't expect I have much to add to the analysis of the most obviously Christian film in recent mainstream Hollywood history. I first saw it at the Chinese Theatre on Hollywood Boulevard—probably the most cinematic cinema in the world—so I was primed to have an awesome experience. At first glance, I didn't think much of it. Nice effects, could have done without the weird robotic spiders. So it slipped out of mind as I slipped out of the theater. Then I took a trip to Nashville, where my friends David and Sarah were wide eyed in wonderment at the movie, and told me breathlessly that they had been to see it on Easter Sunday because they thought it suited the sacramental mood. So I said, "What do you mean?"

And they said, "The thoughtfulness, the philosophy, the Christ metaphors …"

That made me reconsider. Actually, it made me feel stupid, as the scales fell from my eyes and my memory of the film was set free. I immediately went out to see it and haven't looked back. I'm not always happy to do this, but as far as *The Matrix* is concerned, I admit my error; I was wrong. It's amazing.

The terror of artificial intelligence may have been better handled in Kubrick/Spielberg's *A.I.*, and more exciting in *Terminator 2*, but this part of the story isn't really the issue at hand. We know that somehow the machines have made life a wee bit difficult for everyone out there, turning us all into human batteries or somesuch. And there are these cool guys in gray and black (but for Morpheus, only sleek British Racing Green will do) who live in the "real" world and fly around in a great spaceship (named "Nebuchadnezzar" after the king who turned back toward God when he opened his eyes to what the world is really like) and try to unplug people from the nightmare of being only technically human. And of course this is a metaphor for the way life is and should not be. It's a magnificent film that I could talk about forever; but I'll make it easy for ya: here are the nine commandments of *The Matrix*:

THE NINE COMMANDMENTS OF *THE MATRIX*

1: THE VOICES IN YOUR HEAD ARE NOT REAL

The Matrix starts with Trinity—who somehow looks a lot older than she must be—escaping from the cops and "agents" who run the show. Agent Smith, who turns out to be the nemesis in this story, but a highly entertaining nemesis to be sure, tells a senior officer, "Your men are already dead." And I guess this is the point—we are already dead and need to be resurrected; but before that can happen we need to be *made aware* of our deaths. The contemplative writer Anthony de Mello encouraged people to meditate on an image of their own future rotting corpse, not for morbidity's sake, but because he believed that we can only truly live once we have confronted the inevitability of our death. Trinity has awoken from her living nightmare, and nothing can harm her, because she knows that nothing can be worse than what she used to live in. And the early scenes show how she has trained her mind to control her responses—when she flies through a window, her body wants to lie on the floor, but her mind and voice say "GET UP" so she does. She has managed to find a happy medium between spirit and flesh.

This is the first lesson: Until you learn to discern the voices in your head, you will never find your way. I have written earlier about the need to recognize that we all have various noises competing for our attention. Some of them are affirming, some are helpfully critical, some are condemnatory, some are appetites for fun or food, some are temptations to destroy. They are all real, but only the ones that we *invite* belong to us. There is a new way of seeing the world (and ourselves) that can free us from the shackles of self-criticism and fear. We may all be partly the product of our circumstances, but the good news is that we are much more than that (assuming we are human, which I guess most of us are). We can *choose* something different than what went before. You fear your future because you hated your dad or your parents or your school and think you might turn out like him/they/it? Think again: You have much more to worry about than that. What about the ancestors you never met, whose genes (helpful and nasty) you carry? What about the unremembered moments of childhood trauma that have scarred your soul so deeply you don't even know what they are? You don't believe that *those* things necessarily have power over you, so why worry about your dad? Or maybe you think God will never use you because of some dark secret; I don't know, maybe you kissed a person you loved or killed a person you didn't. What makes you think you're more important than King David? So important that God wouldn't forgive you?

2: THE VOICES IN YOUR HEAD ARE REAL

The matrix has you, says Morpheus (who has come a *long* way from little Larry Fishburne in *Apocalypse Now*), but what *is* the matrix? It's the question that drives you, "Why you hardly sleep, why you live alone, and why night after night, you sit at your computer." What's your question? We all have something that drives us but is so personal, perhaps so inarticulate that we couldn't tell it to others or understand it clearly ourselves. In this sense, the voices in your heads *are* real. But, like Tolkien's ring of power, it wants to be found; the answer is out there; it's looking for you, and it will find you if you want it to.

3: THE FUTURE DEPENDS ON US BEING A TEAM

I was initially concerned about the overriding individualism of *The Matrix*, but, as with so many things, I realize I was wrong. Agent Smith explains how he believes that humans are not mammals—not developing equilibrium; the multiplication and consumption of resources and the destruction of each other is the definition of human nature. Human beings, or at least the way they behave, may well have become a disease, a cancer, but there is a cure. It is not, as many viewers of the movie seem to think, rebellion against the state or any institutions. It is about finding a purpose in community. I think it's a misinterpretation to read the film as an affirmation of superheroic individual spirituality. You are not *"The One."* Neo cannot do what he needs to without the mentoring of Morpheus, the training from Tank, and most of all the love of Trinity. Ultimately, Neo's initiation into the ways of the matrix, his training, and his resurrection is only accomplished when Trinity makes it possible. It's called teamwork. And even if you think you *are* The One, you can't go it alone. Of course it's subversive, but the revolution that will overthrow the matrix is one that requires people to work *together*.

4: NON-VIOLENT SUBVERSION IS THE ONLY WAY TO FLY

The movie was released shortly before the Columbine killings, and some were quick to attribute blame for this to the movie's incredible violence. And there is a danger that we will turn a blind eye to this. If we don't look closely, we may be forgiven for thinking that the solution it prescribes is to "shoot the bad guys." But we find that Neo learns to subvert violence by absorbing it—he doesn't even have to dodge bullets anymore, once he accepts his destiny. His absorption of violence goes along with a resurrection that shames his enemies—making a public spectacle of them, perhaps? And these enemies—the agents—are not flesh and blood, but representations of repressive power. They cannot be dealt with by bullets. It is just the word "no," spoken with authority that makes Neo not need to dodge them. He dives into the heart of his enemy, and bends reality to his good will. The "rules" do not apply to Neo, and in a very real sense, nor should they apply to you, if you want to take spirituality seriously. And the rules of this world never question the use of violence as a means to an end. But you should.

5: IT IS POSSIBLE TO LIVE WITHOUT FEAR

Morpheus says that the existence of the matrix means that everything we think is real is a construct. Merton and Derrida say the same thing in a different way; but whether we learn it from a twentieth-century American monk, a twenty-first century French philosopher, or a twenty-second century virtual reality revolutionary, it is one of the keys to life. We can learn the difference between what really matters and the illusions of created things, to be able to live life with no inhibitions, totally free of worry, but not of responsibility. St. Augustine wrote that to be a Christian was "to love God, and do what you want"; which I guess is one way of saying that if you're seeking to be in touch with the divine, you will find yourself becoming the kind of person God might have made you to be. In other words, to be fully human.

6: WE ALL NEED TO BE CONVERTED

Neo is sceptical of the rebels at first, but decides to trust them when they remind him that he has been down "Adam Street" before, and he knows where it leads. Morpheus reminds him that he knows: There's something wrong with the world, you don't know what it is, but it's there, like a splinter in your mind.

He knows he needs to wake up, to recognize the matrix that surrounds us—"the world that has been pulled over his eyes to blind him from the truth of his own slavery." But he can't be told what the matrix is—he has to see it for himself; and the traumatic baptism that follows taking the red pill is the price he has to pay. Taking the red pill has become a bit of a cliché in Christian circles; let's at least try to live up to the metaphor. Taking God seriously is a bit like the taking the pill—it is painful to realize that we have been traveling the wrong way and that the world is upside down. And sometimes discipleship ain't much easier. We may wish, like some in *The Matrix*, that we had never taken the pill in the first place; taking the blue pill may well be the way to a kind of peace. And some people aren't ready to be "unplugged"; this journey needs to be handled with care. But there is a time for philosophy, and there is a time for decision. There is a difference between knowing the path, and walking the path. The red pill is there to be swallowed, not admired.

7: TIME IS NOT ALWAYS AGAINST US: IT CAN BE REDEEMED

We may feel that time is always against us—but *The Matrix* shows it doesn't have to be; time has already been redeemed.

8: YOU WILL NOT BE TESTED BEYOND WHAT YOU CAN BEAR

Blink and you'll miss it, but Agent Smith explains that the first matrix didn't work; humans needed suffering in order to believe that it was real. Ironically this flaw in the system is the key to its destruction. And there is always a way out.

9: ULTIMATELY, THE CHOICE IS YOURS

Perhaps the most important line in the whole film is, "The matrix cannot tell you who you are." And neither can I. When you realize that something has gone terribly wrong with this world, and our place in it, when you realize, as Neo does that "the memories are not real," you will be distressed or upset. But this kind of revelation is given to you because it is what you need to know. Like Abraham, who believed he was supposed to sacrifice his son, even though that was never God's intention, we sometimes need to be brought to a place where we imagine the worst before we can take reality seriously. It's the ambition for change—the sense that something can be done—that shapes you, even when you don't end up doing the thing you expected. But if your response to revelation about the true nature of the universe is to disappear into a fog of despair or self-indulgent nihilism, beware.

In purely cinematic terms, *The Matrix* is amazing; for a start, the set design and art direction are incredible—for a film about the theory that nothing is real, this has an awesome sense of place. It's also literate and witty, the photography is magnificent, and even Keanu finds the perfect blank on which to project a performance. The scary thing is, one day it will look old-fashioned. In the final scene, Neo looks around, surveying those he's come to save; perhaps he hasn't grasped the magnitude of his responsibility, but then again, neither have we. He may not even know what he's really saying when he declares: "I came here to tell you how it's going to *begin*; I'm going to show them a world without you—a world where anything is possible." It's our task to be agents of change in this world, to do justly, to love mercy, to walk humbly with our God. We will never get it perfectly right; I mean what is perfectly right anyway? How could we possibly know? And *everybody* falls asleep sometimes. But *The Matrix* might just help us wake up.

AND SO WE END WHERE WE BEGIN

THERE'S A SCENE TOWARD THE END OF WOODY Allen's *Manhattan* where he records himself rhyming into a tape recorder all the things that keep him alive when the odds are against him. Things like the Marx Brothers, won ton soup, Central Park, his girlfriend's face … It is one of the most affecting movie moments I know. This kind of "blessing count" is how I want to end our journey together through the landscape of cinema spirituality. So, if I were lying on a sofa in Allen's apartment in Manhattan (which I guess I never will be, although I am writing this in New York—check out the Bowery Poetry Club off Bleecker St. next time you're there; great place to write and listen), here's what I might recount:

Some things that make me grateful to be alive: Randalstown forest on a crisp morning, followed by fresh coffee at T&G's; stealing prawns from the Christmas dinner table every year since I was five; Tony Bennett; Dad's triumphal laugh when England score a rugby try; some old hymns; *A Prayer for Owen Meany*; Mum's skin when I kiss it goodbye; arriving at

Greenbelt every August and never getting a tent site close to the venues; the fourth movement of Mahler's fifth; tigers; Delgany and everything it meant to me; *Singin' in the Rain* (probably the most purely pleasurable film there is); the island of Iona; being forgiven for all the mistakes I've made and knowing that there is forgiveness for all that have been made toward me; fantasizing about using the gym more often; the experience of taking off in a plane; Ellen Burstyn; long, languorous, smoke-imbued and wine-imbibed dinners with friends; the inside of Krakow Cathedral; North American independent bookstores; my grandmother's calming voice; Van Morrison in all kinds of moods; the contemplation of writing; and the feeling when the lights go down in a cinema ...

We are fortunate to live in a time when music, film, and literature are more accessible to the general public than ever before. Thankfully, some of the books, records, and movies out there have something valuable to say about spirituality. The messages may not be explicit, they may even take a little bit of digging to find, but they are there if we are attentive. Any film that makes us reflect on choice, or confession, or our mutual brokenness as fallen people, or our need to accept responsibility and its consequences, or the power of love, or the need to engage in remembrance instead of denial, or that reminds us that forgiveness is a free gift, must be welcomed. We must always be attentive and sensitive to the unknown pain of those around us, so I want to draw this book to a close with a quotation from a great man, who understood the pain of exclusion and unforgiveness. His education in a Northern Irish school may or may not have increased his wisdom, but nevertheless, what he says is true and worthy of reflection: "Repentance can change even the past," Oscar Wilde said.

This is a miracle. *What* is a miracle? I grew up in the Christian charismatic movement, so I have a great deal of unusual stories bouncing around inside my neurosis—stories of teeth turned to gold, of legs lengthened, of wheelchairs left behind ... Whether these stories are literally true, and why people believe them is a matter for another book, but it has always confused me how some charismatics downplayed the fact that anyone who was miraculously healed would, of course, eventually die again. The real miracles—the miracle of everyday life, of breathing and seeing and tasting and natural lakes and caves and art and love and sex and friendship and work—we took for granted. This made falling over in a meeting with lots of noise around you seem more valuable than communing over black coffee with friends on top of a Swiss mountain. A pity, that.

There was a time when people would have thought that moving celluloid pictures, animated by light, telling stories, was impossible. We would do well to remember this, and in our remembering, be grateful for what cinema can offer. Cinema, often, is a miracle itself. Jesus once spoke of the "greater things" that His followers would do, which seems strange for a man who had just raised the dead. But people say He said it, so I guess He meant it. What are the "greater things"? Perhaps mercy, justice, freedom, sight to the blind give us some indication, but I suspect words don't do justice to justice. Being fully human is not the same thing as being part of a particular faith tradition, Christian or otherwise. If we think faith is just a matter of believing the "right" things and trying to persuade others to do the same, we've put the cart before the horse. Surely we must realize that we're all such lonely people, and the struggles facing humanity are so inconceivably great, that *belief* alone is not going to resolve our condition. To follow Jesus means to invest the time to create the space for God to make you human again. We should make the time for this. When he was being installed as Archbishop of Canterbury, Rowan Williams said: "We are made to be God's children; we only become truly human when we allow God to re-make us. No one can be written off. We can't assume that any human face we see has no divine secret to disclose."

Film can help us if we know where to look. It's good to use film to escape from pain for a while, but beware of using it to escape from responsibility. Watching a movie about poverty, for instance, and then doing nothing about it is like the pre-Revolutionary French king who had biblical passages about justice read to him while the poor were dying at his gates. Movies can reveal the truth twenty-four times per second[1], and I hope this journey has helped you find some tools to discern that truth. Of course, films are not always allegorical to Christian experience, but they are the most vital art form and must be taken seriously. I did not write this book to give you easy answers but to provoke you in a new way of appreciating film. There's a line in a film somewhere—it might be *The Wizard of Oz*, but they all seem to blur into one now—wherever it comes from, it says: "Some people without brains do an awful lot of talking."

And I guess that must be my cue to let you get back to whatever it was you were doing before you picked me up. If I could leave anything with you, it would be this: You don't have to fight to be loved. You just are. This book, for what it's worth, is my gift to you. It's just a collection of my thoughts, which are no more or less valid than yours, but I hope it's opened some doors. So until we meet elsewhere, maybe you'll take my advice—just watch the movies, start an argument, find the tools to engage, change your life, take a chance, think, enjoy, find liberation, find and lose yourself, be real, be now, be human.

---

[1] Films are projected at a speed of twenty-four frames per second.

If you liked this book,
you'll love